I'LL BE
THERE
FOR YOU

KELSEY MILLER

I'LL BE THERE FOR YOU

The One about *Friends*

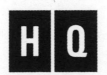

ONE PLACE. MANY STORIES

HQ
An imprint of HarperCollins*Publishers* Ltd
1 London Bridge Street
London SE1 9GF

This hardback edition 2018

1
First published in Great Britain by
HQ, an imprint of HarperCollins*Publishers* Ltd 2018

A catalogue record for this book is
available from the British Library.

ISBN: 978-0-263-27581-0

Printed and bound in Great Britain by
CPI Group (UK) Ltd, Croydon, CR0 4YY

MIX
Paper from
responsible sources
FSC™ C007454

This book is produced from independently certified FSC™ paper
to ensure responsible forest management.

For more information visit: www.harpercollins.co.uk/green

For *my* friends

CONTENTS

INTRODUCTION

The Sweet Spot

A few months ago, I walked into the gym, hopped on my usual machine, and thumbed the worn-out little button on the monitor up to channel 46. It was very early evening—a kind of magic hour at the gym. The place was packed, but oddly quiet, save for the whirring of stationary bike wheels and rhythmic thumping of sneakers on the treadmill. Gyms in New York City have a reputation for being scene-y and intimidating, full of athletic wunderkinds and sweat-free medical marvels eyeing each other as they deadlift a thousand pounds and do pirouettes in the mirror. On the whole, this reputation is shockingly true. But not at 5:30 p.m. At that hour of the day, all is calm and no one is judging. And every TV seems to be tuned in to a basic cable channel, as New Yorkers unwind with some cardio and reruns. That day, I walked in and saw the usual array of familiar faces lined up above high-tech machines: some folks watched *Grey's Anatomy*, others preferred *Law & Order*. Some even tuned in to *Family Guy*, right out in the open. Really, there's no judgment at 5:30. Personally, I always went right to channel 46, where every afternoon TBS ran *Friends*.

I'd started this routine a few years prior, around the same time I started working out regularly. I was in my late twenties, and up until that point, exercise had been the kind of thing I did either obsessively or not at all. Like most young women (at least the ones I knew), I'd thought of working out as something you did to try to look better, or to "cancel out" the dollar-slice pizza you ate on the street with your friends after five glasses of revolting wine. Now, I'd entered a new phase of adulthood. I ordered the good pizza and ate it at home with my long-term boyfriend—and not too close to bedtime, or we'd both need a Zantac. I exercised for actual health reasons, like a grown-up. It was boring and consistent, and I actually *liked* it. There were other things I didn't like about getting older (like always having to keep Zantac in the house), but the gym wasn't one of them. Because there, every evening, I could turn on *Friends* and hop back in time for a moment.

Channel 46 became the nostalgic escape hatch at the end of my grown-up workday. I would pedal away on the Arc Trainer, watching the episode where Monica accidentally dated a teenager, or the one where Chandler got stuck in an ATM vestibule with Jill Goodacre. I didn't even know who Jill Goodacre was, really. I just knew she was a Victoria's Secret model in the '90s, and rewatching the episode was like returning to an era when both she and Victoria's Secret were hot pop-culture references.

I'd never counted myself among the die-hard *Friends* fans, though of course I'd watched it. I was ten years old when it debuted in 1994, and in college when it ended. During those years it was one of the biggest shows on television—one of the biggest cultural events, period—and its enormous impact was baked into my DNA like radiation. I'd gotten The Rachel in middle school, I'd watched the finale with a group of weepy girlfriends, and if pressed, I could *probably* remember all the words to "Smelly Cat." But that was base-level *Friends* knowledge, which was, frankly, hard to avoid having. The show was always there, one way or another. I'd find it on hotel-room televisions in the middle of the night, or hear the theme song in a grocery store and get it stuck in my head for days. *Friends* became an easy reference point in conversations. ("You know, Adam Goldberg. *Dazed and Confused*? He was Chandler's creepy roommate with the goldfish? Yeah, that guy.") I'd never owned the DVDs, but they always seemed to be around, either left by old roommates or brought in by new ones. When the show came to Netflix, on New Year's Day 2015 (after months of hype), I tuned in for a hungover rewatch. So had all of my colleagues, I found out at work the next day. The true devotees hadn't even waited until morning. They'd started shortly after midnight and watched until sunrise. I enjoyed revisiting the episodes occasionally, but I assumed I was a *Friends* fan the way everyone kind of was.

At first, the gym reruns were just an entertaining little addition to my cardio. Part of the fun, though, was watching it the old way—on actual television. I liked the inconvenience of it, even the commercials. I liked not being able to choose which episode I watched. One day, "The One with the Cake" came on again, and I had a thought I hadn't had in years: *Oh, man, I just saw this one.* Even the annoyance was a comforting throwback.

Soon enough, I found myself timing my workouts to line up with the reruns. I knew the TBS schedule by heart, the distance between work and the gym, and the exact time I had to leave the office in order to make it in time. A few years later, I was a full-time freelancer, working from home, and it became even easier. All I had to do was wake up earlier so I could wrap up work by 5:00 or so, and I would make it to the gym just in time for "The One with Ross's Sandwich." By now, I could admit the truth: 5:30 p.m. had become my new prime time, and *Friends* was once again Must-See TV.

★ ★ ★

Let's be clear: I did other stuff, too. I had a life. I was a writer, living in New York City. I had my own nice apartment (not Monica nice, but no one had that). I got to live in it with my very nice boyfriend, who soon became my very nice fiancé. I had my hardships, like everyone does, but I had much more to be grateful for. You couldn't have paid me to go back and re-live my twenties—especially not those early years, eating drunk pizza on the street. So why, as I inched into my thirties, was I suddenly clinging to a twenty-year-old show about twenty-something people?

I didn't figure it out until that day a few months ago, when I breezed into the gym, turned on *Friends*—and it wasn't there. Something had happened. Channel 46 was no longer TBS, but some god-awful sports network. I frantically clicked through the channels, mentally drafting an email to gym management about the great wrong they had done in changing cable providers. I looked around at my fellow rerun-watchers, expecting a row of outraged faces, but found none. Maybe I'd been wrong about the 5:30 crowd and the slightly embarrassing bond I thought we shared. Was I the gym weirdo? A good ten minutes passed as I stood motionless on the machine, absently thumbing the buttons and staring, wide-eyed, into space. (Yes, for sure, I was the weirdo now.)

In that moment, I thought of all the other times I'd gone back to *Friends* reruns: sick days, sleepless nights in unfamiliar hotel rooms, the day I got rejected by [insert job and/or roman-tic prospect]. It was a soothing balm on a lousy day—that much I already knew. But I'd also returned to *Friends* during periods of deep sadness and anxiety: while mourning the death of a grandparent, or waiting to hear back on biopsy results. On days like that, *Friends* wasn't numbing, but comforting and warm. I leaned on the familiar jokes and unabashed sincerity. And I was not the only one. In the weeks after my little mental meltdown on the Arc Trainer, I spoke to others who said the same. Usually, it would start with my shame-faced confession: "So, turns out I'm emotionally dependent on a sitcom! How've *you* been?"

Many of my peers responded with stories of their own *Friends* phases. Some recalled watching it after 9/11. A lot of people mentioned the 2016 election or the 2017 mass shooting in Las Vegas. *Friends* was what they turned on when they just couldn't absorb any more news coverage. For those who grew up on the show, it was a reminder of that earlier, simpler time—not in the world necessarily, but in their own lives. Many watched the show during personal low points or times of high stress: break-ups, unemployment, the sleep-deprived first months with a new baby. Why *Friends*? I'd ask. Was it because the show touched on all those topics, but in an optimistic way? Were they seeking out that emotional resonance? "Uh, no," they told me. "It's just a funny show."

These people use the term *comfort food* when talking about *Friends*. They refer to its lightness, its detachment from reality. They watch it because they *can't* relate. It's ridiculous! Six adults with perfect hair who hang out in a coffeehouse in the middle of the day? Who's paying for those giant lattes? *Friends*, for them, is pure escapism.

For others, it's something else entirely. As I began to write this book, I spoke with more people, from all over the US and the world, about their relationship to *Friends*. And everyone seemed to have one, even if they'd never been a fan—even if they'd never seen a full episode. My friend Chrissy, who grew up as a dual citizen in both America and Switzerland, is one of the latter. *Friends*, she said, was equally huge in both countries, despite the cultural differences. "For Europeans who had never been to the US, *Friends was* America," Chrissy told me. I thought she was referring to things like sweatpants and not being able to afford health care, and other parts of American life that they don't really have in Europe. Again, I was cor-

rected. "It was the friendliness," she told me. "Americans smile
the moment you meet them. They talk to you like you already
know each other." To the Swiss, she said, American tourists
came across like suspiciously nice aliens. *Friends*, with its high-
energy humor and chummy characters, helped make sense of
that. Maybe Americans were just an overly friendly bunch. Or
maybe just New Yorkers.

I spoke with style editor Elana Fishman, who was raised in
South Florida and now lives in Manhattan. Fishman *is* a die-
hard *Friends* fan, and she, too, got her sense of New York life
from the show. She spent her high-school years watching the
DVDs with her sister every afternoon, and while she understood
that *Friends* was a fantasy, there was something about it that felt
true. "On some level, I thought, 'Okay, this is not at all realistic—but what if it *could* be?'" she told me. Fishman dreamed
of going to college in New York, then starting a journalism
career there. *Friends* gave her excitement and hope; it wasn't
an escape from reality but a glimpse into the future. Her life
wouldn't be *exactly* like *Friends*, she knew. But maybe it would
be close. "[I thought,] 'Maybe I'll move to New York, make a
best friend who has a rent-controlled apartment in Greenwich
Village, and we'll live there! And it'll be great! And we'll have
the guys across the hall who are our best friends.'" Those things
could happen. It would be pretty fortuitous for all of them to
happen all at once, but not impossible. And really, only one of
them mattered. "I didn't have a lot of friends in high school,"
Fishman added quietly, trailing off into a chuckle. "So, watching *Friends*—it was like a double comfort. I was going to make
it to New York, and find that group of friends." She laughed
again. "I know, it's sad!"

I don't think it's sad. I think it's right on the money. I think
it's the very reason *Friends* remains one of the most-watched
shows on television, to this day. A reported 16 million Amer-

icans watch the reruns weekly. That's as many or *more* viewers than some of the episodes got during *Friends*' first run. And that's just the people watching it on TV. Netflix has retained the streaming rights since 2015, and since its wildly popular US debut, the company has been rolling out the series to 118 million (and counting) subscribers worldwide. In those markets, too, the *Friends* fandom remains huge and steady, and in some, it's actually growing. In 2016, ratings were up by 10% in the UK, where the reruns air on Comedy Central—a channel whose primary demographic is aged 16–34. Teenagers—who weren't even born when *Friends* went off the air—lie around on the couch, watching it after school. Young adults come home to their cramped apartments late at night (perhaps still full of street pizza), bring their laptops into bed, and fall asleep to an episode. And not-so-young adults, like me, watch reruns on exercise machines.

Friends has managed to transcend age, nationality, cultural barriers, and even its own dated, unrelatable flaws. Because, underneath all that, it is a show about something truly universal: friendship. It's a show about the transitional period of early adulthood, when you and your peers are untethered from family, unattached to partners, and equal parts excited and uncertain about the future. The only sure thing you have is each other.

Cultural critic Martha Bayles calls it "the sweet spot"—a fleeting period of enormous freedom and encroaching responsibility, where friends band together in families of their own making. "In most countries, young people have neither the resources nor the adult approval to experience the sweet spot," she writes in her book, *Through a Screen Darkly*. Yet *Friends* is just as popular with them. It is, she writes, "a chance to live vicariously in the sweet spot." Indeed, even for those of us who had it, the sweet spot was never *as* sweet as it was on *Friends*. Our problems were never solved so tidily, our hair was never that good, and again, nobody had that apartment. The truth is, not even our friendships were that perfect. Some of us were lonely in those years, and some of our friend-families were dysfunctional. For others, the real sweetness came later. But what we all can recognize—what is absolutely spot-on about *Friends*—is the unmistakable, life-changing love that can only exist between friends. It is the net that catches you when family disappoints or falls apart. It is the ballast you can wrap your arms around when romance falters. Friends are the people who walk steadfast, hand in yours, through the rough patches. And then it happens—your grip loosens, the path widens between you, and one day, you look around and find you're walking on your own, out of the sweet spot and into the rest of your life.

That's what I realized, that day at the gym. I was thirty-three, engaged—not all *that* certain about the future, but no longer totally lost. That phase of my own life had been ending for a while. Over that last few years, close friends had moved away for work or gotten married. People had children and mortgages and career ladders to climb. I had a gym membership, for God's sake, that I actually *used*. None of these were bad things. This next stage was exciting in a whole new way. But entering it meant leaving another, as well as the relationships I'd had there. Not the people—I would always have them. But it would be different. We couldn't go back to being twentysomething friends any more than we could go back to summer camp or high school (and yeesh, would we really want to?). Life happens, friendships change—and change is the worst. So, no wonder I'd gone back to something familiar. *Friends* was a way to revisit the time in my life that was fading, slowly but steadily, into memory.

True, it was just an old sitcom. Yes, in most respects, it bore no resemblance to my own experience. But in the only way that mattered, it did. It was a show about friendship. And like old friends, it never really went away.

PART 1

1

The One That Almost Wasn't

On September 22, 1994, NBC aired the pilot episode of a half-hour comedy now titled *Friends*. It began as plainly as the title implied, with five twentysomethings lounging at a coffeehouse, talking about nothing much. For the first three minutes they didn't even have names. Then Rachel Green burst into Central Perk, hoisting up her sopping wet wedding gown, her hair utterly unremarkable. She introduced herself to the gang, and the gang to all of us. The story had begun.

It was a fairly inauspicious beginning. As with many television pilots, this episode was nowhere near as good as those that came later. "The One Where Monica Gets a Roommate" is pretty much just that: Rachel shows up in the city, having run out on her wedding, to find her long-lost high-school friend, Monica—for some reason. Why? Whatever, don't worry about it. Monica lets her move in, seeing as she has an enormous apartment, smack-dab in the middle of Manhattan, with an empty second bedroom. Don't worry about those things, either. On paper, the *Friends* pilot asks you to overlook a lot of absurdities and holes—as did most sitcoms of its time. On-screen, it's only slightly less clunky. The performances are uneven, and the laughter so much louder and uproarious than the punch lines deserve. Watching it now, one can see the seedlings of the bright and crackling comedy to come. But one can also see, quite clearly, how it could have fizzled into nothing.

"They're 20-something; they hang together; they're wild and crazy and even occasionally funny," the *New York Times* reported in its first tepid write-up of the show. "But would you hang with them? As with all gang shows, it depends on how the individuals develop. In any case," the four-sentence blurb concluded, "this is mainly a show about demographics."

Ouch. It wasn't the friendliest welcome to the fall lineup, but it wasn't entirely wrong, either. The show was about demographics— one in particular. *Friends* was centered around six Generation X Manhattanites, not exactly a group in which the majority of Americans could see themselves reflected. This was just one of many reasons the show should have, and so easily could have, failed. Today, it's impossible to envision a television landscape in which *Friends* did not succeed, so far-reaching was its influence. But so much had to happen to get that single, just-fine pilot on the air. So much had to go right, and so many other things had to go wrong. It took a fortuitous blend of timing and luck and snap decisions—and a good deal of behind-the-scenes finagling between the power players, not just at NBC, but Fox and CBS, as well. And after that, it would take even longer for the show to prove itself as something more than a bubbly, blond *Seinfeld*.

In the end, the *New York Times* was right about *Friends*, but for the wrong reasons. It wasn't a show about the tribulations of these specific few. It was the opposite. It had a theme so broad and loose that it pushed the boundaries of low-concept and was hardly concept at all. As the creators themselves put it, *Friends* was about "that time of your life when your friends are your family." Or, at least, it would be.

★ ★ ★

On a rainy Wednesday afternoon in 1985, Marta Kauffman was standing at a bus stop in lower Manhattan. She was wet and miserable, and she had a decision to make. "I kept thinking, 'I need a sign, 'cause I don't know what to do,'" she would recount, decades later. Twenty minutes passed, and the bus never arrived. Typical. Then a taxi pulled up right in front of her—not at all typical on a rainy New York day. She didn't think twice, just grabbed it, gave the driver directions, and leaned back in her seat. Suddenly, it occurred to her: *a sign*. She sat up, and there it was, right in front of her face. She knew exactly what to do.

Marta Kauffman and David Crane met in 1975, at Brandeis University. In 2010, Kauffman and Crane were interviewed by the Television Academy Foundation, where their story would be preserved for future generations of creatives and cultural historians. By then, the creators of *Friends* had long since ended their landmark show as well as their professional relationship. But their legendary rapport and synchronicity was undiminished. This was a duo that, from their early days in Hollywood, were known for their preternatural chemistry, finishing each other's sentences and pitching network executives with uncanny energy and ease. In that 2010 interview, when asked to tell the story of how they first met, they replied in tandem, without skipping a beat: "He was a street urchin," Kauffman began. On cue, Crane concluded: "And Marta was a whore."

Onstage, that is. They were both acting students at the time, and had been cast in a production of the Tennessee Williams play *Camino Real*. It would be nice to view this first meeting through the lens of destiny, imagining a young Kauffman and Crane instantly recognizing themselves as kindred from the start. The truth, though, has a lot less fairy dust. The truth sounds a lot more like everyone else's college theater stories: they met, did the play, and then never really hung out after that.

Two years passed. Kauffman went abroad for her junior year, and by the time she returned to school, she'd decided to try working behind the scenes. She enrolled in a directing course, which Crane was taking, too, having recently come to the realization that, as an actor, he was "really not good." Kauffman didn't yet know this, so when she was assigned to direct a production of *Godspell*, she asked her old castmate to be in it. "And he said, 'No. But I'll direct it with you?'"

Two directors on one show can often become a too-many-cooks situation, particularly when the cooks are two young, ambitious theater students. Dueling egos and clashing creative visions can spoil the production and make mortal enemies out of the competing codirectors. But, at least in their recollection, Kauffman and Crane's first collaboration was precisely the opposite. It was easy and it was a *blast*. Having been relative strangers before, they now fell into an instant and easy rapport. Already, they were completing one another's sentences, working in sync like seasoned producing partners. "It was one of those relationships where you very quickly realize, *This is fun*," says Kauffman.

They had fun codirecting *Godspell* and so decided to do another play, and then another. There was no formal agreement, but Kauffman and Crane now realized they both enjoyed creating theater, maybe more than performing—and they enjoyed it even more when creating it together.

"I don't even know which of us said it," Crane recalled. But, on a whim, one of them suggested they write something. The way he tells it, the decision to become writing partners went something like: "Yeah, let's write something! It'll be a musical! Sure!" Kauffman shrugged and nodded. "We have a barn."

Neither had ever written a play, let alone a musical. So they did what one is supposed to do in college: experimented. They booked a theater space and commissioned classmates Seth Friedman and Billy Dreskin[1] to help out.

This play would become the first Kauffman-Crane production, titled *Waiting for the Feeling*. (It was exactly what it sounds like, according to Kauffman: "An angst-driven, collegiate, 'comedy'" about how hard it is to be a college student.) Still, the experience confirmed what they'd first come to realize while directing *Godspell*. They clicked. They were good (if still juvenile) writers. They understood each other, but also complemented one another. Crane was analytical, his focus homed in on the words on the page. Kauffman was better with emotion, and enjoyed the creative work of taking a story from script to stage and, later, to screen. Down the line, during the production of *Friends*, Crane preferred to stay in the writers' room, tweaking jokes and refining stories, while Kauffman did much of the creative producing on set, checking wardrobe, watching camera blocking, and hashing scenes out with the actors.

What made Kauffman and Crane such a strong team was the fact that they could put their heads together and create something, and then step apart to execute their vision in slightly separate roles. They had talent and dynamism and extraordinary work ethic, but they also had trust. On this foundation, the pair would go on to forge a lifelong friendship, and a twenty-seven-year creative partnership, which would forever alter the trajectory of both network and cable television programming. It was a natural, comfortable interdependence. Together, they just worked.

When people wonder about that ineffable magic that made *Friends* such a hit, much credit (if not all credit) is given to the cast. But Kauffman and Crane were the primary ingredient, no

---

1 If the name "Billy Dreskin" rings a bell, it's because Kauffman and Crane would use it to name an off-screen character in Seasons One and Two. He's first mentioned in "The One with Two Parts: Part 2," where Monica tells Rachel's father that, in high school, Rachel had sex with Billy Dreskin in her parents' bed. The real-life Dreskin was a rabbi by this time, and apparently his congregation was none too thrilled about this shout-out.

question. It was not only the fortitude of their professional relationship, but the intimacy and trust within their personal one.
They were the original friends.

Kauffman and Crane moved to New York after college, pursuing the musical-theater career they'd begun at Brandeis. They
wrote their next show, *Personals*, along with former classmate
Seth Friedman. It was a musical revue about the people behind
newspaper personal ads, featuring music and lyrics by none other
than Alan Menken and Stephen Schwartz—already musical-
theater stars, and on the verge of becoming musical-theater
legends, as well as the musicians behind virtually every Disney
animated feature of the 1990s. *Personals* made the rounds on college festival circuits, and even a USO tour, before landing off-
Broadway in 1985, where it starred a twenty-six-year-old Jason
Alexander. The production was bursting at the seams with talent, and yet reviews were almost comically mixed. "Entertaining and ingenious," declared the *New York Post*. "Unfailingly
mirthless," countered the *Times*.

Still, Kauffman and Crane had laid solid groundwork for what
they planned as a lifelong career in the theater. Only in their
late twenties, they'd already written and mounted a handful of
off-Broadway plays and musicals—some with Kauffman's new
husband, composer Michael Skolff—many of which were well
received. If they weren't yet an established hit, they were on
their way, with no plans to change course.

Then television agent Nancy Josephson came to see *Personals*. She, too, was a relative newbie, on the cusp of titanic success—much of which would arise from her decision to contact
Kauffman and Crane, and eventually sign them as clients. That
night, after seeing the show, she reached out to the playwrights.
Had they ever considered writing for TV? Not really. Did they
want to give it a shot? Why not.

Josephson tasked Kauffman and Crane to come up with ten

television concepts to shop around. Crane is the first to acknowledge that some of the show ideas were, in a word, "crazy." Others were just bad. But Kauffman and Crane were undaunted, perhaps because, being so far removed from Hollywood, they had no real sense of the competition they were up against. At that point, television would be at best a side gig, with both of them still committed to the theater. They flew out to Los Angeles for meetings occasionally, but remained firmly rooted in New York. And then, out of the blue, someone bought one of their scripts.

"Talk about your first work not being your best work," Crane said, shaking his head. "It was called *Just a Guy*. And it was really just about a guy… I don't know, it was really lame." But it was a milestone—a massive turning point in their career. "We sat in the rental car, screaming," Kauffman recalled. *Just a Guy* was never produced, but now they could say that they'd sold something. "And then we were able to sell a few more scripts that didn't get produced," said Crane. On the one hand, they'd spent years doing unpaid work on unproduced scripts, flying back and forth across the country, and this was the big payoff: five minutes of screaming in a rental car, and a fee that, after commission, probably wouldn't cover rent on either of their apartments, let alone both. On the other hand, they were TV writers now, officially. In selling one lousy script, they'd shot past the thousands of other writers out there trying to do just that.

It was the third of three key events in their early professional partnership—the one that made them pack up and leave their lives in New York, to try this TV thing, for real. The first was simply meeting Josephson, and agreeing to her suggestion that they give TV a shot. (When later asked about her role in their career, Josephson took no more or less credit than she was due: "I saw the play and thought they should work in TV. I guess I was right about that.")

The second moment happened after Josephson told them it was time to formalize their writing team. By then, Kauffman and Crane were doing some work as a pair, and some as a trio, with their friend Seth Friedman, who had cowritten *Personals*. Then Josephson brought them a potential gig working on a screenplay. It would turn out to be just another script that never got produced, but the nameless project became a turning point, nonetheless. As Josephson was finalizing the deal, she told Kauffman and Crane they had to decide whether or not they would do this job with Friedman, or work together as a pair. If this was a partnership, it was time to make it official, once and for all. They had twenty-four hours to make the call.

That evening, Kauffman found herself in a taxicab, inching her way home through the driving rain. A sign, she thought. "And I sit up, and I look at the license of the cabdriver. And his name was David Yu." That was it, as far as she was concerned. From then on, it was David and Marta. They were partners. And soon they were off to LA together, for good.

"The meeting that you think is not going to yield anything is the one that's going to change your life." When asked for his advice to aspiring TV writers, this was David Crane's reply. "If success should happen, you have no idea how it's going to happen." He and Kauffman were brought into the television world because of their exceptional creative and story-crafting abilities. They then spent years ideating, pitching, *maybe* selling but never producing, and heading back to the drawing board, hoping the next one would be a hit. In other words, they were following the traditional path toward (fingers crossed) success. But in the end, success turned up in an unexpected detour from that path. It wasn't one of those myriad pitch meetings that got Kauffman and Crane their big break. It was simply the fact Universal Studios had a bunch of old black-and-white TV shows lying around, and was looking for a way to make money off them.

The way the story goes, in the late 1980s, director/producer John Landis had a bungalow on the Universal lot. He hadn't had a hit in a couple years, and so studio chief Sid Scheinberg charged him with the task of coming up with a show using Universal's enormous anthology of midcentury television footage. As Kauffman recalled, they'd brought in "thousands" of writers to invent series ideas around this archival material. Game shows, *Mystery Science Theater*–style shows, and none of it had worked. By the time they reached out to Kauffman and Crane, she said, "they were scraping the bottom of the barrel, talking to two musical-theater writers." They were in Los Angeles, about to fly home to New York after wrapping up yet another fruitless pitch meeting, when Josephson called and asked if they could squeeze in one more before going to the airport. As Crane recalled, "We went in, and they showed us six minutes of black-and-white clips and said, 'What would you do?' And we said, 'We have absolutely no idea.'" Another flop, but, oh, well. Every other writer in town had flopped, too, and anyway, this meeting was little more than a pit stop on the way to the airport. They got on the plane, took off, and that's when something occurred to them. "By the time we got off the plane, we had an idea," said Crane. It wasn't even a pitch, but just a vague concept about a guy who'd grown up watching old TV shows, which popped into his head like funny little thought bubbles. Or something like that. They got home, dropped their bags, and called the studio. "And they said, 'Come back.'"

Kauffman and Crane's airplane pitch would become *Dream On*, a cult HBO comedy series about a divorced father who, like so many of his generation, had been raised in front of the television. In each episode, his fantasies and thoughts appeared, literally, on-screen, via clips from his favorite childhood TV shows. Airing from 1990 to 1996, *Dream On* was a quirky mix of nostalgia and humor. Most importantly, it was, as the critics put it, "adult."

Dream On was one of HBO's first forays into scripted series, debuting at a time when premium cable was stuck in a danger-ous rut. The draw of these channels was the luxury of being able to watch feature films at home, without commercial interruption. Since launching in 1972, HBO had been on a steady, exponential rise. "But then the bubble burst," the *Los Angeles Times* reported. VCRs, pay-per-view, and new basic-cable movie channels like TNT and AMC were now incentivizing viewers to ditch pricey premium subscriptions. In 1990, HBO's customer base grew by only 1.8%, with 4.5% of existing subscribers canceling every month. In creating original programming, HBO couldn't just deliver a show that was good. If they wanted to survive, they had to give people something they couldn't get on network television. Two things, really: sex and swearing. Kauffman and Crane turned in their first draft to Executive Producer John Landis, who sent it back with two notes: "It needs to be funnier, [and] it needs to be dirtier."

Other than that, Kauffman and Crane could pretty much call the shots. They had zero experience and total creative authority. They were thrilled, but panicked, and rightfully so. Shortly before beginning production, recalled Crane: "We were actually talking to a couple writer friends, going, 'Okay, so you hire writers…and then you sit around talking about what the episodes could be? And then does someone go off and write it? Or do you write it as a group?'" The general feedback from their fellow writer friends was something along the lines of "I hate you."

So they winged it. They had a staff of three writers and a warehouse in North Hollywood, where they whipped up a show that they thought was funny, and hoped everyone else would, too. In the end, they didn't win over everyone, but more than enough. *Dream On* was HBO's first definitive hit, as well as Kauffman and Crane's, though today its legacy has been largely lost in the shuffle. Watching it now, it feels very much like a relic of its time: one part a standard story of a divorced dad muddling through middle age, and the other part a naughty cable show, where everyone swears like a sailor and walks around with their nipples out. But look beyond the titillation and it's a quiet triumph.

Dream On was often mixed with the critics; the most typical complaint was that the language and sexuality seemed a little too deliberate, which, of course, it was. But it was a solid success, and signaled a sea change for premium cable, and for HBO in particular. *Dream On* was quickly followed by shows that further cracked the mold of traditional television formats, allowing for both sophisticated and oddball comedy, nuanced and polarizing drama, and the kind of stories that simply didn't sell before, because no one knew if an audience would buy them. It proved that television didn't have to cast the widest net possible in order to be successful. A show could be smart and specific and sellable, all at the same time.

Dream On is not often mentioned alongside those other early series—*The Larry Sanders Show, Oz, The Sopranos, Sex and the City*—which would come to define HBO as a leader in innovative, high-quality entertainment. Indeed, it doesn't belong on the same list as those series. But there is no doubt that *Dream On* was the launch pad for them all. In the wake of all the behemoth successes that came after it, *Dream On* has faded into relative obscurity—an artifact from an era when it was still risqué to drop an *F*-bomb or display two whole butt cheeks in the same frame. But without it, there would be no *Sex and the City*, and almost certainly no *Friends*.

With *Dream On*, Kauffman and Crane had a hit under their belt, an Emmy nomination,[2] as well as the experience of running a show. Most importantly, they now had Kevin S. Bright. "When we first started, technically speaking, we weren't partners. I was their boss," Bright later explained during his own interview with the Television Academy Foundation. Along with John Landis, Bright was an executive producer on *Dream On*. But it became clear very quickly that Bright was a natural—and necessary—collaborator in the Kauffman-Crane partnership.

---

2 Though not a win. "We were up against the *Seinfeld* masturbation episode," Crane recalled. "It was, like, why are we here?"

"He's really good at a lot of stuff that a) we're not great at, and b) we *really* don't care about," Crane explained. Bright knew how to pull together a great crew, manage all the nuts and bolts of producing, and usher a show through postproduction. "[*Dream On*] was a show that lived and died in the editing room," explained Crane, and that was entirely Bright's domain. Plus, they just clicked. "We had shorthand with each other," Bright explained with a shrug. "We were three ex–New Yorkers."

Two years into *Dream On*, the three of them formed Bright/Kauffman/Crane Productions, the company that would produce not only *Friends*, but *Veronica's Closet, Jesse*, and, finally, *Joey*. Shortly thereafter, their deal with Universal was up for renewal, and while *Dream On* was riding high on its surprise success, the studio didn't seem all that eager to make them an offer, or even meet with them. "It was one of those things that happens in television, where the company you're working for feels you owe them," said Bright. "Rather than they owe you for creating success for them." Every other studio was very much interested, though, and after meeting with Les Moonves (then president of Lorimar Television, which soon combined operations with Warner Bros.), they signed a development deal, and left *Dream On*.

The team had only two real deal breakers in mind when it came to future projects: first, no single-star shows. *Dream On's* premise had required lead actor Brian Benben to appear in nearly every scene of every episode, an exhausting demand that often made shooting difficult for him and therefore everyone else on the production team. That was a relatively easy ask given that few network shows relied so heavily on a single character. The second ask was trickier. "We said to [Moonves], 'The only thing we don't want to do is a family in a living room with four cameras.'" It was 1992, the golden age of families in living rooms: *Blossom, Roseanne, Full House, Home Improvement, Family Matters*, and *The Fresh Prince of Bel-Air*. Networks were minting money with these multicamera comedies, and not much else. If you weren't a family in a living room, then you'd better be football.

Thus came Bright/Kauffman/Crane's next show, and first major flop: *Family Album*. It was one of two series they developed during their first year with Warner Bros., the other being *Couples*—a single-camera comedy about three couples living in the same apartment in New York City. That show, they said, was the obvious winner. It flowed right out of them, Crane recalled: "We wrote it in, like, a week! We love it… It's smart, it's single-camera, it's got everything we want." *Family Album*, on the other hand, was multicamera, family-focused, and in terms of writing, "[like] pulling teeth." No one wanted a show like *Couples*, no matter how good it was. They wanted, as one network executive told them, "a white-collar *Roseanne*."

Backed into the living-room corner, they did their best. "We did everything right. We drew on our own lives. It was about this family from Philadelphia. We had characters based on our parents…and yet, for some reason, the DNA was wrong, and it was incredibly hard to write." Still, *Couples* was passed over,[3] while *Family Album* was picked up and ran on CBS. For six weeks.

Family Album was no one's dream project, but its cancellation was still a blow. "Around that point we were feeling not so much like the cable wunderkinds anymore," recalled Bright. "We were more like the cable disappointment." *Dream On* had been a hit, but one hit (and a surprise niche hit at that) is a meager track record. "It was interesting to us how fast the hype about you can change. 'Golden children, eh. You're golden children with tarnish now.'"

That same year, *The Powers That Be*, a show that Kauffman and Crane had created (but hadn't run) for Norman Lear was canceled, too. While they'd hardly written a word of it beyond the pilot episode, they were still credited creators, and thus now had another failure with their name on it.

---

3 *Couples* later reemerged as a television movie, which aired on ABC in July 1994.

Back to the drawing board, again. Sitting in their office at Warner Bros., the three ex–New Yorkers started thinking back to the days before they came out to Hollywood, when they were just out of college and a little lost—but not alone. Kauffman and Crane thought about their old friends from the theater days, and how they'd banded together as a makeshift family, in those years before they'd made their own families, before careers had taken shape, and adult life was still amorphous. "We were looking at that time when the future was more of a question mark. Maybe 'cause that's what we were feeling in that moment," said Kauffman. Maybe there was something there. After all, she thought, "everybody knows that feeling."

Weeks later, it was done. Kauffman and Crane delivered a seven-page pitch for a show they titled *Insomnia Café*.[4]

"This show is about six people in their twenties who hang out at this coffeehouse," they wrote. "It's about sex, love, relationships, careers…a time in your life when everything is possible, which is really exciting and really scary."

The following pages went on to describe potential storylines and character sketches—all drawn from friends in their social circle back in New York, with a little bit of their twentysomething selves thrown in. But ultimately, it was that single and incredibly simple concept that sold the show: "It's about friendship, because when you're young and single in the city, your friends are your family." It was straightforward and endearing, and in 1994, it was exactly what NBC was looking for.

"We wanted to reach that young, urban audience, those kids starting out on their own," remembered Warren Littlefield, former president of NBC Entertainment, in his 2012 book, *Top of the Rock: Inside the Rise and Fall of Must See TV.* He'd been studying the ratings one morning, reviewing numbers in the

---

4   "We were driving along—I think it was Beverly Boulevard—and we saw a place called the Insomnia Café," explained Kauffman. "And I remember we were talking about [how] that would be a cool place to have one of our main sets… We liked the idea of something being overcaffeinated."

major markets—New York, Dallas, Los Angeles, Saint Louis. "I found myself thinking about the people in those cities, particularly the twentysomethings just beginning to make their way… It was very expensive to live in those places as well as a tough emotional journey. It would be a lot easier if you did it with a friend." He'd been hunting for a *Friends*-esque concept ever since, "but none of the contenders had ever lived up to our hopes." Then Kauffman and Crane showed up.

In the historic pilot season of 1994, their pitch remains legendary. "The pitch was like two old friends telling you a story. The jokes were already there," added Karey Burke, who was an NBC executive at the time. "It was theater."

It's a testament to just how good the pair was at pitching that it was such an easy sell. Because, beyond that famous log line and the six character sketches, they really didn't have much else—including a plot or even a solid premise, according to Crane. "I remember pitching it and we were saying, 'Yeah, and basically we're just in their lives. And here are the six characters, and they're specific. But yeah, we're in and out of their apartments and they go about doing stuff. That's your show.'"

NBC bought it—not only a script, but a pilot, as well. At the very least, this would not be another idea sold, bought, and left unproduced. The show's title was changed from *Insomnia Café* to *Friends Like Us*,[5] and Kauffman and Crane sat down to write. In three days flat, the script was done. As with *Couples*, the writing came easily and it came out good. But *Couples* had also been a great pilot that went bust, so they wrote this first script with the understanding that it most likely would be the last. "At the point where you're doing pilots," said Crane, "you don't think you're going to spend the next ten years of your life doing this." No one was all that worried about answering questions like: If Monica is a chef, then why is she home for dinner every night?

---

5   A suggestion that came from David Crane's partner, Jeffrey Klarik, a television writer-producer himself, who was working on *Mad About You* at the time.

Why doesn't anyone lock their doors in this downtown Manhattan apartment building (except when someone is locked out for storyline purposes)? How the hell did a recently homeless, evolution denialist, aura-cleansing weirdo like Phoebe wind up hanging out with these bourgeois squares? As Crane pointed out, at this stage of the process, it just doesn't matter much because, in all likelihood, your show won't survive long enough to answer these questions. "We had absolutely no idea what this show was going to be. For us, it was just another pilot. We'd just had a series canceled. We were thinking we'd never work again, so we were scrambling... [It] was feeling good, but it was just another pilot. Or it was just another pilot until Jimmy Burrows wants to direct it. Excuse me, James Burrows."

If you've watched any network television programming since 1975, then James Burrows is a name you've likely seen thousands of times, but never noticed. He is a director and producer, who has worked on shows including but not limited to: *Taxi*, *Cheers*, *Wings*, *Will & Grace*, *Frasier*, *Dharma & Greg*, *3rd Rock from the Sun*, and *NewsRadio*. As Littlefield describes him in *Top of the Rock*, Burrows is "the most successful director in television comedy—ever." After reading Kauffman and Crane's pilot script, Littlefield called him up. "I literally had no time," Burrows later told the *New York Times*. "But I read it, and I said, 'I can't let anyone else do this.'" He agreed to direct the pilot, but nothing more.

With Burrows signed on, things got more serious. He embraced the loose, low-concept structure of the show, and later, when directing the pilot, would offer several crucial tweaks that made the show stand out. But even with a knockout script and the best television comedy director on board, some NBC executives still had serious "concerns" about the show.

First of all, everyone was too young. What about adding an older character? Someone who could pop in every now and again to give some sage advice to these young folks. Maybe it could be the guy who owned the coffeehouse—or a cop! "You know the children's book *Pat the Bunny*? We had Pat the Cop," said Kauffman. They would eventually write a script incorporating the character, and hated it so much that they called the network and begged them to can the idea, promising to incorporate the parents more or bump up older guest-star appearances. The network agreed. Then there was the issue of the coffeehouse. "You gotta remember what time it was," said Kevin Bright. "Starbucks hadn't really taken hold yet." Neither had the mid-'90s trend of coffeehouse culture, complete with enormous mugs and acoustic guitar music, which *Friends* would soon launch into mainstream popularity (well, *Friends* and Jewel).[6] The network suggested the coffee shop be swapped out for a diner—much like another NBC sitcom. "They came to us and said, 'Why don't you have a diner, like *Seinfeld*. Everyone knows what the diner is.'" It wouldn't be the last time they'd have to fight against being pressed into *Seinfeld*'s mold, but Kauffman, Bright, and Crane pushed back on this, too, believing that audiences would somehow figure out what a coffeehouse was. The network relented, with the caveat that they change the color of the couch.[7] Sure.

One last adjustment was made, changing the title from *Friends Like Us* to *Six of One*,[8] and finally, they were cleared to start shooting the pilot. And then came the infamous slut survey.

The pilot episode featured a storyline in which Monica goes on a date with Paul (Paul the Wine Guy, of course), a man she's had a crush on for ages. During their dinner, he tells her he hasn't been able to have sex with a woman ever since his wife

---

6   It was indeed present in New York City, though. "The coffee shop on *Friends* was put together as a compilation of coffee shops I had visited and taken pictures of in Manhattan," said Kevin Bright. "Just the little pieces of things—like there was one of those coffee shops that actually had a real wood bar as their coffee bar. So, we took that from there."

7   According to Kauffman, the bright orange-red sofa was originally beige, before the network requested the change. Arguably, a very good note.

8   ABC had recently debuted a sitcom called *These Friends of Mine*, and the titles were deemed too similar. That show would later be retitled *Ellen*.

left him. Monica winds up sleeping with him, and the next day finds out that the whole story was a lie he uses to try to get women into bed—leaving her crushed. After a run-through for network executives, West Coast President Don Ohlmeyer spoke up. "At first, he didn't like the storyline, because one of our main characters is sleeping with a guy on the first date," recalled Crane. "[He said,] 'Well, what does that say about her? Doesn't that say she's a whore?'"

At which point, said Kauffman, "fire came out of my nose." She immediately excused herself from the room, incensed, and left Crane to handle the situation. After talking through it, Ohlmeyer came around—but only because Monica winds up feeling hurt and humiliated after the encounter. Her so-called transgression was allowable, only because she was punished for it. As Ohlmeyer put it (according to Kauffman and Crane), "She got what she deserved."

Nevertheless, at Ohlmeyer's insistence, they handed out a survey to one of the test audiences, after another run-through. In the politest of terms the survey asked: What did they think of Monica having unmarried, filthy, and scandalous sex with a man on the first date?

I'm paraphrasing—but just barely, according to Kauffman. Presented as it was, she recalled, the survey might as well have said, "For sleeping with a guy on the first date, do you think Monica is a) a whore, b) a slut, c) too easy." It was clear that Ohlmeyer wanted this storyline cut, and believed the audience would back him up (the other executives apparently didn't agree, but neither did they get in his way).[9] In the end, though, his survey backfired. The audience responded to the scandalous storyline with a resounding *so what*? They didn't care. Monica was a hit.

---

9   It's worth noting that NBC did insist the writers revise an earlier script wherein Paul has an (unseen, unmentioned, but strongly implied) erection. In 1994, even an implied erection was a standards violation.

On May 4, 1994, "The One Where Monica Gets a Roommate"[10] was shot on Stage 5 of Warner Bros. Studios. After wrapping with eight hours' worth of material (two hours of footage from each of the four cameras), it was rushed to an editing studio, where Bright began cutting it into a twenty-two-minute episode. "Kevin worked with the editor, like, forty-eight hours straight," said Crane. It was one of the very last episodes shot that pilot season, and there would be no time for additional notes. Bright sent off the finished pilot, got in his car, and started driving home to get some sleep. His car phone rang.

Don Ohlmeyer had one more note: "Pace it up." The beginning was too slow. That opening sequence of conversation clips in Central Perk was plodding and not grabby enough. Ohlmeyer had called Kauffman and Crane, who desperately explained that the opening conversations were just that—just talking. It had always been written that way, and at this point it was already shot; there was no way to "pace up" plain-old back-and-forth talking without literally speeding up the soundtrack. Ohlmeyer replied with an ultimatum: "If you don't somehow pace up the beginning, this show is not going on the air." In a panic, they called Bright, who turned his car around and went back to the editing suite.

That's how *Friends* got its first title sequence—not the one in the fountain with its famously catchy theme song. That came later. "The opening sequence was something that almost never was," said Bright. Initially, it was set to air without one at all. *Friends* was on the air at the time, using only a brief, animated title card. Networks thought of long openings and theme songs as an opportunity for viewers to change the channel, thus Kauffman, Bright, and Crane had been told in no uncertain terms that their show couldn't have one. But now it needed one.

Bright asked if he could have an hour to turn something around. He called the music editor and asked her to cut together

---

10   The episode was given this title after the fact. Originally, it was simply "The Pilot."

a forty-five-second version of REM's "Shiny Happy People," using only the chorus. "And then I said to the editor, 'I want you to scan through the show, and I'm just gonna say stop. Whatever image we stop on, pull that image.'" One hour later, they sent back the pilot with this cobbled-together compilation of screen grabs and REM. They didn't cut a single moment of the actual show, but forty-five seconds of pop music was good enough for Ohlmeyer.

After several rounds of testing the pilot with audiences, NBC's attitude about the show was one of hesitant glee. It didn't test well, but testing is a notoriously unreliable diagnostic—and, internally, everyone could see there was something good and exciting here. So the network decided to take a gamble. They called the cocreators and told them they were giving the show the 8:30 slot on Thursday nights, placed right in between *Mad About You* and *Seinfeld*. In 1994, there was literally no more prime spot in prime-time television. There was just one final note: the network wanted to change the title again, and simply call it *Friends*. Bright's response: "If you put us on Thursday nights, you can call us *Kevorkian* for all I care."

Everything that came next is, without a doubt, a success story—if not a straightforward one. It took a fortuitous blend of talent, left turns, and elbow grease just to get the show up to this, its starting point. All that is thanks, almost entirely, to the wisdom and relentless work of Marta Kauffman, David Crane, and Kevin Bright—with the support (and occasional roadblocks) of numerous collaborators and one incredibly powerful television network. But if there was a magic formula to *Friends* that launched the show from a promising but tepid pilot into a stratospheric hit, then the final key ingredient was the cast. On its own, the show is good—exceptionally so. But, as David Schwimmer realized the first day he came to work and met his five new counterparts, "the miracle is the casting."

2

The One with Six Kids and a Fountain

On a summer night in 1994, six young actors boarded a private jet in Los Angeles and flew to Las Vegas for dinner. It was director James Burrows's idea. The pilot episode of *Friends* had been shot and delivered, but not yet aired. NBC was so enthused about the first script that they'd already ordered a full season of episodes. Poor testing aside, Burrows had the unshakable feeling that they had a hit on their hands. On top of that, they had six overexcited pilot stars knocking around the Warner Bros. lot, unsure if their show would go anywhere, but nevertheless riding high on all the hype. Burrows called Les Moonves: "Give me the plane. I'd like to take the kids to Vegas."[11]

On the hour-long flight, Burrows showed the cast their episode, for the very first time. When they landed, he took them all to dinner at Spago, Wolfgang Puck's flagship restaurant and

---

11 It wasn't quite as easy and glamorous as it sounds. Burrows sometimes tells a slightly different version of this story wherein he comes off sounding less like the Godfather and more like Dad. "These kids, they all wanna go to Vegas." Moonves told him too bad, he couldn't just lend him an airplane. Burrows countered, "I'll pay for dinner." Fine.

legendary '90s celebrity hotspot. ("It was so *fancy*," Jennifer Aniston recalled nearly twenty years later, grinning at the giddy memory.) The whole group was overwhelmed and dazzled, itching to go out and do whatever it was that hot young television actors were supposed to do when they flew into Vegas on private jets. Then, in the middle of dinner, Burrows held up his hands and said what he'd brought them here to say: "This is your last shot at anonymity."

Burrows had agreed to stay on for a few more episodes, and would eventually direct the majority of Season One. But he'd already seen firsthand the audience response. "They loved these characters. They laughed at these characters. They were six young people who were handsome and pretty *and* funny." This dinner, he told the cast, would be their last night out as ordinary people, their "last fling" with normality, before the swarming fans descended. Burrows looked around the table at six blank faces, and hit the point again, perhaps a little too hard: "From now on, your lives are over."

They didn't buy it. "Everyone was like, '*Wow*, oh, my *God*,'" remembered Lisa Kudrow. "I sat there going, 'Well, we'll see.'" Matt LeBlanc was incredulous, but then he remembered who he was talking to.

All due respect to Burrows, it was a fairly ridiculous prediction—optimistic, to say the least. Most new shows didn't (still don't) survive, and even the hits didn't hit *that* hard. Complicating things further, his cast was in a tenuous position, with some of them committed to other series. If one of them had to drop out, they would lose that preternatural chemistry that so electrified studio audiences. In all likelihood, this "last shot" in Vegas would be their first and only taste of celebrity life. The cast accepted this "warning" with respect, but with a grain or two of salt, as well. So, Burrows—the man they'd come to nickname "Papa"—gave in, and asked if they wanted to go gamble.

By the following year, his prophecy would have come true

and then some, with all the cast members earning six-figure fees for a single Diet Coke endorsement, on top of their growing per-episode salaries. But that night in Vegas, Burrows said, "They didn't have a pot to piss in." They each wrote Burrows checks for a couple hundred dollars and he gave them some cash to go hit the casinos. "We were having so much fun, I didn't care what was happening," recalled Aniston. They had jobs and they had some pocket money and no idea of what was to come. Aniston, at least, also had no idea how to gamble. "I barely understood what cards were."

But that night she learned, and in the months to come, poker would become a mainstay on the *Friends* set. Burrows let the cast borrow his dressing room (the largest on set) so they could play during rehearsal or shooting breaks. This would eventually become the basis for the Season One episode, "The One with All the Poker."[12] But that night in Las Vegas, it was Burrows's way of bonding the cast off-screen—almost corralling them into real-life friendships. He knew—everyone knew—from the first read-through, that they clicked as actors. But chemistry would only go so far. If, and hopefully when, the show took off, he knew they'd have to like and support each other, as colleagues and collaborators. No one had successfully launched a comedy ensemble of this size. Burrows understood that if *his* ensemble was going to pull it off, they'd have to step into the spotlight as a team.

David Schwimmer was the first to be recruited. He was the only one, in fact, for whom a character had been written specifically, and the only one who was offered his role sight unseen. He said no.

Schwimmer was born in the Flushing neighborhood of Queens, New York, in 1966, but moved with his parents (both

---

12   It would also be reflected in a popular promotional poster, featuring the cast in a poker-game setup, which graced many a bedroom wall in the 1990s.

lawyers) and older sister, Ellie, to Los Angeles at the age of two. From the start, he recognized himself as an outsider in this industry town, a feeling he would never shake, even when he became one of the most successful and recognizable people in it.

At Beverly Hills High School (the legendary high school that would become fodder for numerous film and television series, including *Beverly Hills, 90210*), Schwimmer was both a nerdy, metal-mouthed outcast and a bully, by his own admission. He joined the drama club, where he found his friends (including actor Jonathan Silverman, who would become the breakout star of *Weekend at Bernie's*) as well as a passion for theater. One night, his parents took him to see Ian McKellen's one-man show, *Acting Shakespeare*, and upon leaving the theater, Schwimmer knew without question that he wanted to be an actor himself. "I watched this guy without any props, or makeup, or changes of clothing, or anything—I watched him simply sit in a chair and stand occasionally, and transform into about twelve different lead characters from the greatest of Shakespeare's plays. And I couldn't believe it, it was like a magic trick," he said. "I think that was the moment for me, really."

But outside of that one extracurricular, he was miserable and itching to leave. His was a family of bone-deep New Yorkers, and while his parents' careers flourished in Hollywood (his mother famously handled Roseanne Barr's first divorce), they never let their children forget that there was a much bigger world outside the sunny bubble of LA. Arthur Schwimmer and Arlene Colman-Schwimmer were fun parents but not lax ones; Schwimmer later remembered his childhood household as one full of laughter and after-dinner card games, but also a constant focus on academic achievement. His mother, in particular, imbued in David a social conscience, particularly when it came to issues of gender equality[13]—an ethos that would later emerge at a pivotal point during *Friends* production.

But back then, Schwimmer was a theater kid, not an aspiring TV star. He loved his close-knit family, but not his hometown. "When I was there I always felt: this is not me. I'm surrounded by people with a different value system. And I just wanted to get out of California." When he was a senior, producers from the hit Broadway production of Eugene O'Neill's *Brighton Beach Memoirs* came to LA to audition replacements for the show. The Beverly Hills High drama teacher submitted both Schwimmer and his friend Silverman for the lead role of Eugene Jerome, originated by Matthew Broderick. But Schwimmer's parents soon intervened. They were die-hard theater fans themselves, and supportive of their son's ambitions—but not at the cost of higher education. "No, you're not going to Broadway," they told him. "You're going to school."

Silverman won the part, and Schwimmer went off to Northwestern University. Despite his initial disappointment, Schwimmer's college experience became one of—if not *the*—most crucial points in his life as an actor. Just like Marta Kauffman and David Crane, Schwimmer made his closest friends and theatrical collaborators in college, and with them he founded the Lookingglass Theatre Company, shortly before graduating in 1988. Thirty years later, the nonprofit ensemble company continues to mount productions, often with Schwimmer at the helm as director or producer. From those early days, Schwim-

---

13 Much more could be written about Arlene Colman-Schwimmer, a woman who has devoted her career and personal life to the cause of feminism. Among other things, she was the leader of two women's law associations, the original incorporator and chairperson of the National Women's Political Caucus, and a former officer of NOW. In law school, she was one of seven women in a class of 349. "The criminal law professor called on the women only to recite the sex crimes—in order to embarrass us," she later recalled. When she expressed interest in pursuing a criminal law career, she was told outright "to find a husband and have babies." Colman-Schwimmer would go on to have a long and incredibly successful career as a divorce lawyer (one of the only "acceptable" specialties for a female lawyer at that time), and later started her own practice focusing on sex discrimination and family law.

mer's passion for American social-justice causes transferred to
the stage, where he explored contemporary plays about race
and economic inequality, alongside classics like *The Odyssey*
and *Our Town*. The Chicago theater scene as we know it today
was young (Steppenwolf, the influential theater company, having only been founded about a decade prior), but it was growing fast. Moments away from graduating one of the country's
most respected acting programs, Schwimmer found himself on
the swell of a thrilling new wave of American theater. And, at
last, he'd found a community of which he felt a part, blissfully
removed from Hollywood in every sense of the word.

Then came the senior showcase, the traditional conclusion to
every college theater program. As usual, a handful of agents and
managers flew in from New York and Los Angeles to watch
the graduating students perform and keep an eye out for fresh
talent. Schwimmer performed a selection from Tom Stoppard's
Rosencrantz and Guildenstern Are Dead, after which one of the
LA-based managers approached and gave him the I'm-gonna-
make-you-a-star speech. In the grand tradition of earnest and
perhaps *slightly* self-serious college theater majors, Schwimmer
rebuffed the idea of movie stardom. For the most part. The
manager pressed, assuring Schwimmer that if he just came back
to LA, he'd be cast in a heartbeat, make buckets of money, no
problem. "Mind you, I was incredibly naive, and I believed her
when she said I would make a very good living, very quickly,"
Schwimmer said. It is hard to imagine any twenty-two-year-
old—even one who'd spent senior year securing 501(c)(3) status
for his nonprofit theater company—not being drawn to the daz-
zling promise of instant, enormous fame. In the end, though,
Schwimmer says he did it for the money. He had a plan.

As Schwimmer explained to his theater company, he would
go to LA with this manager, make a quick million dollars, and
bring it back to Chicago so they could use it to build their own
theater. It would take, like, six months—maybe eight. "This is

how naive—and also full of myself—I was," Schwimmer re-called decades later. Back then, he and his classmates were the big fish in a small but prestigious pond. Again, as Kauffman and Crane had done just a few years earlier, Schwimmer took a sabbatical from the theater world—certain it would be a brief and lucrative one.

It was neither. In the end, only the manager turned out to be temporary. In those first eight months, Schwimmer did get a role in a television movie, as well as an agent, Leslie Siebert (who is now a senior managing partner at the Gersh Agency, and still reps Schwimmer today). But nothing else. Discouraged and humbled, Schwimmer went back to Chicago and joined his company at Lookingglass.

For years, Schwimmer hopped between Chicago and Los Angeles, where he'd pick up the occasional bit part on shows like *NYPD Blue* and *Blossom*. Mostly, though, he waited tables for half a decade. "I worked at nearly every Daily Grill in Los Angeles," he said. His first real break was a small four-episode role on *The Wonder Years*. The night the first episode aired, Schwimmer was working the dinner shift at a Daily Grill on La Cienega Boule-vard, which had a TV behind the bar. "Hey, Schwimmer, you're on TV!" called his friend working the bar, and Schwimmer spent the next half hour giddily sneaking glimpses at the show while bouncing back and forth between dinner-rush diners. "So, I'm waiting tables and catching myself on TV for the first time. And then back to, 'Hey, do you want blue cheese or Thousand Island?'"

Then, in 1993, Schwimmer once again found himself up against his high-school friend Jonathan Silverman, when both were called to audition for the same part on a new pilot. The show was Kauffman and Crane's ill-fated *Couples*, and again, Sil-verman got the part. But Kauffman and Crane loved Schwim-mer's audition, and when *Couples* fizzled and they began sketching out characters for the *Insomnia Café* pitch, it was his performance that inspired the character of Ross. "David had this wonderful hangdog vulnerability," recalled Kauffman. "And he just stuck in our minds."

In the meantime, Schwimmer had landed a role on *Monty*, a new Fox sitcom starring Henry Winkler, about a conservative, Rush Limbaugh–esque radio host and his left-wing liberal family. It was, without question, the biggest job he'd ever gotten. He was a series regular with a five-year contract, and money in the bank for the first time. And it was a nightmare. "As beautiful a guy as Henry Winkler was, the experience wasn't very empowering for me," Schwimmer later explained. "I'm a very collaborative person, and if you're going to work with me as an actor then I want to *bring* something to it." He'd try to throw out ideas and discuss with the writers, but nobody wanted to hear it from an actor (maybe Winkler, but not this kid). Naively, he'd expected television would be like ensemble theater, with everyone pitching in creatively and working as a team. Instead, he was just an actor working alongside—not *with*—everyone else. They shot thirteen episodes, but to Schwimmer's great relief, *Monty* was canceled after the first six aired. The LA experiment was over. Schwimmer went straight back to Chicago, telling his agent not to send him anything, and certainly no more TV jobs. After *Monty*, he was done. The Lookingglass company mounted an adaptation of Mikhail Bulgakov's Stalin-era novel, *The Master and Margarita*, at Steppenwolf, with Schwimmer in the role of Pontius Pilate. Having gotten as far away from network television as possible, Schwimmer got a call from Siebert. Yes, she knew he didn't want to do any more sitcoms, but there was this new script he just had to read.

No.

But these were the writers from that great pilot *Couples*. And they wrote this part *for* him.

Incredibly flattering, but no. Thank you.

And it's an ensemble.

At this, Schwimmer paused. His only real priority was working with a true ensemble. Knowing that, and the fact that this part had been written just for him, it seemed absurd and disrespectful not to at least consider it. He agreed to read the script, but nothing more. Kauffman and Crane were friends with Robby Benson, an actor/director[14] who Schwimmer greatly admired. The writers asked Benson to give Schwimmer a call and see what he might do to persuade him to come back and meet with them—just a meeting! It wasn't as if this show would actually go anywhere. It was just a pilot, come on! Still, he hedged a bit. Finally, they brought in the biggest gun possible, and asked Burrows to call. Schwimmer got on the plane.

Matthew Perry was broke. While Schwimmer was being wooed via telephone, hemming and hawing over the role that had been tailor-made for him, Matthew Perry was frantically calling his agents, begging them to get him a gig. Didn't matter what kind of gig as long as it was shooting *now*. His business manager had just called to inform him that he had no money. No, he wasn't running low on money—he was out. He needed a job, ideally today.

At twenty-three, Perry had been a working actor for almost ten years. Though born in Williamstown, Massachusetts, he was raised in Ottawa, Ontario, primarily by his mother, Suzanne Langford, a journalist and one-time press secretary to Canadian Prime Minister Pierre Trudeau. Perry attended the same grade school as the PM's son, and future Canadian leader/beloved political dreamboat, Justin Trudeau. (In 2017, Perry famously confessed on a late-night talk show that in fifth grade, he and his friend Chris Murray beat up Trudeau because they were jealous of his athletic ability.[15]) His mother later married

---

14 Depending on your generation, you may know him best as the romantic lead of *Ice Castles* or the voice of the Beast in Disney's animated feature *Beauty and the Beast*. He would later direct six episodes of the first three seasons of *Friends*.

15 Ever the charmer, Trudeau replied on Twitter: "I've been giving it some thought, and you know what, who hasn't wanted to punch Chandler? How about a rematch @MatthewPerry?" To the internet's great delight, Perry concluded the "incident" with a Chandler-style response: "I think I will pass at your request for a rematch, kind sir (given that you currently have an army at your disposal)."

journalist Keith Morrison (best known to Americans as a long-time correspondent on *Dateline NBC*). As for his father, Perry said, he mostly saw him on TV.

While Perry spent most of his youth in a community far removed from show business, his father was one of the most recognizable faces on television at the time. John Bennett Perry was the iconic "Old Spice Man," appearing in ads throughout the 1970s and '80s. He notched small roles in numerous films and television episodes of the era, as well, but to this day he remains famous as the dashing but rugged symbol of commercial masculinity. At fifteen, Perry went to live with his father, and was none too thrilled to find himself the son of a sex symbol. "I would never bring a girl home, because all the girls would just go, 'Who's *that* guy?' 'That's my dad. I know. When you guys are done, I'll be in therapy.'"

Perry had moved to the States to further his tennis career. In Canada, he'd become a nationally ranked player among boys under fourteen. When he got to LA, however, he discovered that being one of the best tennis players in Ottawa was about as impressive as being one of the top-ranked ice hockey players in Southern California. He was a natural athlete, but simply couldn't compete, so he shifted his focus on his second favorite extracurricular activity: acting. It was a natural move for an LA teenager, especially one with built-in connections. And as he himself would readily acknowledge, Perry was always a performer, a competitive or even desperate seeker of the spotlight. "I was a guy who wanted to become famous," he told the *New York Times* in 2002. "There was steam coming out of my ears, I wanted to be famous so badly."

With his father's agent representing him, Perry booked one-off roles here and there, on shows like *Charles in Charge* and *Silver Spoons*. In 1987, he landed the lead in a long-forgotten *Second Chance*, a Fox comedy about a man who dies in a hovercraft accident in 2011,[16] meets Saint Peter, is deemed not bad enough for hell but not good enough for heaven, and so instead is sent back to earth in the 1980s in order to help his teenage self make better decisions. How's that for a log line? The show was briefly pulled off the air after poor ratings (astonishing, I know!), retooled slightly, and brought back under the title *Boys Will Be Boys*. The new version still didn't work, and today, the show is best known simply for featuring one of Matthew Perry's first lead roles.[17]

After that, Perry continued to bounce between guest spots, appearing once or twice on dozens of the most popular series of the 1980s and '90s, including one episode of *Dream On*, where he met Kauffman, Bright, and Crane. He wasn't famous but he was visible and busy and making a decent living. At least he thought he was, until his phone rang one day and he found out he was broke.

But at least he was broke during pilot season. Shortly after calling his agents, Perry got an offer to do the pilot of yet another Fox sitcom with a premise that sounds more like an ill-advised audience prompt at an improv comedy show. *LAX 2194* was about airport baggage handlers working at Los Angeles International Airport, in the year 2194. "I was the head baggage handler," Perry recalled. "And my job, in the show, was to sort out aliens' luggage." Ryan Stiles and Kelly Hu costarred as futuristic US customs agents,[18] and for reasons I cannot begin to imagine, the producers decided to cast little people as the aliens.

Despite the bright red flags, Perry said yes to the role. He had to. Sure, it might complicate things in the long term; if the pilot turned into a series, then Perry would be locked into play-

---

16 Apparently, in 1987, it was still assumed we'd have replaced cars with hover-crafts by 2011.

17 In an incredibly bizarre coincidence, it is also known for having "predicted" Colonel Muammar Gaddafi's death. But that's a whole other kettle of fish. For further reading, see the internet.

18 Again, the sitcom version of "the future" is one in which we've invented hovercrafts and learned to coexist with extraterrestrial beings, and yet we still have to deal with the same old bullshit at the airport.

ing a twenty-second-century baggage handler. But that seemed extremely improbable to everyone except, presumably, the network executives who'd greenlit the pilot. *LAX 2194* would keep Perry out of the running for other roles, but only for one pilot season. What he didn't know was that, over on the Warner Bros. lot, his name was on a list of actors to be brought in for another show. And it was close to the top.

Perry did know about the pilot itself, though—everyone did. "It was the script that everybody was talking about," he recalled. He knew, too, that he was perfect for it. All his friends were being brought in to read for it, and Perry kept getting calls from them saying, "There's this guy on this show that is *you.*" The role of Chandler Bing wasn't written for Perry, the way Ross had been for Schwimmer, but it might as well have been, so close was the resemblance. Chandler was a mix of silliness and bone-dry sarcasm, a mask over his insecurity, which slipped just often enough to let you see the genuine, sweet guy beneath (in desperate need of therapy). Yeah, Perry thought, that sounded familiar.

Kauffman, Crane, and Bright felt the same way about Perry. Too bad he was already on that alien airport show, or whatever it was. Perry would have been perfect, but they didn't want to bring on any cast members in second position. "Second position" casting is a common but extremely awkward scenario in the television business: an actor who's already working on one pilot or series gets cast in another pilot—with the assumption that the show they're already working on will get canned, freeing them up for the new gig. On the other hand, if the actor's first-position show *isn't* canceled, then they're stuck with it, and their second-position show has to be recast and reshot. It's a necessary evil in an industry where projects fail far more often than succeed, but still, no one wants to cast their pilot with someone they have second dibs on.

Anyway, Kauffman and Crane thought, Chandler would be

one of the easiest roles to cast. So much of the character's humor was already built in; he had jokes, and lots of dialogue an actor could work with. But after three weeks and countless auditions, they still hadn't found him. Perry himself had coached several candidates, many of whom were his friends. He even tried to teach them some of those specific mannerisms and speech patterns that became so iconic to the role. Could it *be* any more obvious?[19]

Also obvious, to Perry at least, was the fact that *LAX 2194* was not a winner. Particularly not during this pilot season, which was packed with an unprecedented number of hits-to-be—*ER*, *Party of Five*, *Chicago Hope*, *Touched by an Angel*—and future beloved cult hits like *My So-Called Life* and *The Critic*. He called his agents constantly, begging them to book him a *Friends* audition. Yes, he'd be in second position, but surely he was a safe second.[20]

Meanwhile, the *Friends* creators were on their third week of Chandler readings. While no one fit the bill exactly, actor Craig Bierko came the closest. He was a good friend of Perry's, and had been well-coached by him. Bierko had also been on *The Powers That Be* (the disastrous show Kauffman and Crane had created for Norman Lear), and they knew him to be a great actor and a good guy. He wasn't a perfect fit, and some at the network thought he was downright wrong, but after nearly a month of auditioning every other available actor, it was time to move on. They offered Bierko the part and sent him the script. He declined.

Bierko has since gone on to have a successful career of his own, and while he will always be known as The One Who Turned Down *Friends*, he readily acknowledges that he only got

---

19 Perry himself had adopted this cadence from his grade-school classmates Brian and Chris Murray (of the Justin Trudeau incident). "[They] were like, 'Could that teacher be any meaner?' And I was like, 'Whoa. In twenty years, I'm gonna buy a Malibu house 'cause of that.'"

20 "Safe second" is a less official term, but just as necessary an evil as "second position," and it's exactly what it sounds like. Ex. A show about baggage handlers? Oh, sure, bring him in. He's a safe second.

the offer by doing a very good Matthew Perry impression. He had the chance to take the starring role in another pilot, which simply seemed like a better opportunity than being one of six in an ensemble. With the second-best Chandler out of the picture, Perry was finally able to nag his way into the room. His agents called to tell him he had an audition, and when Perry hung up the phone, a feeling came over him. "I instantly knew my whole life was going to change—which has never happened before or since then. I knew I was going to get it. I knew it was going to be huge. I just knew."

Perry read for Kauffman on Wednesday, then Warner Bros. on Thursday, and once more, for NBC, on Friday. But as Kauffman remembered, it was a done deal from the first line: "He came in, and that was it." Second position or not, he was worth the gamble. On Monday morning, Matthew Perry came to work. He was Chandler Bing.

Phoebe Buffay should have been a casting nightmare. She was a trapezoidal peg in a round hole. The character's over-the-top bohemian vibe, combined with a backstory of hideous trauma, set her so far apart from the rest of the group that her presence itself begged the constant question: *Why is she here?* It should have taken months to find an actress who could juggle all of Phoebe's oddities, maintain her level of woo-woo while remaining tethered to reality, and manage to convince an audience that she had a deep connection to these people with whom she had nothing at all in common. Then Lisa Kudrow walked in and just did it. Done.

During *Friends'* heyday, much to-do would be made in the media over Kudrow's prowess at playing ditzes despite the fact that, in reality, she's an intelligent, highly educated woman. In later years, when Kudrow launched another successful career as a writer and producer (*and* actor), the narrative flipped. *Turns out Phoebe's actually smart!* In both eras, Kudrow succeeded, in large part, due to one very wise decision: she didn't listen to any of that. She just showed up and did her job.

By her own admission, Kudrow was a markedly serious young woman—so much so that her parents were concerned she'd never have a social or romantic life. She grew up in LA, but, like David Schwimmer, was raised in a family with no interest in Hollywood, and certainly not celebrity culture. She describes her mother, Nedra, a travel agent, as "the classiest lady that I'd ever encountered." Nedra was reserved and refused to gossip, qualities that Kudrow always aspired to. On the other hand, her father was a talker. He had a performative nature, which he passed on to his children, of which Lisa was the youngest. Dr. Lee N. Kudrow was a renowned physician and researcher, specializing in headache medicine. From an early age, Kudrow intended to follow his example and go into medicine herself— not just because she greatly admired her father's work, but because it seemed respectable.

At an even *earlier* age, Kudrow had wanted to be an actress. In nursery school she'd memorized and recited *Alice in Wonderland* to her family, and through her adolescence she did school plays and summer theater programs. But in high school, things changed. "That's when I started thinking, 'What kind of adult am I going to be?'" She loved performing, but the idea of calling herself an actress didn't sit right. She had the (not entirely wrong) idea that actors were looked down upon, in the wider world, and perhaps she looked down on them, too. Plus, she had other interests. Kudrow was an excellent student, particularly adept at biology. She would become a doctor, she decided. "I thought, 'Yeah that's good. That's the kind of mom I think your kids will be proud of.'"

Not many people enter high school considering the respect of their future children, but that's the kind of teenager Kudrow was. She stuck to the plan through college. After graduating from Vassar with a BSc in biology, she went to work with her father on a study of hemispheric dominance and headache types,[21] hoping that having her name on a published paper would be helpful in applying to graduate school.

But something changed that summer. She'd be driving around, listening to the radio, and an ad for some new sitcom would come on, reminding listeners to tune in that night. They'd play a clip of dialogue from the show—some joke with a big punch line, followed by a wave of laugh track. "This thought would pop into my head: 'God, punching that joke so hard. Just throw it away. Lisa, remember to throw it away—it'll be funnier.'" What? Where did that come from? It was spooky, but she couldn't stop it. All of a sudden, Kudrow had this bossy little acting coach in her head. Every time she watched a TV show or heard an ad on the radio, it would pipe up: "Okay, remember to do it *this* way when *you* do it."

Kudrow pushed back against herself. *Remember your kids? You're not going to be an actor.* "I just kept trying to shove that away," she recalled. Then one more voice chimed in, suggesting she give it a shot. This time, she listened—because that voice belonged to Jon Lovitz. Lovitz had been her older brother's best friend since childhood, and she'd seen up close how long and hard he'd struggled to break into show business. But that summer, Lovitz was cast on *Saturday Night Live*. "And I realized, oh, my God. So this is something that actually can work out. For real people." Maybe even people with kids.

Lovitz urged Kudrow to check out LA's legendary improv comedy school, The Groundlings. Just take a class and see what happened—no harm in that, right? *Right*, Kudrow thought. She was twenty-two years old. She didn't yet have children to raise or a mortgage to pay, or any of those looming adult responsibilities she'd been preparing for since ninth grade. This was the time to take risks. *If not now, when?*

---

21 Translation: whether or not left-handed people are more likely to get cluster headaches.

Nervously, she approached her parents with the news. "Fantastic," they said. "When do you start?" She was surprised at the time, but on reflection, Kudrow suspected they were worried about her. Of course they were proud of how hard she'd worked and how career-focused she was, but there was more to life than mortgages and hemispheric dominance. Like, say, dating. She needed *something* to help her lighten up. Improv classes? "Thank God, yes, go. Right now. We'll drive you."

That was it for biomedical research. Kudrow went from taking classes at The Groundlings to teaching them part-time. Still, it took a while to step out of her comfort zone, even as she began to build a roster of characters. The first one she ever performed was a biology professor. "I started with what I knew," she recalled. And then she pretty much continued as such, creating a host of very smart, very serious academic types, whose humor lay in the fact that they didn't realize how boring they were. Kudrow was great at playing these roles and, ever the A-student, she stayed in her lane—until the day her teacher, Tracy Newman,[22] nudged her out of it. "We've never seen a dumb character from you," she told Kudrow. "We need to see an airhead. Just go for it."

She quickly whipped up something based on girls she'd known in high school, and soon discovered she could play dumb as well as smart. One airhead led to another, and she wound up getting cast in her first play, *Ladies' Room*, written by Robin Schiff (another Groundling), for which she created the character Michele. She had about five minutes of stage time in *Ladies' Room*, but Michele would later reemerge as one of Kudrow's most beloved film roles, in *Romy and Michele's High School Reunion* (also written by Schiff).

Kudrow kept a day job, doing administrative work in her fa-

---

22 A writer and producer herself, Newman would go on to win an Emmy for cowriting the landmark episode of *Ellen* in which DeGeneres's character came out as a lesbian.

ther's office, while she began to pick up more auditions here and there. The Groundlings gave her a degree of visibility, but she was never touted as one of the group's superstars (or else she didn't see herself as such). Still, as she landed her first, small television gigs, Kudrow began to form a new career goal: she wanted to be on a sitcom.

Almost immediately, the dream came true. In 1993, Kudrow got a principal role in one of the hottest new pilots of the year—one that had all the elements working in its favor: it was the spin-off of an incredibly popular sitcom, it featured an established TV star, and Burrows was attached to direct. Lisa Kudrow had won the part of Roz on *Frasier*. Four days into production, she was fired.

"They originally wanted Peri Gilpin," Kudrow would later explain of the *Frasier* debacle. The part of Roz had actually been written for her, though Kudrow didn't yet know that. And thanks to her training, Kudrow had gotten very good at auditioning—sometimes to her detriment. She could nail a scene in the room, even if she knew in the back of her mind that she wasn't right for the role, and would never be able to sustain the performance long-term. Unfortunately, she learned that lesson on *Frasier*. Kudrow tanked the first table-read. "Then at the rehearsals Jimmy would say, 'It's not working, don't worry about it, don't even try.'" She was sure Burrows hated her, that everyone hated her. The chemistry just didn't work, and as production fumbled forward, Kudrow felt all eyes on her. Whatever magic she'd had in the audition room, it was long gone. Kudrow was quickly fired (and nicely fired, she insisted) and replaced by Gilpin.

Maybe it was a sign, Kudrow thought. She'd gotten her big shot and blown it so tremendously, so publicly. This whole city—this whole planet—was full of people who wanted to make it, and never would. *Maybe you're one of those people*, she thought. *Maybe you're just not meant to do it*. Her old friend and director,

Robin Schiff, tried to pep her up, giving her the classic when-one-door-closes-a-window-opens talk. The city was also full of scripts in development and shows in production, windows aplenty. Kudrow waved off the platitude. Then she got another call, from actor Richard Kind—who gave her the opposite of a pep talk: "I heard what happened and I *can't* believe it... How [do] you get out of bed every morning, get dressed, walk out the door, and show yourself in *public*? I wouldn't be able to do it."

It was *so* melodramatic that Kudrow snapped out of it. She'd lost a TV show, not a lung. She would survive this and, in fact, she was doing okay. Every day, she did go out in public, taking morning walks to the pastry shop, Michel Richard, where she'd treat herself to a *pain au chocolat* and a coffee, and then stroll around the neighborhood. Her brown hair began to lighten in the sun, and something about it made her feel better. She went to a colorist, asking her to match the new golden highlights in her hair, and over the course of six months, as she muddled through the post-*Frasier* funk, Kudrow became a full-blown blonde. "It literally lightened me up," she said. It was an internal shift as much as a physical one, and with one door firmly closed and behind her, she was on the lookout for her next big window.

Any window, really—didn't have to be a big one. Kudrow was in better emotional shape but financially not so much. She began looking around for another day job when her agent called one morning. Danny Jacobson, the cocreator and executive producer of *Mad About You*, wanted her for a waitress role. (Kudrow had previously appeared in a Season One flashback episode, and though it was a tiny part, she'd made a strong impression.) It was a last-minute thing, and the nameless character had just a couple lines of dialogue, so she wouldn't have to audition or anything, but she'd get a guest-star credit. "I don't think you should do it," Kudrow's agent told her. It was disrespectful, calling her in for a no-name role without even sending her sides to read, and anyway, "you'd have to be there, like, in an hour." Kudrow jumped in the car.

The no-name waitress was a hit, and by the end of the week, Jacobson asked if she might be available for a few more episodes. Soon, she had a name—Ursula—and even a small fan base. Sometimes people on the street recognized Kudrow as the clueless waitress from *Mad About You*, and *TV Guide* gave her a "cheers" in the Cheers & Jeers section. That alone felt like a watershed moment to Kudrow. She was back! It was happening! If nothing else happened, she would always know that she had been a popular, recurring (not regular, but whatever) character on what everyone agreed was the *best* comedy on network television. If this was the top, great. And it probably would be, so she'd better do her damnedest not to screw this up.

Pilot season came around again, and like everyone else, Kudrow heard the chatter about this hot new script about a group of friends who hung out in a coffee shop. Jeffrey Klarik was a writer on *Mad About You*, as well as David Crane's boyfriend. Kudrow didn't know that at the time, but later she'd speculate that Klarik was the reason she wound up getting called in for Phoebe, and went straight to the producers to read. As Kauffman recalled, when Kudrow began to speak, it was in Phoebe's voice, just as they had written it. "It was *exactly* what we heard."

Next, she was sent to read for Burrows—and Kudrow knew it was over. He hated her, she was sure. During the disastrous *Frasier* pilot, it was Burrows who'd first recognized that *she* was the disaster. So, fine, this would be the end of the line for *Friends*, but who cared? She still had *Mad About You*. Knowing she had nothing to lose, Kudrow breezed through the audition for Burrows, who nodded and dismissed her, saying only, "No notes." In truth, Burrows had no notes because, like everyone else, he saw immediately that Kudrow was Phoebe. The only problem was that she was Ursula, too.

It wouldn't be unheard of for a series-regular actress to occasionally pop up in a recurring role on another show. But *Mad About You* and *Friends* were on the same network, the same night, and scheduled back-to-back at 8:00 p.m. and 8:30. And, of course, they were both set in Manhattan. It just wouldn't work to have the waitress from Riff's zipping downtown every night to live her double life as a West Village massage therapist. Thus, Phoebe became a twin.[23] Kauffman and Crane came up with the idea, and ran it by Danny Jacobson, who—to everyone's surprise—said sure, no problem. "I don't know that *we* would have said yes to that," Crane recalled. Again, it didn't hurt that Klarik was there to help mediate. And *Mad About You* was a rock-solid hit. *Friends* was just a promising newbie that was lucky enough to be riding into Thursday night, cushioned cozily between one popular comedy and one *spectacularly* popular comedy.

Courteney Cox had just done a stint on the latter, playing Jerry's girlfriend, Meryl, on one episode of *Seinfeld*.[24] The show was in its fifth season and had never been bigger. That year, it took an astonishing leap from #25 in the Nielsen ratings to #3, and gained almost 10 million new viewers. Cox had played roles on other series before—some of them popular. But *Seinfeld* was a whole new ball game. This show had discarded the so-called rules of television comedy, delivering weird, niche storylines using pitch-black humor and a cast of caustic characters, but it was just so damn good. Still, good quality doesn't always translate to good numbers, nor longevity. The real miracle of *Seinfeld*— a show "about nothing," which should have appealed to no one—was that it had all three. But *how*? Everyone was trying to pinpoint it, that magic *Seinfeld* formula. After a few days on the

---

23 Kudrow's own older sister, Helene, often played the stand-in for Kudrow during Phoebe-Ursula scenes.

24 Titled "The Wife," this is the episode where Jerry's girlfriend poses as his wife in order to use his discount at the dry cleaner's. It may be better known as the episode where George gets caught peeing in the gym shower.

set, Cox had discovered at least one absolutely crucial ingredient. She would bring it with her to her next job, and there, too, it would change everything.

Cox was called in early on during the *Friends* casting process. She was nowhere near as famous as she'd soon become, but she was an established television actress, and much more recognizable than any of her future costars. She'd been working since her late teens, first dabbling in modeling in Manhattan, the summer after graduating from high school. Cox grew up in Mountain Brook, Alabama, but had family connections in New York, thanks to her stepfather, Hunter Copeland. His nephews were drummer Stewart Copeland (of The Police), and music promoter/booking agent Ian Copeland, whom Cox would later briefly date. Cox returned to New York after her freshman year at Mount Vernon College, where she'd been studying architecture. She took a summer job as a receptionist in Ian's office, and continued to pick up modeling gigs[25] and go out on a few commercial auditions. It wasn't much, but to a nineteen-year-old, it was a more than enough to convince her that this was the place to be. "I just thought, I can always go to college," Cox recalled, adding that she did sometimes regret not going back later. None of the *Friends* cast truly "stumbled" into acting, but Cox was perhaps the least likely star, if only because of her practical nature. In many ways, she was a less extreme version of Monica: sharply focused, no nonsense, and even puritanical.

But she was also young, and just as Kudrow had, Cox realized that if there was any time to give this business a shot, it was now. Furthermore, she was getting jobs, she'd been signed to Ford Models, and her nebulous career was picking up speed. Maybe

---

25 As ever, it wasn't quite as glamorous as it sounds. Cox's bread-and-butter jobs were things like book covers, where she'd sit and be illustrated into a spooky scene for the front of a paperback thriller. "But I loved it!" she said. "Because it was a good way to try to afford to live in New York City, which was not easy."

this *was* the practical choice, at least for the moment, Cox said to herself. "I just thought, I'll take this ride."

Cox began taking acting courses and speech classes, to get rid of her Alabama accent. She got a two-day job playing a debutante named Bunny on *As the World Turns*, and a commercial for New York Telephone. Then one day she was sent out on what she thought was a commercial audition, and wound up in a room with Brian De Palma.

The audition turned out to be for a music video—the one that would make Courteney Cox a famous face (if not yet a famous name). She was cast in the video for Bruce Springsteen's "Dancing in the Dark," where she played a fan who gets pulled out of a concert crowd to dance on stage with The Boss himself. It was her third job.

It's hard to overstate the cultural relevance of music videos and MTV in the mid-1980s, but suffice it to say that Cox could hardly have landed a bigger big break. The video was everywhere, and so was she. It was almost as if Bruce Springsteen *had* plucked her out of obscurity and made her a star. From then on, she booked a steady stream of TV gigs, doing guest spots as well as commercials. In 1985, she landed a Tampax ad, in which she famously became the first person ever to say the word *period* on national television. That, too, got Cox a heap of press, as well as fan mail from women's advocacy groups who lauded her for daring to mention the menstrual cycle in such straightforward terms. Cox didn't think it was such a big deal (and, frankly, wasn't that thrilled to be known as The Girl Who Said *Period*) but hey, it was work.

Despite those first few hits, Cox spent much of the next decade living on guest spots, tiny film roles, and the occasional pilot. She starred as a telekinetic teenager in the sci-fi drama *Misfits of Science*, which was canceled during its first season, but gave her just enough financial cushioning to keep going. She landed the recurring part of Alex P. Keaton's girlfriend during the last two seasons of *Family Ties*, followed by another starring role on an ill-fated CBS comedy called *The Trouble with Larry*.[26] Then, in 1994, a full decade after the Springsteen video, Cox got another big break. Three, in fact.

Ace Ventura: Pet Detective premiered in February, to dismal reviews and massive box-office success. Cox played the female lead and love interest, and now her face was everywhere again, if only because it was next to Jim Carrey's. The following month, her *Seinfeld* episode aired. Then her agents called with more big news. The producers from that hot new pilot everyone was talking about wanted her to come in. They had a role for her, and it was great: a cute, funny, slightly spoiled girl from Long Island who ditches her fiancé at the altar and comes to New York to make it on her own.

Yes, Kauffman admitted, "originally, we wanted her to do Rachel." They hadn't even considered Cox for Monica. Kauffman and Crane had written that role imagining a voice like Janeane Garofalo's. Their Monica was tough and defensive—with plenty of heart underneath, of course, but guarded by a hard demeanor and a sharp tongue. Cox had such warmth about her, such a nurturing and almost maternal presence. She just wasn't Monica.

Cox insisted she was. She *got* her, this organized, self-reliant woman who kept herself and everyone else in line. She didn't know yet that Monica had a hypercompetitive streak and a tendency to obsess. Neither did the writers, at that point. Like all the characters, Monica would be shaped by Cox's performance— her particular talent for playing the hard-ass with a heart of gold, and the full-body commitment with which she threw herself (sometimes literally) into physical comedy. In time, these things would add even more color to the character, creating her drive

---

26   Clips of this series are available on YouTube, if you'd like to surmise the network's reasons for canceling it within a month. Personally, I think Wikipedia summary of the show's premise says it best: "Larry returns home a decade after he was dragged off by baboons on his honeymoon. His wife, Sally, has now married another man and has a nine-year-old daughter. Larry falls in love with his former sister-in-law, Gabriella, who hates him."

and high-grade neurosis. But when Cox first read the pilot, all she knew was that she clicked with Monica—in a way that didn't often happen with sitcom characters. Monica wasn't an archetype, but a mix of traits and quirks that Cox herself could relate to. She knew this woman, and she liked her.

"She said, 'No, I'm Monica,' and she was right," recalled Kevin Bright. "Trust the actor." Cox came in to read and hit it out of the park, balancing all of Monica's sharp edges with a warm, welcoming humor and revealing her complexity, rather than walling it off behind sarcasm. She brought a high-energy vibe to the role that hadn't been there before, and would soon become Monica's defining characteristic. She nailed it, and she knew it.

"I remember thinking the role was mine," recalled Cox.[27] She still had to read for the studio and the network, but it was a done deal. Then, on her way in to read for Warner Bros., she stopped in the ladies' room, where she overheard someone talking in the next stall. Cox froze.

While she'd given a fantastic audition, there was one other actress who also seemed right for Monica. Nancy McKeon, who'd played Jo on the long-running series *The Facts of Life*, was called in for a reading, and everyone agreed she'd given a *great* one. On top of that, she had a fan base, having starred in one of the biggest sitcoms of the 1980s. Cox was excellent, and somewhat known, but it might be nice to have a real TV star in the mix. Opinions were split fifty-fifty, so Littlefield left it to Kauffman and Crane. The two of them went for a walk and talked it out. *Friends* was supposed to be a true ensemble. No lead characters and no star actors. Both Cox and McKeon were

---

27 Leah Remini, who'd also been brought in to read for Monica, thought so, too. In her memoir, *Troublemaker*, she remembered leaving the audition and walking out to the parking lot with another actress: "We chatted on the way to our cars, wishing each other the best, and then we saw Courteney Cox walking toward us, then past us and right into the building. Motherfucker! We both knew it right away: she had the part of Monica." Remini would later be a guest star in the "The One with the Birth."

wonderful Monicas on their own, but who would be best for
the team? They decided to bet on Cox.

There's no way to know what kind of show *Friends* would
have been had McKeon won the part. But Cox brought something more than her performance to the set—that crucial lesson
she'd learned on *Seinfeld*. Three days into shooting the pilot, she
huddled up her castmates and laid it out: if they wanted *Friends*
to be even a tenth as successful as that show, they had to become
a unit. The title had changed, but they were still six of one.

"Courteney had said, 'Look, I did a guest star on *Seinfeld*,'" Lisa
Kudrow recalled, "'one of the reasons I think that show's so great
is that they all help each other out.'" She explained how, on that
set, the actors would give each other suggestions and take one
another's notes without offense. Cox urged them to do the same.
"If you've got something that you think is funny for me to do,
I'm gonna do it. We've got to all help each other." And, as she reminded them, this show wasn't called *Ross* or *Monica*. There was no
titular star here—no one who would get all the praise if it hit, or
take all the heat if it failed. They had to carry this thing together.

"Normally, there's a code with actors," Kudrow explained.
"We don't give each other notes under any circumstances, and
we don't comment on each other's performances." It was almost
taboo, what Cox was suggesting, but she knew if they could all
agree to it, then it would make them infinitely better as a cast.
And since she was the most famous one among them, it was on
her to offer that permission. Given her status, Cox could have
done the opposite, behaving like the lead and letting the others
settle into supporting roles around her. Instead, she used her
clout to cement them as a team. Kudrow recalled: "She was the
one who set that tone and made us a real group."

Matt LeBlanc was nervous, even so. Looking at this cast of
characters, he knew there was at least one who could be kicked
out of the group, and it was him. Phoebe was a weirdo, sure—

but Joey was a letch. The original character breakdown described him as a "handsome, smug, macho guy in his twenties." His interests included "women, sports, women, New York, women" and himself. On paper, it might seem funny to have this egotistical creep juxtaposed with two sensitive beta males and three women, but how many times could Joey leer at his female counterparts and make crude jokes before everyone turned on this sleazeball?

It wasn't just Joey at issue, either. LeBlanc was greener than his castmates, a fact that hadn't gone unnoticed during his first audition. "He wasn't quite as experienced, it felt, as some of the other actors," Kauffman remembered. She was right. LeBlanc had a lean list of series credits by that time, and his biggest gig thus far had been a long-running commercial for Heinz ketchup. Even in a cast of relative unknowns, he stood out as a newbie. And it didn't help that he walked into the audition room with a hangover and a bloody nose.

LeBlanc had gotten into acting as a side gig. He'd grown up in Nonantum, or "The Lake,"[28] a predominantly Italian-American village in Newton, Massachusetts. There, he said, "everybody had some type of trade. That's what you did." His was carpentry, which he began studying during high school, and later at Boston's Wentworth Institute of Technology. He left after one semester (thinking that, in this line of work, higher education was basically pointless, "like going to LEGO college"), and started working on a construction crew building houses in the nearby suburb, Natick. He had skill as a carpenter (certainly more than

---

28 This village is now famous for two things: being the hometown of Matt LeBlanc, and having its own mysterious dialect of Massachusetts slang, called "Lake Talk." Some theorize that Lake Talk is a combination of World War II military code and ancient Italian-Romany slang. It includes phrases like "cuya moi" (shut up) and "dikki ki dotti" (unbelievable). In 2014, LeBlanc demonstrated some Lake Talk on Conan, saying, for example: "We were down the corner the other day. There's some quister jivals (pretty girls) down there, mush (dude)." This has nothing to do with anything; I just think it's really cool that there's a secret language known only to the people of one Massachusetts village, and Matt LeBlanc happens to be one of them.

Joey would), and he had a good job. But he was also eighteen and, as he put it, "I got ants in my pants."

A friend suggested he go down to New York and give modeling a shot. He was already in great shape from his labor-intensive job, and it could be a good way to make some money on the side. He went down to the city to meet a photographer, shelling out five hundred bucks for a set of head shots. The photographer was happy to take his money, though declined to inform him that, at 5'10", he would never be hired as a model. Looking around, LeBlanc figured it out for himself, but there was no getting his money back. He headed back down to the street, feeling like an idiot. Then he saw a girl.

Telling this story decades later, LeBlanc had to admit it—the moment that changed his life was a very Joey moment. The girl passed him on the sidewalk and he turned around to check her out. She turned around to check him out, too, and they both started laughing. The young woman was an actress on her way to an audition and invited him to tag along. She'd later introduce him to her manager, who thought LeBlanc had a great look for commercials and signed him as a client. "I'd just hoped to get laid before I got back on the train," he recalled. "So, I was pretty happy with how that turned out."

LeBlanc did have fast and remarkable success in commercials, doing ads for Coca-Cola, Levi's, Kentucky Fried Chicken, 7 Up, Fruitful Bran, and Heinz in his first three years alone. The ads gave him a degree of experience, and enough cash to pay for real training. He signed up for classes with Flo Greenberg, founder of the Actor's Workshop. After the success of the Heinz commercial, LeBlanc began to get calls from LA, urging him to come out and read for sitcoms. LeBlanc hesitated—not because he didn't want the jobs, but because he felt he just wasn't good enough yet. He still knew more about carpentry than acting.

"Everybody wanted him," Greenberg later said. "He said to me, 'Flo, I'm not quite ready to go. I know that we need to work a little bit more.'" But it was now or never. If he waited too long, the buzz from the commercial would fade and there'd be another hot new face all over the television. He asked Greenberg if she would let him come back and work with her soon. Maybe he'd make some sitcom money and then he could fly back to New York for a whole month to train with her. Would that be okay? She told him, of course, anytime, and then she urged him out the door, knowing this was goodbye. "He was sent for, and he had to go."

Of course, the buzz faded, anyway. LeBlanc was not an instant star, though he did book a series, *TV 101*, starring Sam Robards, which ran on CBS and was canceled in its first season. In 1991, he landed a recurring role on *Married with Children*, playing Kelly Bundy's boyfriend, Vinnie Verducci. He'd play the role again on the spin-off series *Top of the Heap*, and then once more on the spin-off of *that* spin-off *Vinnie & Bobby*—both of which were canceled after seven episodes. Next came some music-video gigs, a couple episodes of Showtime's *Red Shoe Diaries*, and a few more Italian Guy characters. If he was bothered by getting pigeonholed into this macho, leather-jacket niche, he didn't complain. It was a stereotype, yes, and often quite an ugly one with undertones of criminality and misogyny that had plagued the Italian-American community since long before *The Godfather*. But again, it's unlikely that any of that crossed LeBlanc's mind as a young twentysomething with bills to pay, and absolutely nothing to pay them with. Beggars can't be choosers, and by early 1994, that's pretty much what he was. The commercial money was gone, and one day he checked his bank balance and knew he'd have to find another guest spot (or a day job) immediately. So when his agent called saying he'd been asked to read for a pilot role—another chauvinistic, leather-clad Italian Guy—LeBlanc said yes, *please*. He had eleven dollars.

Then LeBlanc had a really stupid idea—and not a Joey-style stupid idea that ends in laughter and knee-slapping. It was his buddy's suggestion actually, but LeBlanc went along with it, perhaps because he was so excited just to have a potential new gig. The night before the audition, LeBlanc was hanging out with another actor, running his lines. His friend had a thought: This was a show about young, close friends, right? So, maybe they should quit practicing and instead go out and "prepare"— by getting shitfaced. Just like real friends do, right? Right!

Cut to the next morning: LeBlanc woke up on his friend's couch, stumbled into the bathroom, tripped and fell face-first onto the edge of the toilet seat. A few hours later, he was standing in an audition room, in front of Kauffman, delivering a monologue about women and ice cream.[29] Kauffman looked at him—at the enormous bloody gash running the entire length of his nose. "What happened to your face?"

This anecdote would become *Friends* lore in years to come— the story of how Matt LeBlanc Joey'd his way into stardom. But back then, it seemed to underscore LeBlanc's youth and inexperience. Still, Kauffman and Crane loved his reading. LeBlanc had made the choice to play Joey as dim-witted, though they hadn't written him as such. It worked so well, giving Joey a sense of innocence and sweetness, which tempered his machismo. And LeBlanc had a knack for playing dumb—no easy feat in comedy. It wasn't broad or childish; LeBlanc just played him a little ditzy. That was great for the character, but if this guy was a nitwit in real life—and what with the toilet injury, he wasn't coming off like a genius—they'd be sunk. Hank Azaria had also come in to read for the part (and would later be cast as David, Phoebe's beloved Scientist Guy), and he seemed a safer bet. They were leaning toward him when Barbara Miller, then the head of casting at Warner Bros., stepped in. "I'll never forget this," Kauffman recalled. "She said, 'This is the actor who will get better *every* episode. He can do it.'"

---

29   "Welcome back to the world! Grab a spoon!"

★ ★ ★

Late one night, Warren Littlefield pulled into a Chevron gas station on Sunset Boulevard. Filling up his car, he looked up and saw a familiar face. It was Jennifer Aniston, a young actress he knew well, having seen her in a handful of failed NBC pilots. The biggest role she'd had thus far was in their series adaptation of the hit film *Ferris Bueller's Day Off*, in which she'd played the lead's sister, Jeannie.[30] With thirteen episodes shot, it had been her longest running sitcom yet. But it was weak and panned from the start, the show's flaws made even more glaring when compared to its brilliant source material. *Ferris Bueller* had been canceled during its first season, and now Aniston was adrift. By the night she ran into Littlefield at the gas station, she was beginning to run out of steam. Even worse, she suspected the industry was beginning to tire of *her*, too. "I was the failed sitcom queen," she'd reflect, twenty years later. Sooner or later she'd be out of chances, so maybe she should just beat them to the punch and quit. Aniston had nothing to lose, and so she approached the president of NBC, standing at the gas pump, and asked him outright: "Will it ever happen for me?"

It was a question that, up until that point, Aniston hadn't worried too much about. She was an actor, had always been one—just one of those people born with the performance instinct. To her luck and/or detriment, she was also born the child of actors. Her mother, Nancy Dow, had only a handful of television credits, but her father, John Aniston, was already a frequent soap-opera actor by the time she was born, and would eventually become well known for playing Victor Kiriakis on *Days of Our Lives*.[31] On top of that, her godfather was Telly Savalas, a

---

30   The character originated by Jennifer Grey in the film. Grey later appeared as Rachel's estranged best friend and would-be maid of honor, Mindy, in "The One with the Evil Orthodontist."

31   A role he originated in 1985 and, as of this writing, is still playing.

television legend and friend of her dad's. Aniston was born in Sherman Oaks, California, but her parents divorced when she was nine, and she grew up primarily with her mother, in New York City.

Aniston was sent to the Rudolf Steiner School, which used the Waldorf education method—meaning, no TV allowed. Sometimes she could barter a few hours of television, especially if she was home sick, but that only made it more thrilling to her. Sometimes she even caught a glimpse of her dad, now a rising soap star. It's no surprise that, as Aniston's own acting ambitions developed, they were aimed squarely at the television. She recalled: "I wanted to be in that box."

As a New Yorker, she was a theater lover, too. Her mom took her to see *Annie* on Broadway, as well as shows that were less "age appropriate" but highly regarded, like Mark Medoff's play *Children of a Lesser God*. By high school, she knew the acting thing wasn't just a phase. Aniston was accepted at New York's High School of Performing Arts (aka the *Fame* school), and from that point on, she said, "I didn't think I could do anything else, honestly." Her father was less than thrilled, knowing that committing to this profession would more than likely lead to heartbreak or, at best, great disappointment. Yes, he'd eventually found a degree of success *and* a steady job, but both those things were vanishingly rare. And even if she was as lucky as he, it wouldn't inoculate her to heartbreak or struggle. By then, her parents had gone through a rough divorce, and despite having a soap-star dad, Aniston grew up perpetually broke. She'd see those girls from the Upper East Side, with their perfect clothes and their hair just so, imagining with envy what their lives must be like. It was those girls she'd think of, almost a decade later, when she saw the breakdown for a character on a new pilot she was up for: a pretty, stylish, spoiled young woman who had everything and never had to work for any of it.

But that was still years down the line. First came the receptionist job at the ad agency, and then scooping ice cream at Sedutto's, and the two days she spent as a Manhattan bike messenger before realizing what a terrible idea that was. There were the way-off-Broadway plays and other not-quite "acting" gigs. One day when she was eighteen, she got a job reading a Nutrisystem ad on Howard Stern's show—having no idea who Howard Stern was. ("It was quite a rude awakening, shall we say.")

Her father now lived in LA, and every summer she'd fly out to visit him. At first she insisted she'd never actually move out there. Like so many New York actors (all New Yorkers, really), she had a sense of snobbery about Hollywood. New York was where *real* actors lived, honing their craft in black-box theaters, paying dues while waiting tables, and then drawing hoards to Broadway or Shakespeare in the Park. But while she loved her rinky-dink theater gigs, they didn't pay the bills. And unlike Matt LeBlanc, who'd barely been in New York a day before booking his first commercial, she never even came close. "I couldn't book a commercial to save my life," she said. Even with her waitressing job, she was barely getting by. The older she got, the more she felt drawn to the west coast, where there were jobs aplenty and the streets were paved with scripts.

During her next visit with her dad, Aniston decided to extend the trip. She extended it again. Finally, she caved. She borrowed a hundred bucks from a friend to get a set of head shots, and started going out on auditions. In the meantime, she got a telemarketing gig, selling timeshare properties in the Poconos—a job at which she was terrible. "I'd just apologize profusely and hang up the phone," she said. "Thank God that only was two weeks." By then, she'd booked her first TV job.

Aniston costarred on *Molloy*, alongside Mayim Bialik (who was post-*Beaches* but pre-*Blossom*). It was canceled seven episodes in, and thus began Aniston's four-year reign as the failed sitcom queen. And, for a while, that was fine by her. It wasn't The Dream, but she was still getting paid to act. She'd shoot a few episodes, the show would get canned, and she'd walk away with a few months' rent money and look for the next gig. It beat the hell out of bike messengering. But eventually Aniston realized she was going in circles, not actually making progress. She did have a few small successes along the way: a guest spot on *Quantum Leap*, a sketch comedy show called *The Edge* (which lasted for eighteen episodes), and the dubious honor of starring in *Leprechaun*. This film would eventually become a cult classic, and the basis for an endless series of sequels. But, like black-box theater, cult classics don't pay the bills, either—nor do they typically pave the way for mainstream stardom. Not that it seemed in the cards for her, anyway.

"Will it ever happen for me?" Aniston asked Littlefield that night at the gas station. "God, I wanted it to," he recalled. But he just didn't know. Then he got a script from Kauffman and Crane.

Rachel was always going to be the hardest part to cast. Bright, Kauffman, Crane, and everyone else knew it. "The role is potentially so unlikable," Crane said. "She's spoiled and whiny and upset, and she's crying, and no one likes to see that." They auditioned *everyone*, said Kauffman: "Thousands and thousands of women came in." Nothing.

In the meantime, Aniston booked another gig—not just a pilot, but a series, in which she was cast as a one of the leads. *Muddling Through* was shot in the winter of 1993–94, then shelved until it was scheduled as a summer series on CBS—which, if successful, could be extended into the fall. The show revolved around Connie Drego (Stephanie Hodge), a woman returning home to run her family's motel, after doing two years in prison for shooting her cheating husband (not fatally, in the butt). Aniston played her eldest daughter, Madeline, who'd married the cop who arrested her mother. Now the whole family would have to find a way to muddle on through this awkward scenario and come together to run the motel. The show wasn't in the same league as *Friends*, but it wasn't an obvious stinker, either (certainly no *LAX 2194*).

Kauffman and Crane were still adamant about not casting actors in second position, but Aniston was an exception. Not because she was a big name, but the opposite—because she was indeed the failed sitcom queen. She'd done so many NBC pilots that the network knew her well, and despite her series track record, they still believed in her as an actress. Aniston already had Littlefield's approval, meaning that, if Kauffman and Crane liked her reading, she wouldn't have to audition for the NBC execs. That would be one less hurdle for the producers (a big one), and at this point they still hadn't officially nailed down most of the cast. Each actor had to get the okay from them, from Warner Bros., *and* from the network, so until the contracts were signed, anything could change. They asked Aniston to come in and read—for the role of Monica.

Aniston took one look at the script and thought, *No, not Monica. Rachel.* It wasn't that she related to Rachel, but that she knew her instantly. "She was everything I wasn't," Aniston said. "A rich, spoiled princess from a family who had everything." Rachel breezed into that coffee shop and made herself the center of attention, without worrying for a second about rejection or failure or credit card debt. She expected to be welcomed and so she was. She expected coffee, and so it appeared in her hand ("Sweet'N Low?"). Aniston thought of those Upper East Side girls who walked around Manhattan like they owned it, or they *could* with one swipe of their Amex. She knew Rachel like the back of her hand, because she'd grown up watching her, fantasizing about what it would be like to step into her fine shoes.

Courteney Cox had a degree of clout when she'd asked to read for another role, but it was a gutsy move for someone in Aniston's position. Still, the producers didn't have a Rachel, and

they hadn't seen anyone who'd even come close.[32] So they agreed
to let Aniston give it a shot. "We saw Jennifer," remembered
Bright. "It was like—*wow*. After all these months and hearing
so many people read it, this was the person." Aniston embodied
Rachel so perfectly, embracing both her naïveté and her self-
centeredness, without making her a brat. Okay, maybe she *was*
a brat, but not a mean girl. She was selfish, absolutely, but never
vicious. There was something about Aniston's Rachel that made
you forgive her, even while rolling your eyes. You wanted to
see her get knocked down by reality, because she sure as hell
needed it—but you also wanted to see her get up, and grow up.

"She was, head and shoulders, the best one," said Crane. It
was a gamble, but they had to take it. Aniston got the call that
very afternoon. With Littlefield's support, Bright, Kauffman,
and Crane cast Aniston as Rachel, then held their breath to
see what happened with *Muddling Through*. "We asked to see a
couple of episodes," said Bright. "It didn't have 'failure for sure'
written on it, like the baggage-handler show. But we felt it was
kind of weak."

Meanwhile, *Friends* was looking stronger by the day. Once
the cast was at last assembled and the contracts signed, they sat
down for the first table-read. That was the moment everyone
realized the real casting miracle: these actors weren't just perfect
for their parts, but for each other. There was a palpable energy
between them as they began to read. "We were like six pieces
of a puzzle that just felt like, okay, this works," David Schwimmer recalled. They got the show on its feet, running through a
rehearsal on the Central Perk set, and when Kauffman saw them
together, doing that opening scene for the first time, a chill ran

---

32 There was a brief moment of panic when, out of the blue, David Crane got
    a call from an NBC executive who told him she'd offered the role to Jami
    Gertz (best known for films like *The Lost Boys*, *Less Than Zero*, and, later,
    Twister). "We held our breath for twenty-four hours until she passed," said
    Crane, adding that Gertz was a wonderful actress, "but not Rachel."

down her spine. "I remember the atmosphere being electric. I knew we had something special."

Still, special doesn't always mean successful. Lisa Kudrow was just as bowled over by her castmates and the magic she felt between them. "Oh, my *God*," Lisa Kudrow thought. "Well, this is kind of fun and exciting." But a sure thing? No way. "There was absolutely no reason to think it was definitely going to go." A great script and a great team were just two of many more things that had to go right, and like everyone else, Crane was shocked every time they did: "We were always surprised when it kept, like, *happening*."

Even once the pilot was shot and well received, there were still months of uncertainty to come. They'd been given a full season, and so they kept moving right along, shooting "The One with the Sonogram at the End" and "The One with the Thumb." Meanwhile, *Muddling Through* came on the air in July 1994. As expected, it wasn't an immediate hit—nor was it an obvious flop. Burrows approached Aniston on set one day and said, "You know they're going to pick that show up, just to try to mess with *Friends*." He still had that gut instinct about *Friends* blowing up big-time (and CBS did, too, it soon became clear). But Aniston was incredulous, telling Burrows, "*No*, they would never do that."

That's exactly what they did. Aniston was at the up-fronts with the rest of the *Friends* team when CBS came out and announced they were picking up *Muddling Through*—for three episodes. Even Littlefield was shocked. That was a joke of an episode order, and a move that made the network's intentions obvious. CBS wasn't pinning any real hopes on *Muddling Through* being a wild success. They just wanted to throw a wrench into NBC's buzzy new comedy by keeping Aniston occupied *just* long enough that she'd have to be recast.

It worked. Bright, Kauffman, and Crane started scrambling

around for a new Rachel.[33] They kept right along shooting with Aniston in the part, hoping like hell that CBS would cave. But the *Muddling Through* team reassembled and started shooting the three episodes of their new "season." Aniston spent three weeks driving back and forth between Warner Bros. and Sony Studios, where she begged the producer of *Muddling Through* to please, please, just let her go, she was dying to do *Friends*. He waved it off, saying, "*This* show is going to make you a star. I saw that friendship show."

She bided her time and did both jobs. When it came time to shoot the cast photos for *Friends*, Aniston was gently asked to step out of some of the shots. That would make it easier if (when?) they found her replacement. And they were still looking. "I remember a girlfriend calling me saying she was auditioning for Rachel, and do I have any advice?" Aniston recalled. It was a nightmare. It was just what her father had warned her about. "So heartbreaking."

Meanwhile, the *Friends* team were having no luck recasting the role. More importantly, they really didn't want to. Not only was she the one and only Rachel in their minds, they'd already shot four episodes. Reshooting a pilot was rare but reshooting four episodes was basically unheard of. David Crane even went in to meet with Barton Dean, the creator of *Muddling Through*, begging him to let Aniston go. No dice. But Warren Littlefield had enormous faith in his show and in this performer (and just as firm a belief in *Muddling Through*'s comparative weakness). He'd decided to take another very expensive gamble on *Friends*, back the producers up, keep Aniston in the cast, and wait.

On reflection, it might have been an even riskier move than Littlefield imagined. CBS was clearly willing to gamble, too,

---

33   Lisa Whelchel, who'd played Blair on *The Facts of Life*, said she was asked to come in for Rachel during this period. She remembered telling her husband after reading the pilot script, "This is the funniest script I have ever read and this is going to be a huge hit." But she felt that acting on the show would conflict with her Christian beliefs, and so declined the opportunity, saying, "I can tell it's going to be just all about, you know, sex."

and had they raised the stakes again, that might have been the end of *Friends*. At the very least, it would have been the end of Aniston's tenure as Rachel. Even if the show had survived her sudden departure, it would be a whole new *Friends*, with different storylines, and different romantic pairings. In fact, there probably would be no Ross and Rachel, and—for better or worse—there would have been no hoards of women walking around with her haircut. But Littlefield, NBC, Warner Bros., Burrows, Bright, Kauffman, and Crane all knew the cast they had was perfect—lightning in a bottle. So, they bet the house. And they won. In September 1994, CBS aired the final episode of *Muddling Through*, and the show was finally canceled. Two weeks later, *Friends* premiered on NBC.

On a chilly summer night, not long before that premiere, the six cast members stood shivering, calf-deep in water that was, technically, heated, but still pretty damn cold. It was 4:00 a.m., and things hadn't gone as planned.

The opening title sequence was supposed to be shot on a building rooftop, overlooking a section of Los Angeles that could sort of pass for New York. The gang would be having a little roof party, like typical young New York folks. But wind and potential weather issues had made the rooftop scenario too expensive, so Kevin Bright and Marta Kauffman had looked around the Warner Bros. Ranch in Burbank to see if there were any decent spots they might use. In the middle of the lot, there was a small park. On one side sat the suburban facade of the *Bewitched* house, and on the other was a fountain built in the 1930s, overlooked by a row of city-esque row houses. Bright turned to Kauffman and shrugged: "This could be a park in the village. You could buy that." Kauffman nodded. They could blow out the lighting in the building windows, make it deliberately unrealistic, like a Magritte painting or something. Maybe they could bring the couch from the coffeehouse set, and put it on the lawn. "And then something with the fountain, I don't know what," said Bright.

Bright, Kauffman, the cast, and crew headed out to the ranch for a late-night shoot. They danced and did silly poses around the set, some of which were choreographed and others improvised. Between takes, Kauffman approached them. "Hey, guys, we have an idea…"

Hours later, they were soaked and freezing, huddled up together and trying to maintain their game faces. "Everybody had pruny fingers," Matt LeBlanc recalled. When Kauffman had asked them to jump in the fountain, "they were very game," she said. (What other choice was there?) But by the end of the night, countless takes behind them, they were just cold.

"I don't think we were in the mood—or could even *look* like were having fun anymore," said Lisa Kudrow. They stood there, mutely awaiting instructions, in their wet black-and-white party clothes, when Matthew Perry broke the silence: "I don't remember a time when I *wasn't* in the fountain." Kudrow burst out laughing, and so did the others. In the decade that followed, the cast came to rely on Perry for moments like this. It was his thing—breaking the silence with a perfect one-liner in the middle of a difficult shoot or a long night on set when everyone was tired and cranky. "He's the class clown, for sure," said LeBlanc.

That night in the fountain, they just couldn't stop. They were exhausted, verging on hysterical, but here they were, in it together, literally. Perry kept it going, making jokes about how unbel*iev*ably uncomfortable they all were. Someone quickly got the camera rolling, capturing the six of them laughing like maniacs. Bright and the editing team would cut this into the iconic opening sequence, most of which turned out as planned—choreographed dance moves and glances at the camera. But those quick little snippets toward the end, when they're splashing around, absolutely drenched and giggly—that's just them, goofing around and trying to keep each other awake.

Ten years later, while doing press for *Friends'* final season, Perry was asked to reflect on the fountain shoot himself. This time he declined to make a joke. He remembered all the laughter, sure—it was a special night (if slightly freezing). But to him, that memory marked the beginning of a venture that would alter the course of all their lives. What the cameras captured was the moment before everything changed. "You've got six people in a fountain at four in the morning who are about to embark on a journey," said Perry. "And they just have *no* idea what is in store for them—other than it's going to be fun, and *maybe* it will work."

PART 2

3

The One with Marcel and George Clooney

David Wild was sitting with the cast in a Chicago hotel room. They had flown in to appear on *The Oprah Winfrey Show*, and Wild, then a senior editor at *Rolling Stone*, had joined them. He'd known they were a hit before the cast themselves did—even before viewers really understood that their new favorite series was everyone else's, too. Or at least he'd made a very good guess.

Wild and his wife had watched *Friends* from the start, and liked it well enough. But the hum of excitement around the show seemed to suggest something bigger than just a successful sitcom. It was too soon to start using words like *phenomenon*, but that's what he was thinking. He'd told his bosses as much, early on during the first season. "I had suggested to *Rolling Stone* that there should be a cover story. That I thought something was happening with this show," Wild told me. They weren't sold at first. The 1994–95 television season was unusually packed with shows that were both good and popular, and it was too early to pick a front-runner. Furthermore, there was a whole hell of a lot happening on TV besides scripted shows. Jurors had just been sworn in on the OJ Simpson trial. Princess Diana and Prince Charles were in the final act of what seemed to be the world's longest divorce. Tonya Harding was Tonya Harding. Audiences were enthralled with the seedy and scandalous—and *Friends* was so clean you could eat off it.

Still, Wild thought, there was something equally compelling about these six fresh faces and their sweetie-pie show. The season progressed and, despite fluctuating ratings, it seemed more and more viewers agreed. In the spring of 1995, during the final week of shooting, Wild got a call from the higher-ups: "Yeah, you know what? You should go ahead and do something."

Season One of *Friends* is a great one, for a sitcom. It's not a great season for *Friends*, by a mile. The show would soon find its footing with more serialized storylines, and the cast would only get better with time, both as individual performers and (more importantly) as an ensemble. Even so, the early episodes did a great job of introducing us to the gang and making us want to hang out with them again.

The plot would thicken up nicely, but at first it was fairly simple. Twentysomethings navigating the usual travails of youngish adulthood, most of which can conceivably be worked out in twenty-two minutes: Rachel can't do laundry, so Ross teaches her how. Joey and Chandler's crappy kitchen table breaks, so they buy a new one—a foosball table! The girls have a moment of existential dread, realizing that youth is past and life is chaotic and they "don't even have a pla," let alone a plan. So, they get drunk, problem solved. As the eldest, Ross's life is more complicated, what with the divorce from his first love, Carol (who is both newly pregnant and has just come out of the closet), *and* the arrival of his first crush, Rachel. His is the only real throughline of the season, and its conclusion with the birth of his son is a perfect setup for things to get just a little more grown-up in Season Two. For now, it's a lot more thumbs in soda cans, wacky romantic mixups, and monkeys.

The characters haven't totally gelled at this point, which actually works in their favor: Phoebe is an oddball, but her extreme quirks are used for punch lines rather than plot (as is she, more often than not). We're still a year away from the debut of "Smelly Cat," as well as Phoebe's eclectic family. Monica is a little type A, but she isn't yet a neatness obsessive who cleans the toilet seventeen times a day ("Even if people are on it!"). In Season One, she's just the grown-up of the group—a familiar figure in any real-life social circle: the friend who has at least some of her shit together, and always has milk in the fridge.[34] We can easily recognize or relate to Season One Monica, and so when her neuroses get dialed up later (often to great comic effect), we're already along for the ride.

It makes sense, too, that people in this age range would not have fully formed identities. "The time in your life when your friends are your family" could also be called "the time in your life when you have no idea what the hell you're doing or why." The entire series is catalyzed by one young woman realizing just that. "It's like all of my life everyone has always told me, 'You're a shoe! You're a shoe! You're a shoe! You're a shoe!'" Rachel tells her father over the phone, hours after running out on the fiancé she doesn't love and the life she doesn't want. "What if I don't wanna be a shoe? What if I wanna be a purse? Or a hat? No, I don't want you to buy me a hat, I'm saying that I *am* a hat. It's a metaphor, Daddy!" With these few lines, Rachel gives us plenty of reasons to dislike her, and one reason to give her a chance: she wants to change. She doesn't know if she's a shoe or a hat, but she's going to figure it out.

Joey, on the other hand, is a little *too* recognizable, as a creep. Seven minutes into the pilot, he's already hitting on Rachel— and not in a goofy way, because he's not really a goof yet. He's a letch, perpetually showing up in leather or slicked-back hair, in a way that kind of reminds you of Fonzie, and *then* makes

---

34 The den mother as James Burrows suggests. "The pilot is very 'Monica's Kids.'"

you wonder if Fonzie was actually a creep, too. The sweet side
that somewhat tempers Joey's behavior hasn't emerged, and his
occasional cluelessness doesn't make him seem like an innocent
so much as a guy you can't trust to keep his hands to himself.

It even made some of the actresses a little nervous around
LeBlanc initially. "I was scared of that type of guy," Aniston
told *People* magazine during the first season. That Guy exists,
after all, and having played several variations on him, LeBlanc
knew himself that it would be an issue.[35] Not being That Guy
himself, he wasn't worried about his castmates; they soon came
to see him as "the brother type," he told *People* in the same interview. But if the show continued, he knew that Joey would
wear out his welcome sooner rather than later. Audiences would
tire of obvious gags, like the one where the girls are bent over
during a game of Twister, and Joey can't help but waggle his
eyebrows at Ross (who responds by lowering his own eyebrows
and tilting his head: *Really?*).

The issue had worried LeBlanc from the start, but he wasn't
going to be the one to point it out. As production progressed,
though, he knew it was only a matter of time before the writers realized the Joey problem. LeBlanc approached Kauffman
and Crane with a proposition: "Could it be that Joey thinks
of these three girls as little sisters, and wants to go to bed with
every other girl but these three?" (LeBlanc did *not* add, "Because I'm afraid that you're going to run out of stories for me.
I'm gonna have to move out from across the hall." He floated it
as a creative suggestion, rather than, as he later put it, a desperate act of self-preservation.) Thankfully, Kauffman and Crane
immediately got it. Joey began to evolve into a better friend,

---

35 Schwimmer and Perry also confessed they had preconceived notions about
    LeBlanc, based on his looks and his modeling career. "I was, like, 'This guy's
    kind of a dick,'" Schwimmer told *Entertainment Weekly* in 1995. "I thought,
    'Oh, great, here's this guy I'm going to work with for maybe five years, and
    he's fucking Joe Cool stud.'" Realizing perhaps that he was being kind of a
    dick himself, Schwimmer added, "Well, he's turned me around completely."

and a more dynamic character.[36] He was still a womanizer, without a doubt. But from then on, when it came to his female counterparts, he became more of "the brother type" on screen as well as off.

That character shift eliminated another element of *Friends*, which Kauffman and Crane had initially planned to include: a Joey-Monica love story. While developing the show, the creators saw them as a natural pairing, simply because "they just seemed like the most sexual of the characters," explained Kauffman. But that idea had long since gone out the window with the discovery of Ross and Rachel.

Friends did not invent will-they-won't-they as a sitcom storyline. That credit is typically given to *Cheers*, and the sparring, on-again/off-again lovers, Sam and Diane. As *Esquire* Senior Culture Editor Tyler Coates told me, "If it wasn't for Sam and Diane, there wouldn't be Ross and Rachel." Indeed, *Friends* took crucial lessons from its predecessor when stepping into this territory. Sam and Diane were a compelling pair, but a polarizing one because of their fundamental differences. Opposites attracted, but once they got together, sexual tension was just tension.[37] *Friends* took a different approach entirely. There was no conflict between Ross and Rachel, and no mystery. In the very first episode, he asks if he might ask her out sometime, and she says yes. There is zero question of "if," only "when."

Kauffman and Crane let the question linger in the air throughout the first season, but they were in no rush to answer it. *Friends* established itself as a true ensemble show, with everyone given equal amounts of screen-time (if not *quite* equal amounts of

---

36 Joey's real turning point in this season is "The One with Two Parts," in which he dates and is dumped by Ursula, Phoebe's twin sister. It highlights his friendship with Phoebe, but it also allows us to see him heartbroken—alerting us to the fact that he does have a heart.

37 Sam and Diane are "hate-fuckers," argues journalist Taffy Brodesser-Akner. "Hate-fuckers are good for a one-liner, but they tend to suck all the joy out of the room as we debate if their insults and bickering and overall disdain for each other is something enjoyable to be around. It is not."

story). By necessity, the romance couldn't dominate, because the point of Season One was to make us, the viewers, fall in love with all of them.

By the spring of 1995, the courtship was going well. After the pilot, ratings had taken a month-long nosedive, and everyone held their breath. But with Episode 7, "The One with the Blackout," they rebounded, and held relatively steady ever since. That night was not only a turning point for *Friends*, but the moment many point to as the true beginning of Must-See TV. "Blackout Thursday" was a crossover stunt, orchestrated by NBC, to hype its Thursday night lineup of comedies, all of which took place in New York City: *Mad About You*, *Friends*, *Seinfeld*, and *Madman of the People*. The night kicked off at 8:00 p.m., with *Mad About You*'s Jamie Buchman (Helen Hunt) accidentally causing the power outage while fiddling with the cable hookup on her building's roof, leaving everyone in NBC's New York in the dark.[38] They all emerged unscathed and with a slew of new viewers, with *Friends*' audience up by 5 million.

The show got an even bigger boost with its next crossover/cameo episodes, "The One with Two Parts: Part 1," and "The One with Two Parts: Part 2," which aired during February sweeps. It was a double-down move, pulling in faces from two different NBC hits and airing in two segments, at 8:30 and 9:30, with a *Seinfeld* repeat sandwiched in between for good measure.

The first part actually opens *on* the set of *Mad About You*, with Chandler and Joey dining at Riff's, the restaurant where Ursula is a waitress. (Thus begins her brief romance with Joey.) Later in the episode, Jamie Buchman and Fran Devanow (Leila Kenzle) wander down from their Union Square neighborhood and

---

38 Except for *Seinfeld*'s characters, who were miraculously spared. The *Seinfeld* team didn't want to participate in the blackout stunt, and since *Seinfeld* could pretty much do whatever it wanted at this point, there were at least a few blocks of Upper Manhattan that still had power that night.

pop into Central Perk,[39] where they encounter Phoebe, naturally assuming she's Ursula. High jinks didn't really ensue, but the audience cheered nonetheless.

In Part 2, the audience *screamed*. This episode begins with Rachel and Monica in the emergency room, because Rachel has fallen headfirst off the balcony while taking down the Christmas lights, thus spraining her ankle. How she managed to do that is unclear, but who cares because her doctors are GEORGE CLOONEY AND NOAH WYLE FROM *ER* OH MY GOD.

ER debuted the same week as *Friends*, and unlike the comedy, it was an immediate and unstoppable hit. In its first season, *ER* became the second most-watched show in America, right behind *Seinfeld*. By the second season, it was #1. *ER* also enjoyed glowing critical praise from day one, whereas *Friends* was likened to "a thirty-minute commercial for Dockers or IKEA or light beer, except it's smuttier." Its *best* reviews merely argued that "there's really nothing to dislike." *ER* and *Friends* had neighboring sets at Warner Bros., and the casts had become friendly, if only because they were the two hot new shows on the lot. Indeed, the *Friends* cast were subject to some of Clooney's earliest work as an on-set prankster, coming back to their dressing rooms to find he'd defaced the signs on their doors. Not his most sophisticated gag, but hey, they were kids.

Clooney and Wyle appeared as doctors on *Friends*, but not as their *ER* characters—presumably because their show was set in Chicago. Clearly, this was not an era of subtlety on TV, but asking viewers to imagine that doctors Ross and Carter flew

---

39   "What is this place?" Jamie asks, looking around as if she's wandered into a mosh pit instead of a coffee shop. It's a one-minute cameo that sums up everything about the difference between *Friends* and *Mad About You*. Jamie's only a few years older than the Friends, but she is a Baby Boomer, while they're all solidly Generation X. Jamie lives on Fifth Avenue and 12th Street—maybe a ten-minute walk from Central Perk, but a very different neighborhood. She's a character created in 1992, before coffee was cool. She makes coffee at home, like the married, professional, grown-up she is, then she puts on a blazer and goes to work. No wonder she's baffled by this funky living-room-cum-café full of kids just sitting there, being.

into New York just long enough to pick up a shift and a double date would have been a bit much. It was weird enough to see these guys yanked out of their high-drama, single-camera universe and into a sunny sitcom with an audience shrieking in the background. But it worked. The audience did shriek, because against all odds, the episode is really, really funny. Rachel doesn't have insurance, so she "borrows" Monica's by impersonating her (with Monica's reluctant permission). When the doctors ask them out, the women are forced to keep up the ruse during the date, which culminates in the two of them hurling insults at each other, as themselves. ("I am so spoiled!" "I use my breasts to get other people's attention!" "We *both* do that.") It's sitcom-silly to the point of absurdity, *and* the *ER* guys are there, *and* it's an episode about insurance fraud. And, somehow, it works.

Friends cracked the top ten that night (at #9, but still), and from then on, it began steadily inching its way up. Shortly thereafter, David Wild got the call from his bosses at *Rolling Stone*, telling him to go ahead and do the story.

"I ended up being on set for the last days of the first season," Wild told me. He still hadn't figured out just *what* was different about this show that made him and everyone else like it so much, but the difference on set was immediately clear. "It was not the same vibe you got on a *Melrose Place*, or a *90210*," he said. He'd also covered those shows, and their hot young casts. The Friends were pretty hot and young themselves, but they were old enough to be nervous. "I think they'd all taken a few hits," said Wild, "and they knew what it was like to have a bomb show."

But they had no idea how to handle a hit. While shooting the Season One finale, Wild noticed that the cast and creators didn't seem to be basking in the glow of a successful season. They were too anxious about screwing it up. Wild quoted Kauffman in his story: "At the end of every episode, we always look at each other and say, 'Wow, there's another one that doesn't suck.'" Still, everyone knew there was a big difference between success and just not sucking.

The jury was still out. The more popular *Friends* got, the more it suffered the glare of the spotlight. It was mocked in sketch shows for being too pretty and sweet. It was called out by characters on other sitcoms, like the Margaret Cho vehicle, *All-American Girl*: "It's such an unrealistic show. Six very attractive, clever people who drink lots of coffee and don't have sex with each other. Yeah, *right*."[40] There were the inevitable *Seinfeld* comparisons, which were both valid and way off base. It was a New York–based, low-concept, ensemble comedy about a friend group, but *Seinfeld*'s declared ethos was "no hugging, no learning." On *Friends*, all they did was hug.

The same was true off camera, Wild realized. Rather than turn on each other, as other actors might do under such pressure, the *Friends* cast had deliberately, tightly bonded. It was an agreement they'd come to during early rehearsals—another act of self-preservation, LeBlanc later explained: "It was like starting a bunch of marriages."

That's what struck Wild during the shoot. "It was much more like being with a band than being with a TV cast," he said. However, "I've *never* seen a cast, and very rarely seen a band, stick together to the degree they did." Wild had been a music writer for years before covering television, and noticed that, yes, the Friends did appear to genuinely like one another—but more importantly, they seemed to recognize how much they needed each other. They had to function as a group or else things could go sour fast. They spent meals together, watched the show together on Thursday nights, and did all promotional photos as a group. It was the network's preference, too, because, as individuals, they weren't yet real stars. "The first time I interviewed

---

40 In the early years, everyone was curiously divided on this point. *Friends* was either smut or sterile, according to the critics. They clutched their pearls over this group of men and women talking about sex together, but rolled their eyes over the fact that they didn't actually do it. Hmm.

Jennifer Aniston, for instance, it was at a coffee shop on Beverly," said Wild. "We just sat in front of a coffeehouse, and no one bothered her. At that moment, she was not the biggest star on the earth. She was the star of an NBC sitcom."

Then he flew with them to Chicago. That's when Wild realized they weren't just a band. "They were rock stars. People were *losing* it in Chicago." In late March 1995, the cast appeared on *The Oprah Winfrey Show* in their first major television interview. "This show today is going to be so much fun. You know the hit show *Friends?*" Oprah began, turning to her studio audience, which responded with big, Oprah-audience cheers. "Well, if you don't you have been living under a rock... It's not only the hottest new sitcom, but last week, it was the third most-watched show in America!"

When she brought out the cast members moments later, their faces indicated this was news to them. The actors sat side by side on the stage, hands in their laps, looking appropriately nervous to be in Oprah's presence. "When you hear you're the number-one sitcom of the season, what does that feel like?" Oprah asked. They stared at her in silence for a moment, before Perry jumped in, on cue: "Bad." An obvious joke, but the crowd laughed generously because it was just so Chandler—and because what else could he possibly say? Oprah handed the mic to audience members, who asked what would become the standard *Friends*-interview questions: *Are you friends in real life?* Yes. *Is it fun working with a monkey?* Nope.[41] *Can you sing that song Phoebe played during the blackout episode for us real quick?* Oh, sure.

There was one particular topic the cast had prepared for, but no one in the audience brought it up. So, Oprah did it herself.

---

41 In ten years of interviews, this remained the number-one gripe among the cast. Marcel was played by two monkeys, who everyone agreed were the all-time worst guest performers on the show. The reasons are obvious, but still, that's really saying something considering this series also featured infants, children, chickens, ducks, and dozens of movie stars.

"I'd like for y'all to get a black friend. Maybe I could stop by." The crowd burst into laughter and applause, and the camera cut to Schwimmer, who smiled big and nodded hard. "As a matter of fact," Oprah added with a grin, "I'm thinking about buying that apartment building next door." And then, with *barely* a breath in between, she moved on. "Anyway, when we return, find out if David's character, Ross, is ever going to get Rachel in the sack." Cut to commercial.

Few critics had even mentioned the fact that *Friends* took place in a New York City comprised entirely of Caucasian people. Even those who pointed out the show's incongruities seemed mostly to be bothered by the least consequential problems: *All they do is sit around drinking coffee. Don't they have jobs? Why is Monica's apartment so big?* But even in those early days, the cast was at least aware of the issue, and knew that if it wasn't addressed on the show, they'd eventually have to answer for it.

But today was not that day. In a matter of seconds, Oprah managed to acknowledge the glaring whiteness of America's favorite new comedy, drive the point home, and then move on with a laugh. Green as they were, there is no question that Oprah did the cast of *Friends* a significant favor in doing all the talking on this point. She allowed them to remain beloved rising stars, while signaling to them—and to her millions of viewers—that this was indeed an issue and it would not go unnoticed.

But, even in that moment, it was clear that Oprah truly liked the show, and saw the universality in this specific group. "They remind you of yourself. They remind me of *myself*," she said. Toward the end of the episode, they showed a taped interview with a group of college kids in Chattanooga, Tennessee, sitting in a coffee shop and talking about how much they loved the show, because "it's real life. It really is how *we* are." They had a Phoebe in their group, too! They *loved* Ross. They dressed like Rachel. If they were stuck in an ATM vestibule with Chandler "it would be perfection."

Back in the studio, the cast members shifted in their seats, and Oprah asked how it felt to know they were having this kind of impact with viewers across the country. "Didn't know it 'til just now," Kudrow replied. A charming, doe-eyed answer, but it probably was an honest one. Twenty years later, Kudrow recalled the same thing: "[Oprah] said, 'Did you know about this?'" when the interview clip concluded. They glanced at each other: *Did you know?* "We had no idea." Again, it was 1995. There was no real internet to speak of, they'd hardly left the soundstage for months, and when they did go out in LA, no one treated them like big shots, because they weren't. Still, if *Oprah* says you're famous, then it must be true. And it will be even more true by the time you walk out her door.

Wild observed from offstage, taking notes. This was the turning point, he realized. The cast knew it, too. He watched it sink in, after the show. "Who *were* those people?" Perry asked his castmates, still gobsmacked by the Chattanooga college students. Back at the hotel, they were getting ready to fly home when a couple of women turned up out of the blue. They'd been sent by *The Jerry Springer Show*, which also taped in Chicago, to try to entice the guys to swing by before leaving. They declined, but it was another telling moment. *Rock stars*, thought Wild. *Clean-cut rock stars.* He remembered the story about James Burrows flying them to Vegas for one last shot at anonymity. "I was seeing the other end of that."

From then on, things would be different. Unless they seriously bungled that season finale, they'd be looking at a whole new level of success the following year. It wasn't a sure thing—nothing ever was. But seeing what happened in Chicago, Wild felt it was a very safe bet. "It was not Beatlemania, but it *was* a mania," he said. He flew home, and started writing.

Wild's piece "'Friends': Six Lives on Videotape," was the cover story of *Rolling Stone*'s May 1995 issue. It gave the first up-close look into life behind the scenes of *Friends*, telling the story of six earnest, incredibly likable actors rising to fame, linked arm in arm. The feature was peppered with anecdotes that made the cast simultaneously more glamorous and more accessible: one minute they're mobbed by fans at the airport, and the next they're sneaking out for a smoke break before the Oprah interview. A grumpy security guard approaches, Wild reports, demanding, "Who *are* you folks, and who told you you could smoke here?"

The cover photo, by Mark Seliger, features the cast in 1940s-style getups, piled into a lemon-yellow convertible, which appears to be flying down the road. It's all bright, juicy colors, comic and sexy at the same time. More than anything, it's reminiscent of a Norman Rockwell painting: wholesome and American and immediately familiar.

It was no accident, that styling choice. The image illustrated that feeling everyone was having about *Friends* but couldn't quite put their finger on. The show was unrealistic, even absurd, in that first season. But it was wholly relatable in one crucial way: it was about friends. That was it. It wasn't complicated. Everyone watching the show knew what it was like to have a close friend, or maybe a handful, so tight they felt like family. On the surface, *Friends* appeared so specific and of-the-moment—the cast with their chunky shoes and their crushes on George Stephanopoulos—but really, you could place the characters in any time or place. Sure, we liked their outfits, but we loved them because of their kinship. Watching them ride out a blackout together, or celebrate Thanksgiving with a platter of grilled cheeses—it touched the softest, most sentimental spots in our hearts. Ross and Rachel, that was icing (really good homemade icing, but icing nonetheless). The thing that mattered most about *Friends* was right there in that simple, one-word, unambiguous title.

Just as crucial as the friendship between these characters was the one happening off-screen. The bond between the cast members would serve them incredibly well financially, during their infamous contract negotiations—but that came much later, when the show's success was firmly established. Thanks to the one-two punch of Oprah and *Rolling Stone*, it soon would be.

Wild's piece in particular was more than just great press. It was the first chapter in the behind-the-scenes narrative of *Friends*. It answered the question everyone had—the question everyone *always* has about actors on their favorite TV shows—and it gave the right answer: yes, they are friends in real life.

Off-screen friendship is always a boon to a sitcom, for obvious reasons. It adds a gloss of authenticity to the fiction. It allows us, the viewers, to believe that what's happening on-screen is just a scripted, well-lit version of reality. Off-screen drama can be helpful, too, especially if the show itself is dark and dramatic. But with a show about friends, *called Friends*, we really need to believe they like each other. We have to be able to imagine that when the cameras stop rolling, they just head home to hang out in one another's real-life living rooms. And from the start, the *Friends* cast told us that's exactly what they did. "As completely corny and weird as it may sound to everyone, these people *are* now my friends," Cox was quoted in Wild's piece. Even better, it was her living room in which they all gathered most Thursday nights that first year, to watch their show together. Monica was "always the hostess," after all.

Friends would weather its share of drama and negative press. That, too, was coming, right around the corner. But in the spring of 1995, there was little to complain about (except the monkey). They capped a solid season with a cliffhanger finale. Oprah liked them. This time last year, the cast had been standing in a fountain at 4:00 in the morning, and now they were in a convertible on the cover of *Rolling Stone*, hair blown back, speeding into summer.

"Usually," explained Kevin Bright, "you do the first season, you have reruns during the summer, and you hope to come back in the second season, and up your game, up your numbers, up your popularity with the audience. But there'd been so much buzz around *Friends* that even people who weren't watching it were very aware of it." To say the least. They were everywhere. The Rembrandts' EP of "I'll Be There for You" was released in May—a perfect song of the summer, tailor-made for groups of friends to sing along to, driving with the windows down. On top of the *Rolling Stone* cover, the cast turned up on *People, Entertainment Weekly,* and *TV Guide.* When summer repeats began, millions more viewers tuned in to see what all the fuss was about. That was when *Friends* blew up. "We became the number-one show on television in the summer, with *reruns,*" Bright said.

They'd done it. Everyone was watching. Time to make another one that didn't suck.

4

The One Where
Two Women Got Married

There's a short film on YouTube titled *Homophobic Friends*. Film-maker Tijana Mamula first uploaded it in 2011, and since then, the film has been referenced in dozens of op-eds and think pieces, with headlines ranging from defensive to outraged to ironically amused: "Friends: Could There BE Any More Gay Jokes?"

It's a question that's lingered over the series, in the years since it went off the air. Is *Friends* homophobic? Or is it a product of its time? Mamula's film answers at least one of those questions with an unequivocal yes. Her film is an edited compilation of every gay joke made on *Friends*. It's cut together in the style of an episode, the difference being that it runs almost an hour long. And, in fact, there *could* be more gay jokes. "I discarded a few that were completely repetitive," Mamula told me. Her original cut was ninety minutes. There are the sight gags where Joey and Chandler realize they've been hugging too long, and frantically break apart. There are the easy one-liners ("If the Homo sapiens were, in fact, *Homo* sapiens, is that why they're extinct?") and the flat-out lazy one-liners ("So, how goes the dancing? Gay yet?").

Then there's Carol and Susan. To some, these characters are held as evidence that *Friends* is callous and offensive in its treatment of gay people. Indeed, Ross's first-season arc is essentially one long lesbian joke. At times, there is no joke at all; someone simply uses a term like *lesbian lover* and the audience laughs. In later seasons, these women fade into the background and then disappear entirely, retired like an old bit that isn't working anymore.

But to many other viewers, Carol (Jane Sibbett[42]) and Susan (Jessica Hecht) are proof of just the opposite. They are *Friends'* saving grace—the only real element of diversity in the series. "I loved Carol and Susan," pop-culture journalist Sarah Beauchamp told me. "They were, honestly, some of the sanest characters on the show."

Above all, they were *there*. Real-live lesbians, on prime-time television. Growing up as a gay kid, Beauchamp wasn't much bothered by all the pointed remarks about their sexuality. That was to be expected. Back then, if a gay character appeared on screen, sexuality was their defining characteristic, if not their only one. Beauchamp was just thrilled to see these women— living their lives, raising their child—and know that tens of millions of others were seeing them, too. On January 18, 1996, they even got to see them get married. "As in, 'I now pronounce you wife and wife' married?" Ross asked. And the audience laughed like crazy.

As Kevin Bright said, a show's second season is about stepping up the game, growing the numbers, and generally going big. That's precisely what happened with Season Two of *Friends*. They got rid of the monkey and doubled down on everything

---

42 In all but one episode. Carol was originally played by Anita Barone, in "The One with the Sonogram" at the end. She left *Friends* shortly thereafter and joined *The Jeff Foxworthy Show*.

that people seemed to like about Season One, including the lesbians and the gay jokes. It is impossible to come away from this season and deny that *Friends* relied on homophobic humor. It's also clear that with "The One with the Lesbian Wedding," they did step up their game.

Carol and Susan were loosely based on a real couple, Deb and Rona,[43] who were longtime friends of Kauffman and Crane, from back in their New York days. Kauffman was godmother to their daughters, and vice versa. As she said, they wrote the women into the series because they seemed like a natural fit: "We never did it to make a point. It was just that these were the people in our lives and we thought this would be good material."

In many ways, it clearly did. Watching the two women and Ross sort out the complexities of their new family was both unusual and relatable to anyone who's dealt with kids and divorce. The setup was certainly used for laughs, as well, but the women themselves were never the butt of the joke. More often it was Ross who got nailed by Susan, for being ignorant or squeamish about the lesbian thing. She remained a necessary, deadpan counterpart to Ross throughout the series, though it never got ugly, because it was *Friends*. Ultimately, they were family. One day, Deb told Kauffman she'd been watching an episode with her eldest daughter. The girl looked at Carol and Susan on-screen, with baby Ben, and turned to her own mother. "A family like *ours*," she said. It was the first time she'd seen one on television.

Kauffman and Crane had always wanted a wedding for Carol and Susan, and in 1995, it wasn't unheard of. The first same-sex wedding depicted on television happened in 1991, on the Fox sitcom *Roc*. Led by Charles S. Dutton, the show followed a black family living in Baltimore, and often trod into complex political areas. The episode in question features a gay uncle (played

---

43   Like Billy Dreskin, Deb and Rona get their own little shout-out. "Who should we call first, your folks or Deb and Rona?" Susan asks Carol in "The One with the Dozen Lasagnas" back in Season One.

by Richard Roundtree—aka Shaft) who first comes out to the family, then reveals that his partner is white, and *then* marries him at the end. While the script was full of typical cracks at gay people, it also confronted a hornet's nest of nuanced topics about prejudice and intersectionality—eons before words like *intersectionality* entered the mainstream lexicon. It also didn't pretend that bigotry could be solved in twenty-two minutes. At the end of the episode, the titular character, Roc, admits he's still not totally comfortable with his uncle's sexuality. Rather, he is learning to be "comfortable with being uncomfortable."

In December 1995, *Roseanne* featured a gay wedding, as well—and (as usual) it didn't so much grapple with the issues as flip them a big, fat middle finger. In the episode (titled "December Bride"), Roseanne winds up planning a wedding for a gay acquaintance, Leon (Martin Mull), and his partner, Scott (Fred Willard). When Leon walks into the venue, he is horrified to discover that Roseanne has filled it with drag queens, topless male strippers, shiny purple fabric, feather boas, and, sitting on the altar, an enormous pink triangle. The buttoned-up Leon shouts, "You have somehow managed to take every gay stereotype and just roll them up into one gigantic, offensive Roseanniacal ball of *wrong*!" He's so repelled by the scene that he calls off the wedding and, in a panic, even tries to convince Roseanne that maybe he's not gay, after all. Rattling off a list of stereotypes himself, Leon argues: "I hate to shop. I am absolutely insensitive. I detest Barbra Streisand, and for God's sake, I'm a Republican!" True to form, Roseanne bluntly asks, "But do you like having sex with men? GAY!" It's an episode that openly jeers at gay people and rolls its eyes at homophobes. It *wants* to make everyone uncomfortable. Whereas *Roc* tried to raise and reflect on complicated feelings about gay unions, *Roseanne* simply tried to push every possible button as hard as it possibly could.

Friends didn't want to do either of those things. Crane said so, in no uncertain terms: "I'm not trying to make people comfortable, and I'm not trying to make them uncomfortable," he told reporters in November 1995, a week after shooting "The One with the Lesbian Wedding." Months before airing, the episode had already gotten plenty of hype, particularly due to the casting of Candace Gingrich—whose brother, then House Speaker Newt Gingrich, actively fought for anti-gay-marriage legislation like DOMA, and often likened homosexuality to an illness or addiction, "like alcoholism." Candace was a burgeoning gay rights activist and had been cast as the officiant in Carol and Susan's wedding after meeting Kauffman and Crane at a benefit for GLAAD (the Gay and Lesbian Alliance Against Defamation).

But that was as political as it got. Politics wasn't the point, Crane said. The point was "that gay people have lives, like everybody else. That weddings are a part of those lives. That it's not a gigantic issue. In fact, I wouldn't even say it's the biggest issue in this episode."

Indeed, the wedding storyline gets far less screen-time than the other two in the episode: Phoebe gets possessed by the spirit of a dead woman named Rose, who won't cross over until she "sees everything"; Rachel's mother turns up (surprise—she's Marlo Thomas!) to announce she's divorcing Rachel's father. Sandra Green realizes that, just as her daughter nearly did, she got swept up into marriage with a man she didn't love. "You didn't marry your Barry, honey," she tells Rachel. "But I married mine." This is the central story of the episode, which is sad and somehow perfect. It highlights just how different marriage is for women like Rachel and Sandra than it is for Carol and Susan. It's expected of them—almost inevitable. ("I went straight from my father's house to the sorority house to my husband's house," Sandra says.) That is, of course, an injustice and a trap itself, and Rachel's entire arc throughout the series is about her breaking out of it. But within the context of this episode, it makes another point: for these straight women, it's easier to be married than to *not* be. Even if it's loveless, even if it's for all the wrong reasons. Carol and Susan *do* love each other. They're a family. They have nothing but good reasons to be married. But for them, it's a battle and a constant compromise just to get down the aisle.

Friends was not interested in battles, but it did compromise— some would say too much. Dr. Suzanna Danuta Walters wrote about the episode in her book, *All the Rage: The Story of Gay Visibility in America*. She gave the show credit for being "carefully sensitive," but, she added, the episode "went out of its way to portray the gay wedding as an exact replica of its heterosexual counterpart." With a few notable exceptions: no white gowns, no exchange of vows, and no kiss.

"We were disappointed about that," Jane Sibbett later said in an interview. Same-sex kissing wasn't common on network television in 1996, but it had been done. The actresses suggested they include one, feeling it was only natural for a wedding scene. But the producers were worried that a kiss would go too far for their audience. Instead, the ceremony is punctuated by Phoebe (possessed by Rose) looking at the brides and shouting, "*Now* I've seen everything!" It's painfully obvious today that the writers crafted the entire Phoebe storyline as a setup to this punch line. It's a little sleight of hand, allowing them to avoid a potentially polarizing lesbian kiss, and instead offer a crowd-pleasing lesbian joke. To Sibbett and Hecht, it seemed like a lot of effort to skirt around a little kiss. "How lovely and simple that could have been," Sibbett recalled. But everyone was just too nervous. "And I think maybe they pulled back a little bit."

Everything about Susan and Carol's wedding was designed to be as familiar and unprovocative as possible. Candace Gingrich was there, but not identified, and would likely not be recognizable to anyone who wasn't involved in gay activism. Gingrich was dressed in traditional ministerial robes (though devoid of any religious symbols), in keeping with the rest of the scene. As Dr. Walters points out, the brides walked down the aisle to

classical wedding music, holding bouquets, and on the arms of
men—"one in full military garb, to further the imagery of inclusion." And still there was, as Sibbett calls it, a sense of pulling back. Costume designer Debra McGuire did not make their
gowns in bridal white, but soft silvers and muted earth tones.
She accessorized them each in a decorative hat—the suggestion
of a veil, but not quite. But there was no question that they
would be in dresses. "We took it very seriously," McGuire recalled. "I really loved the idea of these women being women,
of them looking beautiful and feminine, because of the stereotypes about gay women."

This is where *Friends* reveals itself to be truly a product of its
time—a homophobic era in the most literal sense of the word. In
the mid-'90s, the gay rights movement was gaining more traction than ever before. The right to legally marry still seemed a
remote possibility, but civil unions would soon be offered by a
handful of states and countries. A small number of high-profile
politicians and celebrities had come out (this was before Ellen
DeGeneres did but after Melissa Etheridge). It was by no means
an easy time to be gay, but it was a hopeful moment when things
seemed, little by little, to be changing.

And, as ever, people responded to change with fear. In 1996,
the "gay panic defense" was still an acceptable legal strategy.
Jonathan Schmitz—who shot and killed his friend Scott Amedure, after Amedure came out to him on *The Jenny Jones Show*—
successfully used it and was convicted of second-degree murder, rather than first (and was later paroled). President Clinton
instituted "Don't Ask, Don't Tell," a military policy that simultaneously forbade the harassment of *closeted* gay, lesbian, or bisexual service members, and banned them from coming *out* of
the closet. Specifically, they were not allowed to disclose their
sexuality, nor indeed *any* information that might suggest they
weren't straight (what kind of information that might be was

anybody's guess). As the policy stated, openly gay people would put the military at "an unacceptable risk."

At the time, DADT was seen by many as a win for the gay community. Until then, there were no protections against discrimination on the basis of sexuality, and being gay had simply been grounds for discharge.[44] Clinton had campaigned on the promise of finally ending the ban on gay service members—with no such qualifiers about being in or out of the closet. Polls indicated that most Americans supported the move. But Congress and military leaders opposed him, and after months of negotiation, Clinton announced the new policy, calling it an "honorable compromise." And at least *some* gay people agreed. Former army captain John McGuire told the *New York Times*: "People I worked with in the army knew I was gay, but I didn't hold up a huge sign… If you are a gay man or lesbian and join the military, you want to fit in. You want to conform."

That was certainly the case on television, too. Conformity, assimilation, inclusion—whatever you want to call it. It was okay for gay characters to exist as long as they didn't hold up a big, flashy sign. Carol and Susan could be lesbians and even wives, as long as they didn't kiss or touch or cut their hair short. Twenty years later, Jessica Hecht remembered getting the call from a casting associate to come in and read for the role of Susan: "She said they were looking for somebody who could play a lesbian but didn't *look* like a lesbian…somebody who could look good in, like, antique clothes, but not really be too aggressive." The character description put it in no uncertain terms. Susan, it said, was "a lipstick lesbian."

There are, of course, many gay women who do dress like Susan and keep their hair long. Many others prefer short hair

44 I'm deliberately referring to gay, lesbian, and bisexual people rather than everyone under the LGBTQ umbrella, because DADT only applied to them. The military had banned candidates with what it referred to as "behavior disorders," including "transvestism" in 1963, and that ban would remain in place until President Barack Obama lifted it in 2015.

and suits. Actress and comic Lea DeLaria had a small part as one of Carol and Susan's guests.[45] She said of the wedding scene: "They needed at least thirty or forty more fat dykes in tuxedos. All those thin, perfectly coiffed girls in Laura Ashley prints— what kind of lesbian wedding is that? And no one played soft-ball afterward?"

Who knows? Maybe they did. Susan and Carol were not main characters, after all, and they presumably had a whole life and social circle that we never got to see. But that's the point: *Friends* allowed for all manner of gay jokes, but in its brief glimpses of actual gay people, they played it as straight as possible.

I spoke with television writer Ryan O'Connell about this "honorable compromise" so often made on sitcoms. "When you remove any kind of gay quality from a character, it's almost homophobic," he told me. O'Connell wrote for the rebooted *Will & Grace*, another NBC comedy that first debuted in 1998, and returned in 2017. That series *did* have gay lead characters, including Jack McFarland—a singing, dancing, sign-waving gay man. During the show's initial run, Jack was a polarizing character, who many criticized for being *too* recognizably gay. O'Connell summarizes the backlash: "Here's how we went in gay culture: Jack McFarland comes on TV. We're like, 'Yay!' Then there's this movement that says, 'Oh, I don't know. Jack is very stereotypical.'" After that, television saw a wave of gay male characters who were written as the anti-Jack: jocks, cops, conservative Republicans, and other straight-dude archetypes. In reaction to one Jack, says O'Connell, there were years of gay male characters "who had *no* signs of being gay, other the fact that they like men."[46]

---

45 She's the woman who overhears Phoebe say, "I miss Rose," assumes that Rose is an ex-girlfriend, and swoops in to buy Phoebe a drink.

46 O'Connell references *The Unbreakable Kimmy Schmidt* character, Mikey, as the quintessential example: Mikey works in construction, is obsessed with sports, says dopey things in a Queens-Italian accent—he's basically Joey 2.0. "This construction worker that just happens to like guys," says O'Connell. "That fuckin' person feels so false to me. But I know Jack. Honey, I know Jack."

Gay jokes, he says, weren't really the problem with *Friends*. Like Beauchamp, he grew up watching it as a gay kid in the '90s. He heard those jokes everywhere, off-screen and on. "[They] were just so ingrained into the fabric of every show that it didn't even faze me." The real homophobia on *Friends*, and virtually all of its peers, was the constant straightening out of the gay community.

But—and this is not the kind of "but" that erases everything that came before it—with Carol and Susan, *Friends* still stepped up its game. The show did depict the first lesbian wedding on television, in prime time. Kiss or no kiss, that was no small thing. Two network affiliates—WLIO in Lima, Ohio, and KJAC in Port Arthur, Texas—refused to air the episode,[47] but that just wound up backfiring when viewers in their regions raised angry protests, and GLAAD decried the censorship, giving the episode even more press. NBC hired extra temp staff to field phone calls, expecting to hear from thousands of outraged viewers. In the end, they got two calls. Almost 32 million people tuned in to watch "The One with the Lesbian Wedding." It was the highest rated program on television that week, and the first episode of *Friends* ever to hit #1. That is no small thing, either. To have the most popular TV comedy take this risk and not just survive but succeed tremendously revealed that, yes, things really were changing. It made it clear that Americans would not merely tolerate a gay couple on television, but tune in and cheer for them. *Friends* cleared a path for other shows to follow, with far less trepidation.

Furthermore, the story of Carol and Susan and Ross explored another common experience in gay people's lives (albeit through the eyes of a straight character). "I thought it was even better having a character like Ross there," Sarah Beauchamp told me,

---

47   Ron Kelly, the VP and general manager of KJAC, issued a statement saying: "We do not believe the episode of *Friends* meets prevailing standards of good taste in our community." Instead, he said, they would air a preview of the Super Bowl.

reflecting on the wedding episode. "Because he needed to warm up to it and be convinced of it. [In] a lot of families, when a kid comes out, their dad or their mom is getting used to it. So, I liked that they showed that side of it, too."

Yes, Ross spends one and a half seasons moping about his lesbian ex-wife and sparring with Susan—which, Beauchamp adds, is probably how it would go in real life. And it *does* happen in real life, because gay people often have heterosexual relationships before coming out, and that makes for a complicated breakup. "That's something you have to process... Ross definitely didn't handle it well, but I don't know *anyone* who would," says Beauchamp. Even in the idealized world of *Friends*, "I don't think anyone whose wife leaves them for a woman and finds out she's pregnant would be like, 'Oh, great! Let's all co-parent! This is so comfortable for me!'" Ross's initial reaction, she says, was a pretty authentic mix of hurt, anger, and ignorance. "That's reality."

At one point Ross even tries to convince Carol that they should get back together. There's a scene in Season One where the two of them wind up at a hibachi restaurant, reminiscing about old times. "Here's a wacky thought. What say you and I give it another shot?" says Ross. "I know what you're gonna say, you're a lesbian... But there's something right here. I love you." True, he's being unbelievably unfair, and Carol shouldn't have to put up with it. But their deep connection is obvious; they share years of history and complicated feelings, not to mention a child. The talk ends with a brief kiss before she tells him no—of course, no. Jane Sibbett recalled the scene as one of her fondest memories from working on the series: "Because it says so much about our relationship, and that there can be so much love between two people." The scene doesn't come off as offensive, but heartbreaking and intimate.

It's Ross who Carol seeks out the night before the wedding, after her parents refuse to attend and she considers calling it off.

This is the moment when Ross finally comes around, puts his own hurt feelings aside, and steps up. "Look do you love her?... Well, then that's it," he tells Carol. "If my parents didn't want me to marry you, no way that would have stopped me. Look, this is *your* wedding. Do it." He then fills in for Carol's father, and walks her down the aisle (hanging on to her arm just a little too long before letting her go). Is he totally over it? No. He might never be. But it's a turning point for him, and for this newly blended family. Later on at the reception, Susan asks Ross to dance. "You did a good thing today," she tells him.

One act of decency doesn't erase what came before it, but "The One with the Lesbian Wedding" was a good thing, both for Ross and for *Friends*. In light of how much the world has changed in the years since it first aired, the episode stands as an uncomfortable reminder of a time, not long ago, when gay jokes were far more acceptable on-screen than gay people—let alone gay marriage. Even now, when representation is at an all-time high, queer characters make up only about 6% of those on scripted television (most of which are male and white). In 1996, any degree of visibility made an impact. And to give these two women a wedding, to show them surrounded by family and friends, standing up in support of their love—even if just for a minute of screen-time—was an undeniably good thing. "I think for the gay community it was huge, to actually be able to see that," said Sibbett. "I wish that there had been *more*."

5

The One Where We All Got the Haircut

It was summer. It was hot. Madeleine Albright was there, in office, having been sworn in as the US's first female secretary of state. Scottish scientists announced the birth of Dolly the Sheep, the first mammal to be successfully cloned from an adult cell. Somewhere in the Ares Vallis, the Mars Pathfinder had just touched down on Martian soil, marking the first successful rover mission to the red planet. And in a hair salon in Westchester County, New York, I sat in a vinyl styling chair and received my first Rachel.

In this, I was hardly a pioneer. It was 1997, and The Rachel was inescapable. In 2010, a UK study conducted by hair-care company Goody reported that, in Britain alone, approximately 11 million women had gotten the signature cut, and it was *still* the most requested hairstyle in salons. There are no formal estimates on how many women in the US (not to mention the dozens of other countries in which *Friends* aired) walked into hair appointments with a page torn out of *People* and walked out with a top-heavy mop of choppy layers. One can only assume that's because they all did. Fine, *we* all did.

By '97, Jennifer Aniston no longer had a Rachel herself. She'd grown her hair out into a longer, simpler style, removed the blond highlights, and darkened it to a uniform auburn. In all ten years of *Friends*, Season Three was the only one in which she routinely wore her hair pulled back, and did not have a distinctive cut. It was the hairstyle equivalent of a time-out.

It was way too late for that, though. The Racheling had begun and there was no undoing it. At some point during its second season, *Friends* had reached a kind of popularity that bordered on omnipresence. It wasn't just the theme song on the radio and the actors on *TV Guide*. The show became an arbiter of style and beauty. Generational theorists claimed it as the definitive series of Generation X. *Friends* had exploded out of the realm of television and now it was just all over everything.

Marta Kauffman described Season Two as a year of lesson-learning. "We learned a lot about what does work and what doesn't work. What you can do, what you can't."

You *could* have two women get married, for instance. That was a definitive success in terms of audience response and ratings. You could also bring your will-they-won't-they couple together without letting steam out of the tires and losing momentum.

The second season opens with a twist: Rachel now knows that Ross likes her, and she likes him back. But he comes home from a business trip with a new girlfriend, Julie (Lauren Tom). Though the character was clearly created just to keep the central couple apart a bit longer, she also cast Rachel in a whole new, less flattering light. This was the moment, as Phoebe might say, "when she stopped being a princess and became, like, a *woman*." For once, we got to see *her* pine, and be jealous, and make ill-advised phone calls while drunk. The utterly likable Julie brought out an uglier (but extremely relatable) side of Rachel.

Another thing you could do? Have a character of color—with

lines and a name and everything. Julie only appeared in seven episodes, but the character had a huge impact. Even twenty years later, Tom said, "I've had so many young Asian girls come up to me and say that was the first role model that they've had on such a widespread TV show. Where they got to see an Asian girl who wasn't speaking with an accent, who was American, and who was desirable and sexy and funny."

Julie was all of those things, but she was also temporary.[48] Shortly after "The One with the Lesbian Wedding," Ross and Rachel were united at last, in "The One with the Prom Video." This remains one of the best and most archetypical episodes of the entire series. It features the first *Friends* flashback, filling in backstory on Monica and Rachel's friendship. It also gives us Phoebe's iconic speech about lobsters and monogamy. Aniston's hair is at Peak Rachel. And at the center of it all is one of the most acutely emotional moments on a show that is *all* about feelings. Watching the old prom video, Rachel (and everyone else) sees the true depth of Ross's devotion to her. Ross stands exposed and vulnerable, literally backed into a corner. And that's when it clicks for Rachel: he *is* her lobster. She doesn't say a word, just gets up and goes to him.

"I still kind of get chills from it," recalled Kauffman. "When she crossed the room and gave him that kiss, the audience went *insane*."

That's a pretty good word to describe this moment in *Friends'* history, when its popularity morphed into mania. But why exactly did the mania happen? What was it about Ross and Rachel that made viewers go bananas when they finally got together? And what was it about this very simple show about six friends that made it hit so incredibly hard?

Set aside the obvious for a moment: it was well produced and

---

48   The writers gave her a fitting send-off by pairing her up with another temporary character thrown in to keep Ross and Rachel apart: Russ. Yeah, remember Russ? Ross's doppelgänger, also played by David Schwimmer with a bunch of facial prosthetics? That was one of those things that didn't work.

performed, and it aired on a big network during prime time. The same could be said of other series (just ask the die-hard fans of *Freaks and Geeks*, *Firefly*, and *Undeclared*). TV history is rife with one-season wonders, which many would argue were better—shows that should have been bigger than *Friends*, but instead just disappeared.

I spoke with author and preeminent critic Chuck Klosterman, who is himself something of a pop-culture icon of the *Friends* generation. When the series first aired, however, he wasn't watching it. On Thursday nights, Klosterman was tuned in to ABC, watching one of those other series: *My So-Called Life*. "For a bit, it seemed as though these two shows were almost in philosophical conflict," he told me. "That *My So-Called Life* was an attempt to sort of push people toward the problems of reality that exist in modernity. And *Friends* seemed almost purely escapist and fun. And that conflict, if there was one, obviously didn't last long, because *My So-Called Life* immediately went off the air and *Friends* just got more and more popular."

My So-Called Life was a truly groundbreaking drama, following high-school student Angela Chase (Claire Danes) and her friends through the all-too-familiar pangs of adolescence. The show tackled a number of the same topics as *Friends* but in such a different way that it seemed as if these shows couldn't exist on the same planet let alone the same time slot. It featured a gay character, Rickie (Wilson Cruz, the first openly gay actor to play a gay character), who was multiethnic, wore eyeliner, and used the girls' bathroom at school. It, too, explored the deep love between friends, but also the tension and complexity that inevitably arises in those relationships. It even had its own will-they-won't-they couple—Angela and Jordan Catalano (Jared Leto). This couple didn't get together with a tender kiss in front of all their friends. Instead, Jordan and Angela made out in the school boiler room, and then he ignored her for the rest of the episode. As on *Friends*, the romance was utterly compelling, but it was

also shaded in with sadness and frustration Jordan was not Angela's lobster. He was her kind-of-shitty high-school boyfriend.

My So-Called Life was adored by critics and watched by almost
nobody. Klosterman was one of the few who did (before it was
canceled after nineteen episodes). He'd recently graduated from
the University of North Dakota, and was living in Fargo, working at a newspaper that had hired him specifically to address this
new "Generation X" audience that everyone was talking about.
He spent Thursday nights at home, watching *My So-Called Life*
by himself, but on Friday, he'd drive back to his college town,
Grand Forks, where most of his friends still lived. They'd go out
late, come home drunk, and then head back to someone's apartment, where everyone would pile in front of the television. "I
realized they all taped *Friends* on their VCRs and would watch
it when they came back from the bar at night," Klosterman told
me. "That was the first time I saw any of those episodes."

The show became a part of his weekend routine with his bud-
dies. That's what *Friends* was to a lot of folks. "It became this
thing that people watched, seemingly *just* for entertainment—
not seeing anything deeper into it," Klosterman recalled. "But
when something becomes as big as that show did, that changes.
Then it suddenly seems like there was something meaningful
about that decision." At heart, Klosterman felt—and still feels—
that *My So-Called Life* was the better show. Certainly, it was the
one that truly represented Generation X and its values. *My So-
Called Life* reflected people's real lives (and haircuts and clothes
and relationships). And that's precisely why *Friends* won. *Friends*
reflected real life—but just a *little* bit better.

The central theme of TV in the '90s was "aspirational normalcy." That's what media executive Lauren Zalaznick calls
it. Zalaznick oversaw programming and development at VH1
during the mid to late '90s, before moving to NBC Universal, where she famously revamped the Bravo network during
the rise of reality television. Zalaznick has spent her career

connecting the dots between America's national mood and its TV-viewing habits. In the late '70s and '80s, the country saw massive spikes in unemployment and huge economic disparities. TV became all about fantasy, Zalaznick told me. "*Literal* fantasy: *Fantasy Island*. Or fantasies of strength and prowess in *The Six Million Dollar Man*. Or fantasies of wealth and power: *Dallas, Dynasty*."

But by the mid-'90s, the mood had lightened up. The economy was in good shape and growing at a steady clip. Both the Cold and Gulf Wars had officially ended, and though there was still war and poverty and all manner of horrors in the world, many Americans had the privilege of not knowing too much about it.[49] In short, "it was the Clinton years," said Zalaznick. "We decided that the world was pretty good and getting better, and everyone should discover a four-dollar cup of coffee at Central Perk."

It was an era of attainable luxury, when people suddenly started ordering a Venti, fat-free, no-foam latte instead of just *a coffee*. Fashion took on the appearance of normality, as white T-shirts and "relaxed fit" jeans supplanted the bright, boxy, dry-clean-only look of the previous decade. Viewers no longer craved the full-blown fantasy of '80s television, nor did they want thinky dramas like *My So-Called Life* (those were a little *too* real). They wanted comedy, but not absurdity. They wanted characters whose lives they could relate to and whose clothes they could covet (but also conceivably find at a mall). Gone was *Dynasty*'s Alexis Carrington, with her fur dressing gown and her forty-eight-room mansion, and in came Monica Geller, with her GAP cardigan and her two-bedroom, rent-controlled apartment. Unrealistic? Yes. But not impossible.

During that first big wave of *Friends* mania—The Rachel

---

49   Klosterman echoes this sentiment: "Go back and look at the paper in 1996 or 1997. The things people were worried about were, like, 'Are shark attacks on the increase?'"

years—the apartment was everybody's favorite sticking point. "It became an extremely popular thing to say, 'How could they afford this apartment?'" Klosterman pointed out. "But that was also proof that *Friends* was making real traction in society. You can tell a sitcom becomes meaningful when people start worrying about verisimilitude." (Twenty years later, people are still worrying about it. As I write this, there are no less than eight articles on Google News referencing Monica's apartment, all published within the last two weeks.) Of course, *every* sitcom apartment was bigger and nicer than any in real life. Will and Grace had two bathrooms and a walk-in closet. But *Friends* was different from other sitcoms. Indeed, it did epitomize that achievable-aspirational mood of the '90s, but underneath all the aesthetics, it touched on something else that was happening to young adults, both on-screen and off.

"By the '90s, there'd been this change where people in their twenties were getting married later, and were assumed to still be figuring out what their life was going to be," said Klosterman. For previous generations, the expectations were clear: you went to school, perhaps to college, entered a profession, and stayed there. You got married and had a family and, theoretically, stayed there, too. But Generation X (aka the 13th Generation) came of age in an era with no such certainties. Nearly half of them had been raised by divorced parents—more than any other generation before or since. They were a cohort of latchkey kids, who learned from an early age to rely on themselves and their peers—not on family, nor any other traditional institutions. As Gen Xers entered the workforce, they were pegged as aimless, self-involved slackers—an unjust stereotype that was only a little bit true. The 13th Generation was marked by a sense of directionlessness, perhaps because they'd been given so little direction. Furthermore, entry-level positions were harder to come by, as most fields were still dominated by the enormous Baby

Boomer Generation.[50] They weren't lazy but independent and entrepreneurial—less interested in climbing the corporate ladder than in carving a new path.

In 1997, generational historians William Strauss and Neil Howe published *The Fourth Turning*, in which they noted Gen X as "the oldest-marrying generation ever recorded." While others sought the love and stability of family, Generation X did not—at least not right away. They knew better than anyone that families could fall apart. Instead, they relied on "ersatz social arrangements," wrote Strauss and Howe. "Often a platoon of friends."

Kauffman and Crane had identified something both timeless and extremely of-the-moment. In this decade, for this generation, "the time in your life when your friends are your family" was even longer and more precious. And that's why *Friends* took hold in the first place. "A lot of its audience felt like those characters were being projected onto *them*," said Klosterman. It would be easy to posit the opposite: that audiences were simply hooked on this high-sugar sitcom with its glamorous cast and ridiculous apartments that they could never have. But at its core, the show was about something well within their reach. "It's a situation comedy—and the situation they're in was not in any way unattainable. It was possible to have five friends. A person could watch that show and say, 'That's my life.'" If you were the sarcastic one in your group, you could say, "I'm the Chandler." If you'd ever had a crush on a friend (and who hadn't?), then you ached for Ross, and cheered when he got the girl. If you wanted to *be* that girl, you imagined yourself as the Rachel. And then you could literally go out and get The Rachel.

---

50 Which was also a much whiter, predominantly male workforce. Generation X included significantly more women, people of color, and immigrants in its labor force. JUST SAYING.

★ ★ ★

During *Friends'* second season, when the show exploded into a phenomenon, the creators and cast were stunned. "We really didn't know that it was becoming such a part of culture," recalled Lisa Kudrow. They were happy with the rising ratings, but they were far too busy trying to keep them up to stop and congratulate each other. "I was running on panic of *just* not wanting to fail," recalled Crane.

If anyone got it, it was Warren Littlefield. He was the one who moved *Friends* to 8:00 p.m., making it the anchor of Thursday nights. He'd wanted a show that spoke to Generation X, and he'd wound up with something even better: a comedy that spoke to Gen Xers, elicited nostalgia in Baby Boomers, and even reached the not-yet-named Millennials, who couldn't wait to grow up, move to the city, and get an apartment just like that. Littlefield had bet big on *Friends* from the start, and now it had become so huge that it was infiltrating fashion trends and even speech patterns. Could it *be* any more influential? No. If there was ever a time when *Friends* could do no wrong, this was it. But he wasn't about to head over to the set and *tell* everyone that.

The *Friends* team knew what made their viewers happy. So, faced with the pressure of popularity (and the 8:00 p.m. time slot), they decided to give them even more of it. Ross and Rachel finally kissed—done. More guest stars appeared, and not just NBC actors. There were movie stars (Julia Roberts, Jean-Claude Van Damme) and music stars (Chrissie Hynde, Chris Isaak—both of whom sang "Smelly Cat," another fan-favorite that turned up a *lot* in Season Two), and TV legend Tom Selleck assumed the recurring role of Monica's boyfriend, Richard.

Meanwhile, on their own network, the *Friends* cast were now the pinch hitters, sent in to support other comedies on shakier ground. During another crossover night, Chandler turned up briefly in a video store on *Caroline in the City*.[51] Ross appeared in a full episode of *The Single Guy* (which starred David Schwimmer's high-school friend Jonathan Silverman). A few months later, Kudrow made a cameo as Phoebe on *Hope & Gloria*. A print ad promoting the episode featured Kudrow in the foreground, under giant, bold type declaring: "Hope & Gloria make a new Friend!" Hope and Gloria themselves were in the background, about half her size.

It was one of many signals that the show and its cast were breaching a new level of stardom. Cox was on the cover of *People*'s annual 50 Most Beautiful People issue. LeBlanc and Schwimmer shot their first major film roles in *Ed* and *The Pallbearer*, respectively. Aniston and Kudrow did a Got Milk? ad together, while others appeared in campaigns for AT&T (Schwimmer) and Saks Fifth Avenue (LeBlanc). Aniston and Perry played Rachel- and Chandler-esque versions of themselves in an instructional video for Windows 95.[52]

They were having a moment and they seized it—and with good reason. For the first season, the cast had been paid the same amount per episode (reportedly $22,500). But now, their salaries varied widely, with some remaining relatively flat, while others were bumped up to $40,000 or more. (They've never disclosed exact numbers, but Kudrow and LeBlanc later stated that they were the lowest paid. As the show's hit couple, Schwimmer and Aniston were purportedly the highest paid in Season Two. However, in 2017, Cox also acknowledged that she had a "favored nations" clause in her contract, meaning no one could be paid more than she was.) The show was doing better than ever, but as far as they knew, it could fall apart tomorrow. Even if it

---

51   That same night, Lea Thompson (the titular star of *Caroline in the City*) bumped into Chandler and Joey babysitting Ben in "The One with the Baby on the Bus." Thompson's show was nowhere near as big as *Friends*, but she herself was arguably a bigger celebrity than any of the *Friends* cast at that point.

52   It's available online now. I dare you to get through it.

didn't, any one of them could get cut. If audiences cooled on one
of the characters, or if one of the actors proved less marketable,
they knew the network or the producers could write them off
and reshape the show as an ensemble of five. No one was going
broke, but neither was anyone in a position to turn up their
nose at a lucrative ad deal. Especially not a Super Bowl ad deal.

   In January 1996, the Coca-Cola Company announced a new
$30 million campaign, partnering Diet Coke with *Friends*. It
was a huge and unusual deal at the time, combining old-school
product integration and youth culture. "Someone stole a Diet
Coke from Monica and Rachel's apartment," the TV spots declared. The cast appeared, in character, in a mock police lineup
as potential suspects in the great Diet Coke robbery. It was a
watch-and-win campaign titled "Who's Gonna Drink the Diet
Coke?" urging viewers to collect Diet Coke caps (which were
printed with character names) and then tune in to *Friends* on
Thursday nights in January. Every week, a Diet Coke commercial would air during the episode, featuring one of them drinking a Diet Coke, and viewers could match their bottle caps to
win a prize. The *grand* prize would be announced in the final
TV spot, set to air the night of the Super Bowl. In addition to
print and TV ads, the campaign included sponsored viewing
parties on college campuses and Diet Coke/*Friends*–branded
calling cards. Fans could visit Diet Coke's website[53] to see the
characters' "mugshots" and look for clues as to who stole the
soda from Rachel and Monica's apartment.

   "The contemporary personality of the show marries with
the persona and attitude we want Diet Coke to exude," Frank
P. Bifulco, Jr., Coca-Cola's VP of marketing, told the *New York
Times*. Diet Coke was the leading diet soda at the time, but sales
had flattened. Young adults seemed more interested in flavored
waters, bottled teas, and fancy coffee. With this rebrand, the

---

53 As the *New York Times* called it back then, an "area" that could be found "on
    line" on "the Coca-Cola World Wide Web site." Bless their hearts.

company planned to reassert itself as the beverage of choice for Generation X. Like everyone else, Diet Coke was looking for an inroad with these young, savvy people who seemed impossible to impress. This sitcom was the only thing they all seemed to like. As *Entertainment Weekly* put it, the *Friends* campaign was "the biggest marketing event aimed specifically at Generation X."

Coca-Cola even turned over creative direction to the show's producers, instead of their own advertising agency. So, it was Warner Bros. who approached the cast with the deal. "That's where I give Jennifer credit because hers was the voice I remember most clearly," Kudrow recalled. "She said, 'It's too much.' And we could have listened to her. But we didn't." Aniston understood the need to strike while the iron was hot. But thanks to The Rachel, she had a real sense of just how hot they were getting. Every woman in the country was walking around with her haircut. How long before everyone got sick of seeing her everywhere?

All of them were wary of overexposure, and wondered if it was the right move. But turning down Coca-Cola money? That was just plain dumb. Again, the actors were offered drastically different sums, but all of them were looking at paychecks between $250,000 and $500,000. LeBlanc later told the *Times* that they agreed to it on the condition that the TV campaign only run for one month, and only on NBC. "And run it they did," he said.

After five weeks of hype, the final Diet Coke ad aired on January 28, during an hour-long episode immediately following Super Bowl XXX. The ad revealed the grand prize (a trip for two to see a taping of the show) and the soda thief. It was Rachel, of course. All of the cast members were good for the brand, but on Super Bowl night, it was Aniston holding the bottle, tossing her hair back and taking a sip.

The episode itself—"The One After the Super Bowl"—was a watershed moment for *Friends*. It was perhaps the biggest lesson learned during that second year. The show was *stuffed* with guest stars: Brooke Shields, Chris Isaak, Jean-Claude Van Damme, and Julia Roberts (who played a love interest for Chandler, and was conveniently rumored to be dating Matthew Perry). *The Simpsons'* Dan Castellaneta also had a small role, as did comedic actor Fred Willard. Even Marcel appeared again, briefly. One week after "The One with the Lesbian Wedding" became the highest-rated episode of *Friends*, the show smashed its own record again. Almost twice as many people tuned in for "The One After the Super Bowl." To this day, it remains the most-watched Super Bowl lead-out program[54] in television history.

It worked out great for Coca-Cola. Soda sales spiked immediately and kept climbing into the summer. People were into Diet Coke again. But as for *Friends*? They'd had enough. Aniston was right—it was way too much. The pendulum swung hard after the Super Bowl episode, which critics decried as a shameless cash grab that worked all too well. The *Chicago Tribune* dubbed it, "The One Where the Show Crosses the Line from Promiscuity into Prostitution." The cultural phenomenon was now a "national epidemic." *Newsweek* said what everyone was thinking, in a giddy, all-caps headline: "LET THE BACKLASH BEGIN!"

Season Two ended with fewer viewers than it started with. The show still had great ratings, but those fresh faces on the screen had become far too familiar. LeBlanc's and Schwimmer's movies came out, and flopped. Every woman who'd gotten The Rachel now realized what a lousy, high-maintenance haircut it was. Even Littlefield realized that *Friends* had gotten too big too fast. NBC put the word out that there would be no more endorsement deals for the time being, and a lot less press for the actors. "There is a possibility of the show being overexposed," he told *Entertainment Weekly* in the understatement of the century.

---

54   Translation: the show that comes on after the Super Bowl. Aside from the game itself, Super Bowl lead-outs are usually some of the most-watched TV shows of any given year.

Kauffman, Bright, and Crane felt awful—for doing those ridiculous ads, and for persuading the cast to come on board. "That was an absolute low point," Crane later acknowledged. "Everyone came away from it going, 'That was pretty dumb and we didn't need to do that.'" Bright echoed his regrets: "Until you have success, you want it so badly you're not thinking about the way that success is gonna challenge your life," he said. "I think it amounts to 'be careful what you wish for.'"

For the cast, life changed overnight. A year before, they'd been rising stars, but now that fame had calcified into something new: celebrity. It was Burrows's prophecy come true. "If the six of us were together, then that was a disaster," Kudrow remembered. They stopped going out as a group—stopped going out as much, period. LeBlanc was living in an apartment building, and strangers started banging on his door at all hours. "I was like, 'I've got to get a house. I need a house, with a gate.'"

Thanks to Diet Coke, he could afford one.

6

The One After "The One After the Super Bowl"

For my money, the best joke ever made on *Friends* is one with hardly any dialogue. In the Season Three opener, the gang walks into Central Perk to find their usual couch claimed by six other friends. Silence. Everyone stands around, blinking. "Huh," says Chandler. With nowhere to sit, they turn around and shuffle out.

It's one of the most underrated moments in *Friends'* history, because it's a crack at itself. *We know, we're ridiculous. Should we maybe just leave?* It sets us up for a season of reality checks and re-calibration. This was the year that *Friends* became self-aware and a little more grown-up. In subtle ways, the show addressed the public's grievances (*Why do they always get the couch?!*), while giving viewers new reasons to stick around and learn to love it again. Having survived its first great wave of success and the crush of its first backlash, this season marked another milestone: the first *Friends* comeback. Still, there was no going back to a time before Julia Roberts and Diet Coke. The Friends were officially wealthy celebrities—and now, everyone knew exactly how wealthy.

★ ★ ★

In the midst of the Super Bowl media blitz, David Schwimmer's agents had started nudging him to ask for a raise. He'd been designated as the breakout star—maybe not a movie star after *The Pallbearer*, but certainly the actor with the most leverage. There was something discomfiting about that. Schwimmer still believed in the ethos of ensemble theater, and it had served the cast well. Yes, he was Ross, of Ross and Rachel, but the show was *Friends*. They were a team, and had agreed from the start to work like one, off-screen as well as on. How long would that team spirit hold with some of them getting paid like celebrities and the others just like actors? Salary disputes had destroyed plenty of other shows, and with a cast this big it would be all too easy for the higher-ups to play them off against each other during every contract negotiation. Things got messy when big money was on the table. His mother—the Hollywood divorce lawyer—never let him forget it. "Do not be divided," she told him.

Schwimmer went to his castmates with a proposition: it seemed he had a chance to ask for a raise. What if, instead, they all asked for one—the *same* one this time? Just as Cox had done before shooting the pilot, Schwimmer poured his own leverage into the collective pot, using it to unify and strengthen the group.

In June of 1996, the cast approached Warner Bros. asking for an across-the-board raise to $100,000 per episode. On top of that, they wanted a share of revenue when the show went into syndication in 1998. At the time, it was unheard of for actors to get a share of back-end profits, unless they were also part owners of the show (i.e., Jerry Seinfeld). The proposed raises, too, were astronomical in comparison to those of their sitcom peers. Roseanne Barr and *Married with Children* star Ed O'Neill earned six-figure salaries, but they were lead actors and had been on the air for years. Most shocking was the tactic of collective bargaining. No television ensemble had ever negotiated as a group, nor had any cast ever had such power at the bargaining table. If they were serious about this all-for-one-one-for-all approach, then they could walk away and take the entire show with them.

Headlines lit up with reports of the *Friends* cast banding together to make these startling demands, and threatening to strike if they weren't met. It wasn't just trade publications, either, but mainstream outlets from *Us Weekly* to the *Washington Post*. Historically, the general public wouldn't have even known, let alone cared, about the details of television contract negotiations. But this one had become both tabloid gossip and national news. From the outside (and the inside), $100,000 seemed like an outrageous ask. Then again, an outrageous amount of money was coming in. NBC charged advertisers upward of half a million dollars for thirty-second commercial spots during *Friends*. The network in turn paid Warner Bros. $1 million per episode to keep the show on NBC (a few months later, the production company itself renegotiated to a whopping $3 million). Warner Bros. had also decided to sell the syndication rights after just two years—far earlier than usual—and then proudly told the press that when *Friends* reruns began in 1998, they would bring in an additional $4 million a pop. The cast was asking for a bigger slice of the pie (well, six slices), but the pie itself was pretty damn huge.

It was a tense summer. *Entertainment Weekly* reported that the actors were going through with their strike, and that fans were being polled outside the studio, to see which character they would miss the least (it was Joey, allegedly). Now the "salary virus" seemed to be spreading to other shows. The two lead actors on Fox's cop drama *New York Undercover* staged their own brief strike, asking that their salaries be tripled. Instead, producer Dick Wolf filed a lawsuit against them for breach of contract, wrote a script that killed both characters off in a fire, and started casting sessions for potential replacements. The actors dropped it and quickly hurried back to work. Wolf was appalled that NBC and Warner Bros. were tolerating this behavior from their actors, and he did not mind saying so: "What I would have done was come out on the first day, say I was disappointed the cast had decided to negotiate in the press, and I had the unpleasant news that Matt LeBlanc wouldn't be on the show next year." After firing LeBlanc, he said, the rest of them would have shut up and gotten back to work.

They did, in fact, go back to work in August—with LeBlanc, but still without new contracts. Warner Bros. had gone to the actors with a counteroffer of $75,000 per episode (no mention of syndication royalties), but only on the condition that they extend their current contracts from five seasons to six. They didn't bite. Schwimmer was apparently reluctant to commit himself for that long, and (thanks to him) they were now more unified than ever—a mini-union. LeBlanc recalled they made a formal pact: "If they come to *you* behind my back, you tell me. If they come to *me* behind your back, I will tell you. Everyone's in?"

For now, yes. They continued with work, shooting the first half of Season Three as negotiations dragged on. NBC blamed Warner Bros. for bragging about its big syndication deal in the press, emboldening the cast to ask for so much money. The press, meanwhile, pointed out that "both the production company and the network have worked hard over the last two years to promote the cast as a group, perhaps hoping to prevent one person from becoming inordinately powerful," as the *New York Daily News* wrote. "If so, the companies now may be reaping what they have sown." Be careful what you wish for indeed.

Without a doubt, there was division among the six. "I'm not going to say we never had disagreements with the cast—or that the cast never had disagreements with each other," said Kevin Bright. "And yeah, sometimes there was yelling, and sometimes there were people walking off the stage. But it was always solved *on* the stage." Whatever infighting happened during those first big negotiations—and the far bigger ones that came later—they managed to keep it between one another. In the end, Schwimmer said, it came down to a democratic vote: he and the rest of them would extend their contracts to a sixth season, in return for scaled-up salaries every year.[55] After six months of back-and-forth, the contracts were signed in late December 1996.

That was the deal that changed everything, setting a precedent for future negotiations on other shows, and solidifying _Friends_ as something more than a faddish hit. The actors themselves now realized that whatever power they had as individuals was nothing compared to their strength as a group. From then on, they agreed, any decisions they could make together they _would_ make together, whether it came to money, publicity, or their continued participation in the show. Even when it came to awards, they would all submit themselves in the same category: supporting, not lead. They made it known to the producers and the network that if one was fired, they would all leave.

"And then we decided to just pull back and lay low, and stick to the task at hand," said Kudrow. Everyone was in, and for the long haul. Now it was time to earn those enormous, well-publicized paychecks. After all the media hoopla, the task at hand was fairly obvious: try to convince the audience that they were still the same old Friends.

Season Three is _Friends_ at its most grounded. After the previous season of surrealistic highs, this one brings us back down to reality (or as close as _Friends_ ever comes to reality). Monica is fresh off a breakup with Richard, after finding out that he doesn't want children, and realizing how much she herself does. Phoebe finds out more about her complicated family, meeting her birth mother, and struggling to connect with her weirdo little brother. Chandler is back with Janice (Maggie Wheeler), and for the first time, their relationship is more than just an-

---

55 Reportedly, $75,000 per episode for Season Three, $85,000 for Season Four, $100,000 for Season Five, and $120,000 for Season Six. I know.

noying laughs and catchphrases. She's married, with a child, and Chandler soon realizes he doesn't want to be the guy who breaks up a family. The wounds of his own parents' divorce are highly visible this season, and while they're always revealed in a joke, it's easier than ever to see the vulnerability behind his sarcastic front. This is the first year we see Chandler taking a stab at adulthood, and navigating a real relationship. Good thing, too, because by the end of the season, we see a hint of what's to come.

There are plenty of classic *Friends*-isms in Season Three, too. The chick and the duck come in, but unlike Marcel—who just appeared on Ross's shoulder one day—they turn up for a reason. It's a ridiculous reason (Joey is bummed about a girl and buys an Easter chick from a pet shop to cheer himself up; Chandler tries to return it and comes back with a duck, as well) but not as ridiculous as a monkey. Big-name guest stars appear in Season Three, but only about a third as many as Season Two's roster. This year, they're woven into the actual story, rather than just stomping across it, à la Jean-Claude Van Damme.[56] Isabella Rossellini makes one of the show's most memorable cameos, when Ross attempts to flirt with her at Central Perk by telling her she's on his list of "freebies" (celebrities he's allowed to sleep with). This appearance works like a charm because it's actually conceivable that Isabella Rossellini might pop into a hip, New York coffeehouse—*and* that if you hit on her, she'd roll her eyes and leave. It's way more fun to watch Ross get shot down by Rossellini than it is to see Monica go on an actual date with Van Damme.

At the same time, the show seems to cop to some of its absurdities and playfully answer the audience's frequently asked questions. *They just sit around and talk all day. Do these people have jobs or what?* In "The One with Frank Jr.," Phoebe's brother gawks

---

56 The one exception is the Billy Crystal/Robin Williams appearance in "The One with the Ultimate Fighting Champion." They turn up in the opener, have a funny conversation, and then vanish. It makes no sense, but at least they're funny. (Sorry, Jean-Claude.)

at Rachel and Monica, then asks Chandler, "How do you guys get anything done?" His reply: "We don't, really."

Aniston's anti-Rachel hair is the most evident symbol of the Season Three recalibration. It's clear they're trying to keep it as boring as possible—a little less aspirational normalcy and more straight-up normalcy. Aniston herself was pretty sick of being known as a walking haircut. "There's definitely a part of you that says, 'Hmm. Why am I getting noticed for my haircut, and not for my work?'" she said in an earlier interview. The fad wasn't fading anytime soon,[57] and Aniston would always be a hair icon. She'd never shake off The Rachel, but if there was ever any question that she was more than a haircut (and I don't think there really was), then her work in Season Three answered it, loud and clear.

At the center of this season is the ultimate reality check: Ross and Rachel break up. This was the moment Crane dubbed "the lynchpin of the whole season."

I might go so far as to say it is the lynchpin of whole series from that point on. Bringing the will-they-won't-they couple together had been enormously satisfying to watch. Seeing them function as a happy couple was a reward for our patience. But how long before that got boring? How long before that happy couple just got married and moved to Scarsdale? *Friends* did not rely exclusively on Ross and Rachel to keep it afloat, but the *possibility* of Ross and Rachel was an integral part of the group dynamic. If they stayed together for too long, they would sink the entire premise of the show. For the sake of the story (which, thanks to the new contracts, had just been lengthened by another year), they had to break up. But they also had to break up because Ross and Rachel were not, in fact, a happy couple. They were the *worst*.

---

57   Aniston shot *Picture Perfect* during the summer of 1996, when her hair was still very shaggy. It came out a year later, and everyone who didn't get The Rachel the first time around suddenly rediscovered it. That haircut wasn't going anywhere.

Ross and Rachel had love and chemistry and passion—all the right ingredients for romance. On the other hand, they had trust issues and vastly different goals and a lot of growing up to do. In short, theirs was a fairly typical twentysomething relationship. After the delirium of new love began to wear off, their fundamental issues crystallized into bickering and irritation—all very relatable, but no fun to watch. From then on it was just a matter of seeing how long they (and we) could ignore the problem.

The real cracks begin to show when Rachel quits waitressing at Central Perk and starts forging ahead with her career. Ross is totally supportive, until she meets Mark—a seemingly innocuous guy who works at Bloomingdale's and offers to help her get an interview. Now, Ross is less supportive of Rachel because he's too busy being suspicious of Mark. His attitude worsens when she gets the job and suddenly has less time to sit around adoring him because she's out there building a life of her own. Here we see the other side of Ross's nice-guy attributes. His devotion to Rachel becomes possessiveness; his sensitivity becomes insecurity. His detailed fantasies about the two of them moving to the suburbs and having kids now seem like the entitled expectations of a Mad Man, not a Friend.

Ross's icky, throwback misogyny pops up in other ways—like when he absolutely panics over his son having a Barbie, and swaps the doll out for a G.I. Joe—but the rest of the gang are quick to point out that he's being a weenie. Now, though, he crosses the line into extreme jealous-boyfriend territory, showing up at Rachel's office uninvited and sulking when she has to work late. To be fair, she does spend a lot of time with Mark (because he's her coworker), and she does have to work late quite often (because she's in an entry-level position, learning the ropes and paying her dues). If Ross took a moment to stop and reflect on the early days of his own career, he might remember that that's just how it works. But he's far too busy sending stuffed animals to Rachel's office and leaving whiny messages on her answering machine. "It's *just* a job," he tells her. He brushes off her work commitments and dismisses her ambition, increasingly annoyed that it's getting in the way of her *real* job: being his girlfriend. He argues that his own career in paleontology is important and interesting, while nobody cares about fashion. Because this is a network sitcom in 1997, she says, "Maybe we should just take a break," instead of the response he really deserves: "Maybe you should just go fuck yourself."

Everything else about the breakup is brutally real. The miscommunications, the bitter arguments, and, finally, the betrayal that seals the deal. Rachel suggests a break, Ross takes that to mean they're broken up, and before they both come to their senses, he sleeps with somebody else. Over the course of six episodes, Ross and Rachel have devolved from the star-crossed lovers we've been rooting for, to a couple that should have broken up months ago. All that delicious tension between them has turned toxic, and yet it's still devastating to see them finally split. "The One with the Morning After" finds the two of them hashing it out in Monica's living room,[58] trying to decide if they can come back from this. Gone are the grand gestures and cinematic lighting. A romance that began with musical underscoring and kisses in the rain ends quietly, in a darkened living room, the two of them hollow-eyed and weeping. There is nothing to be done. "It's just changed, everything. Forever," she tells him. "Yeah, but—" he looks around in disbelief "—this can't be *it*." But it is.

In retrospect, it's startling to see how brief the relationship actually is, considering how large it looms in the story. There are 236 episodes of *Friends*, and they're only together in about 10% of them. Not until after the breakup do Ross and Rachel really become Ross and Rachel. The real question was never

---

58   With the other four hiding in Monica's bedroom, eating organic leg wax. It's a silly setup, but really, any comic relief will do in this bruiser of an episode.

will-they-won't-they get together, but would they get *back* together, after all that. Now they're older and life is more complicated. There is tension between them again, and it's not based on an unrequited crush but on a messy history. Both they and the rest of the group have to recover from this breakup, and they all come through it together, but changed.

It's after this point, too, that *Friends* really becomes *Friends*. Season Three is more than just a rebound from the backlash. It's the end of the overture, and the start of the first real act. It kills all remaining darlings from the first two seasons and introduces new dynamics that will carry the show through the next seven. The season ends with all six of them at the beach. Ross and Rachel are eyeing each other again. Monica is venting about being single and Chandler jokes about becoming her boyfriend (and it *is* a joke, right?). Once again, the six of them are sitting around the table playing a game. They're still the same old friends. But something's different.

7

The One Where
They All Go to London
(And Everywhere Else in the World)

It is a truth universally acknowledged that Americans don't get British humor. It's too dark and sophisticated for our sensitive palates, or something. Our humor, on the other hand, is deemed as sweet and uncomplicated as a Hershey bar. It's unclear when this schism took place—at some point between the Reformation and the birth of Ricky Gervais—but it remains one of the greatest cultural divides between our wry forbearers and us goody-goodies here in the New World. As Gervais has put it, "America rewards up-front, on-your-sleeve niceness... We avoid sincerity until it's absolutely necessary."

There is, of course, one enormous counterpoint, and that is touchy-feely *Friends*. To this day, it remains appallingly popular in the UK. Reruns have aired almost around-the-clock since the series finale, and as of 2015, the rerun ratings were going *up*.

The *Friends* effect in Britain became apparent soon after the UK premiere, in the spring of 1995. By 1997, when Kauffman, Bright, and Crane were planning Season Four, it had reached a fever pitch. It seemed like the right place and time to try something new. That's how, a year after Season Three's low-key conclusion at the beach, *Friends* capped its fourth year with a true grand finale, in London.

The show had earned back the right to go big again. Following the slow-burn of Season Three, Season Four turned up the heat just so, delivering some of the series' most beloved episodes ("The One with the Jellyfish"; "The One with the Fake Party"), dynamic storylines (Phoebe's surrogacy; the Chandler-Joey-Kathy triangle), and just really, really good lines ("15 Yemen Road, Yemen."). This is the season that gives us such iconic moments as Monica's lesson on a woman's erogenous zones, from one to seven ("seven, seven"), and Joey's catchphrase, "How you doin'?" (before it became a catchphrase). All that before we even get to London, and the big surprise waiting for us there.

Best of all, Season Four includes "The One with the Embryos." More widely known as the one with the trivia contest, it's touted as either the all-time greatest episode of *Friends*, or a close runner-up. Either way, "The One with the Embryos" is a breathtaking high note in the history of television comedy, and a real Must-See TV moment.

The titular storyline began when Lisa Kudrow herself discovered she was pregnant, toward the end of the show's summer hiatus. Though not far along, she told Kauffman and Crane right away, knowing they'd need time to strategize. "We didn't want to do another TV show where you had a woman carrying packages in front of her for nine months, and in big coats," Crane later explained. So, they came back to Kudrow with an idea: Phoebe would become the gestational surrogate for her brother, Frank (Giovanni Ribisi), and his wife, Alice (Debra Jo Rupp), who was older[59] and struggling to conceive herself. Kudrow initially balked, telling them, "It's really early on. I un-

---

59 I'm not even going to get into the whole Frank-and-Alice thing, because, really, what is there to say? They hooked up when he was a high-school student and she was his home economics teacher. You can just file that under Storylines That Would Not Fly Today.

derstand that this serves the story really well, but if, God forbid, something happens to my pregnancy, I'm still stuck playing a pregnant woman." After talking it through with Kauffman, they went ahead with the idea, knowing that, if need be, they would have an out. Phoebe's pregnancy storyline wouldn't begin until halfway through the season, and for obvious reasons, she'd be doing IVF (a procedure that doesn't always work). Thankfully, Kudrow's own pregnancy went smoothly, and by Episode 11, Phoebe was off to the doctor to get implanted.

That's when the contest began. This storyline, too, was drawn from reality. Jill Condon and Amy Toomin Straus, who wrote the episode together, were pitching ideas with the rest of the team when the idea of a who-knows-who-best competition came up. Coproducer Seth Kurland knew a group of writers who'd shared a house after college, and once hosted their own friend-group trivia night—complete with a *Jeopardy!*-style game board. The *Friends* writers ran with it, and started throwing out potential quiz questions, pitting Joey and Chandler against Rachel and Monica. They raised the stakes even further, by adding the ultimate wager: if the girls won the contest, the guys would be forced to get rid of the chick and the duck; if the guys won, they'd get Monica and Rachel's apartment. With that in mind, the writers amplified the contest storyline, making it even bigger and more elaborate.

Bright, on the other hand, was always looking for ways to keep production simple. For one thing, they'd gone overbudget in the early days, thanks to setups that spread the cast out and required additional sets and actors. For another, they'd realized the audience preferred episodes where it was just the six main characters, in the coffeehouse or at home—like the previous season's excellent bottle episode, "The One Where No One's Ready." This at-home contest concept was great. It wasn't until they actually shot it that Bright and the others realized just *how* great.

On shoot night, the audience was hooked from the start, the

studio filled with a crackling energy. Everyone was immediately invested in Phoebe's story, eager to find out whether or not she'd get pregnant. It was a safe bet she would (this was *Friends*, after all), but surrogacy was such an unusual topic for a sitcom that it did seem possible she might not. The contest outcome, though, was anybody's guess. The story started out slow, with Rachel coming home from grocery shopping, and Joey and Chandler trying to guess what she bought. From there, it quickly snowballed into a full-blown, high-stakes competition, and by the time the audience caught on, said Bright, "everybody was on the edge of their seats."

And he took note of that. So did everyone on the stage. By now, this had become standard practice. More so than any other show, *Friends* was guided by its viewers, especially those watching it live. The writers crafted the material, but the crowd decided whether or not it was good enough. If a joke didn't yield the expected laugh, the writers huddled up, rewriting on the spot. The actors tried multiple line readings, listening to hear which one landed best. If the audience seemed uncomfortable or put off by a line, they fixed it and tried the take again—and again, if necessary. This meant shoot nights were a marathon, often going until 1:00 or 2:00 a.m. (and sometimes required swapping out one sleepy audience for a fresh one halfway through). Sometimes producers would turn to the crowd between takes, asking for a show of hands to see how many got the joke. In part, Crane chalked it up to "our people-pleasing need to be liked." But even more important was pleasing their people in surprising new ways. Kauffman pointed out that *Friends* fans had grown increasingly savvy. "They would sometimes laugh at setups to jokes, 'cause they knew the characters so well. They were ahead of us, more than not." If Schwimmer walked in with a hangdog look, they giggled before he could even open his mouth and deliver that mopey, *"Hi."*

The more popular the show became, the harder the writers had to work to meet viewers' expectations, while not pandering. The audience was not only familiar with *Friends*, but emotionally attached to it, and therefore highly attuned to its rhythms and beats. Another Season Four episode had Rachel impulsively proposing to Joshua (a guy with whom she'd gone on four dates) in an effort to one-up Ross (who'd just gotten engaged to Emily). It was meant to be funny—Rachel at her most ridiculous. But in the script, the scene came directly after Ross announced his engagement, and it just seemed sad. The audience felt awful for Rachel and couldn't bring themselves to laugh at her. The writers quickly realized they couldn't tweak their way out of this one, and decided to simply shoot the scene as written, but move it into the next episode, giving Rachel *and* the viewers some recovery time.[60] It was an extreme change to make, but that's how much faith they put in their audience. Kauffman explained, "We had to trust their judgment about things that were working and not working."

That's why "The One with the Embryos" still works so well. Condon and Toomin Straus's script condenses all the best elements of *Friends*, undiluted by anything else. There are no stunts, few guest performers, and nearly every scene takes place in Monica's living room. The trivia game keeps most of the core cast together, just being friends—literally, trying to out-friend each other. As the competition gets more heated, the jokes come faster and funnier. (The finished product looks effortless but Crane recalled they shot numerous variations on the trivia questions and answers, pushing for the biggest laugh possible.) Before we know what's happening, the girls have lost the game and—twist!—they're *really* switching apartments. It wasn't a bluff. This completely outlandish scenario is actually happening, and after everything else that's happened in the last twenty

---

60   You'll notice Rachel is wearing the same outfit in both "The One with All the Haste" and the following episode, "The One with the Wedding Dresses." As if Rachel would ever repeat an outfit.

minutes, it doesn't read as ridiculous. The guys ride in on their big, white dog statue, and lo and behold, it's still funny.

All this, in an episode that *also* discusses surrogate pregnancy, infertility, and IVF. What makes "The One with the Embryos" such an emblematic *Friends* episode is that it balances high-pitch humor with high-stakes emotional drama. In the midst of all the sitcom high jinks, real life is happening, too, and in the end it's Phoebe's story that takes precedence.[61] The episode concludes with her coming out of the bathroom, interrupting the apartment-switching chaos and announcing she's pregnant. In an instant, the contest is forgotten, the fighting ceases, and everyone encircles Phoebe in a spontaneous group hug. As ever, friendship comes first.

Group hugs and babies? It doesn't get more sincere than that. Nevertheless, *Friends* surged in Britain, which, like the US, was beginning to recognize a shift in its young-adult population. "There was this sense that this is the way things are going. The family dynamic has broken up, and now it's all about friends," Toby Bruce told me. Now a television writer and development executive himself, Bruce was a teenager growing up in London when *Friends* hit. While the US television industry was desperately chasing Generation X, the UK's hadn't fully embraced this new cultural moment (nor was TV as massive a medium as it was in the States). The only comparable show on the air at the time was *Men Behaving Badly*, "which was *sort* of a very British version of *Friends*," explained Bruce. *Men Behaving Badly* also followed a small group of twentysomethings living in neighboring apartments, but as the title implies, it was much more beer-soaked and crass. *Men Behaving Badly* reflected the wave of "lad

---

61 Bright, who directed the episode, said his favorite part is not the contest but the scene where Phoebe gives a pep talk to the embryos at the doctor's office. He and his wife had struggled with infertility, and his own children were conceived via IVF a few years prior, he later explained. "And the ability to take a step back and have a laugh about it is a really incredible thing."

culture" that swept through Britain in the '90s. It was popular,
but its success was somewhat predicated on a very specific trend,
era, and audience—whereas *Friends* was on-trend *and* timeless.
"There was a universality to [*Friends*]," said Bruce. "It made you
feel special, but also made you feel a part of something bigger."
Plus, he added, "it was the cool thing from America."

In March 1998, most of the cast and crew flew to London
to shoot "The One with Ross's Wedding." The Season Four
finale was the culmination of Ross's whirlwind romance with
his long-distance English girlfriend, Emily (Helen Baxendale).
This storyline was also adjusted due a real-life pregnancy. The
same week she was cast on *Friends*, Baxendale and her husband
found out they were expecting their first child. Emily was never
going to be a regular character, but her original arc was much
longer. The pregnancy meant speeding things up significantly—
which was fine by Baxendale.[62] She was already a recognizable actress in the UK (best known for the series *Cold Feet*), but
Friends brought with it a kind of hysteria that she was not prepared for. "You couldn't walk down the street to buy a pint of
milk," she reflected, years later. "In fact, you couldn't go anywhere. It was impossible to mix with the crowd, and do what
ordinary people do." Baxendale quickly realized she wasn't cut
out for *Friends* fame, nor Hollywood, especially now that she
was expecting. "You have to be thin out in America," she said.
You also had to have a relentless ambition that Baxendale realized she just didn't. Back home, she could be a working actress
but not necessarily a celebrity. She'd never make *Friends* money,
but she'd be able to run out for milk without getting mobbed.
Eventually, that is.

In 1998, when the *Friends* team arrived in London, the mobs

---

62   Schwimmer was also eager to wrap up this storyline. Years later, he referred
     to it as the one thing he would have changed about Ross's trajectory. "I
     would not have allowed myself to be persuaded to have Ross marry and
     divorce again," he told the *Telegraph*. "The whole arc of the relationship was
     weird then, because for him to be able to move on enough to marry someone
     else and then go back to being in love with Rachel later just went a bit too far."

came out in full force. Fans flooded into the city, some coming from hundreds of miles away. Kudrow's scenes had already been shot back in LA (she was in her third trimester by then, and unable to fly) but the rest were filmed at the Fountain Studios in London, or on location in the city. Some were shot at tourist hotspots and others on inauspicious side streets, but no matter where the production went, the crowds found it. (It turned out that local radio stations were getting tips and broadcasting the crew's location as they moved.) "We felt like the Beatles in reverse," said Bright. While filming a scene with Schwimmer, Cox, and Baxendale, "a thousand people showed up. And they were screaming, of course, while we were shooting." A police officer pulled Bright aside and told him if he just took a quick break and let the fans get one photo, they'd all go away. He asked the actors to turn to the crowd and pose, and to his astonishment, it worked. The screaming stopped, the fans snapped photos, and then politely packed up and let them get back to work. "That's all they wanted was a good shot!" said Bright. Things really *were* different in London.

But *Friends* was still *Friends*, and up to some of its old tricks again. The London episode was chock-full of guest stars, some of whom were best known to UK audiences (*Absolutely Fabulous*'s Jennifer Saunders, a pre-*House* Hugh Laurie), and others who were eye-rollingly famous: Virgin founder Richard Branson, and Sarah Ferguson, Duchess of York. Mercifully, both cameos were brief. The stunt casting played well, and even the duchess (who'd been coaxed into the appearance by her daughters) noticed a boost in her own popularity. In the wake of her divorce from Prince Andrew, she was a frequent tabloid target, but audiences shrieked with delight at seeing her goofing around with Joey and his giant Union Jack hat. "At a time when Fergie-bashing had become a national pastime, *Friends* was a welcome relief," she said.

But the episode's biggest reveal involved no guest stars. It got the loudest, longest audience reaction in the history of the show, Crane recalled: "We revealed Monica and Chandler in bed, and the place went nuts for about two minutes—of screaming. Just screaming."

Bringing Monica and Chandler together was a bold move. Any coupling within the main characters meant a change in the group's well-balanced chemistry. And, unlike Ross and Rachel, there was no romantic history between these two, no secret crushes, no buildup whatsoever. Except that's not quite true.

Looking back at the first few seasons, it's clear the writers were considering this pairing early on. They took their time, throwing out tiny, occasional hints, and then quickly burying them in a story, a punch line, or a much more prominent romantic entanglement. With the nonstop drama of Ross and Rachel, it's easy to miss them, but the seeds of Monica and Chandler (who I refuse to call Mondler) are planted as early as Season One. Monica pines for a baby in "The One with the Birth" and Chandler replies, "I'll tell you what. When we're forty, if neither of us are married, what do you say you and I get together and have one?" During Season Three, he flat out offers to be her boyfriend, and—without even holding a beat to let us wonder if he's for real—Monica laughs him off. She then spends so much time explaining why they will never be together (the number-one reason being that they're such good friends), that we're convinced, too. Or, at least, we're supposed to be. Until this point, *Friends* was never ambiguous about romance. Sometimes the characters were clueless, but we, the audience, were always well aware. The archetypes were obvious: you had your Bad Boys (Paolo), your Ones That Got Away (Richard), your Janices and your Lobsters. In any scenario, the outcome was obvious; we knew Ross and Rachel were meant to be, even for the many years that they weren't. No one was sitting around waiting to see when Monica and Chandler would finally consummate the tension between them, because it wasn't there.

The one exception is Season Three's "The One with the Flashback," when a friendly hug between them lasts just a little too long. For a minute, it seems that something might happen, but then, as ever, Chandler dumps cold water on the moment with a joke. *Friends* lore has it that this episode was written specifically to gauge audience reactions to various couplings: Monica-Joey, Ross-Phoebe, Chandler-Rachel. The Chandler-Monica moment at the end is so small and grounded in comparison to the hilarity that comes before it (i.e., Ross and Phoebe ripping their clothes off on a pool table) that it's totally forgettable. In retrospect, it seems like a big, old wink at the audience. But in the context of the episode, it plays like a *gotcha*.

That's why the reveal in London is a surprise—but a welcome one. Chandler and Monica were not an obvious couple from the start, but the writers had laid just enough groundwork that the pairing didn't seem wrong.[63] It was a perfectly executed twist.

The finale aired two months after the shoot, and thankfully, it seemed the London gambit had worked. Both UK and US audiences tuned in en masse, and critics didn't seem bothered by the guest stars and royal cameos—if only because the episode's cliffhangers were bigger than its stunts. (Chandler and Monica?! Ross said Rachel's name!) Some English reviewers were justifiably irked by the depiction of Brits as a bunch of stuffy, humorless "would-be-speaking-German-if-it-wasn't-for-us" snobs. But even that low blow couldn't dampen the show's popularity abroad. Nothing could—not the sentimental storylines nor Fergie nor even the mention of World War II. Even when it behaved like a loudmouth tourist, *Friends* was still the cool show from America.

Its reach was growing, too. By then, the show was on the air in more than twenty countries, including Brazil, Australia, Bulgaria, Sweden, and most of western Europe. It would even-

---

63 Unlike certain other pairings within the group, but let's not talk about that now.

tually expand to one hundred and thirty-five. Many countries soon produced their own *Friends*-esque programs, to varying degrees of success. India's *Hello Friends* lasted for less than two years, while Spain's *7 Vidas* became one of the country's longest-running comedies.

As in the States, the *Friends* effect emerged off-screen, as well. Coffee-bar chains began popping up in tandem with the show's expansion (years before Starbucks took over the world), even in traditionally tea-drinking markets. Sahar Hashemi, cofounder of London's Coffee Republic, said when they first opened, "People didn't know what it was." This was a country that hung out at the pub, not the café. The first location opened in 1995, the same year *Friends* arrived, and soon patrons began to catch on. "We were just known as a '*Friends*-type' coffee bar," Hashemi said. In India, Café Coffee Day launched in 1996 and quickly expanded to over a thousand locations. Until then, coffee was only common in certain southern regions, and tea had been the country's staple beverage since the days of British rule. Now, another great force from the West was coming in through India's television screens.

Some saw *Friends* as a breath of fresh air. Journalist Shoaib Daniyal later argued the show helped India shake its "colonial hangover." It was another invasion of sorts, he wrote in 2014, but it was also a massive hit with younger viewers. "Everyone in school seemed to watch *Friends*," he recalled. Growing up, he and his peers embraced the show's American lingo, as well as its openness about dating and sexuality. "In fact," he wrote, "*Friends* is probably the single biggest reason for the change in India's attitude to sex."

Daniyal clearly saw this as a positive shift, though that was demonstrably not true for everyone in India—a country with its own complex, historic values around marriage and sexuality. Filmmaker Paroma Soni, who also grew up watching *Friends* in India, voiced concern about its influence. In a 2018 video piece, she pointed out that *Friends* is rife with sexism and problematic relationship models. "I fear that shows like *Friends* legitimize negative stereotypes, giving them an American stamp of approval," said Soni.

In other countries, too, the show was met with an unsettled mix of excitement and worry over its distinctly American depiction of young-adult life. Indeed, the more populations *Friends* reached, the more pressing the question became: Was the *Friends* effect a good thing? If so, for whom exactly? One thing was sure: it was powerful. One had to look no further than the hoards of teenagers, like Daniyal, lining up at Café Coffee Day. "That *Friends* could dislodge chai," he wrote, "is another telling marker of its deep influence."

To be clear, plenty of Indians still drink chai (and at least *some* Americans don't drink coffee). It would take a fairly large leap to say that *Friends* alone incited the rise of contemporary coffee culture. Truly, there are few trends (aside from The Rachel) that *Friends* actually created. But there are countless trends that *Friends* picked up and amplified, then spread across the globe.

Fashion is perhaps the clearest example of the show's impact. "*Friends* is a good example of things that were trendy but not necessarily on the cover of *Vogue*," fashion historian Dr. Kimberly Chrisman-Campbell told me. "It's a good record of *real* fashion." There were far more style-conscious shows (like *90210*) and films (like *Clueless*), which dressed their characters in slightly toned-down versions of designer looks. *Friends*, on the other hand, presented a punched-up version of "real" clothing. It skipped over the most extreme and specific trends of the era (like grunge or goth) and always kept it casual: cropped T-shirts, khaki pants, strappy black dresses, endless combos of jeans and sneakers. At the same time, there were six characters with six slightly different looks, said Dr. Chrisman-Campbell. "You could identify with one of them, even if you couldn't identify with all of them." But you couldn't picture any of them on the cover of *Vogue*. Maybe in a GAP ad.

In 1999, however, a version of them appeared in French fashion magazine *Madame Figaro*. The editorial spread, titled "Let's Be Friends," featured a group of six models (three men and three women) who bore a striking resemblance to the cast. The set-ups, too, were inspired by the show: in one shot, the models stood around a foosball table; in another, they sat piled in front of the TV, eating popcorn; several shots featured them playing American football (on what is clearly a European football field). Though it had the look of a high-end fashion shoot, the models were dressed...well, like the Friends, in T-shirts, flip-flops, even a classic Chandler sweater vest.

Nancy Deihl, the director of Costume Studies at New York University, referenced this photoshoot in her book, *The History of Modern Fashion*, as an example of *Friends'* global impact on the industry. "There was this gradual casualization that started to happen," she told me. As the show spread to new countries, suddenly the whole Western world began to dress like twenty-something semiemployed Americans hanging out in a coffee-house. In part, Deihl said, it was that charismatic cast that sold the look: "Fashion is so much more than clothes. It's *ways* of wearing things, and it's gesture, and it's the way people behave."

But there was something else that *Friends* was selling, along with all those cropped T-shirts and mochaccinos. It was the idea of America—and of New York, specifically. "New York never really goes out of style," said Deihl. "But *Friends*, *Seinfeld*, and *Sex and the City*—they really did a lot for the fashionability of New York for younger people. In a way, they counteracted the idea of New York as this place that was unreachable, or too elite, or too expensive. And, as we know, it can be all of those things. But the way it was portrayed in those shows, it was like the promised land."

PART 3

8

The One Where Everything Changed

I was at my friend Connie's apartment one night, talking about *Friends* and weddings. It was the fall of 2017; I had just been married a month prior, and she was weeks away from her own wedding. Among my peers, Connie was the biggest *Friends* fan I knew—and that's saying something. After her fiancé proposed with a ring, she decided he, too, should have something beautiful to mark the occasion. He opted for an engagement tattoo, and Connie knew immediately what the design would be. "The purest idea of love that I have," she told me. "A lobster."

Connie was a die-hard, from the beginning. "I watched it *obsessively* growing up," she told me. As a kid in Minnesota, she'd painted her bedroom walls purple and spent weekends at the mall, hunting for Rachel-esque baby-doll tees. She, too, hoped to one day move to Manhattan and get a job in fashion, and *Friends* made it all seem so doable—adulthood, career, New York. "It was my first representation of people in their twenties, living in a big city, who genuinely liked each other... There was no sense that moving to New York City was going to be scary. Everything worked out."

When Connie got her first New York apartment, she bought a picture frame to hang on the door, like Monica. "Except I did it with the intercom, because I couldn't drill a hole into the door." In those early days, Connie constantly turned to *Friends* reruns for comfort and reassurance. Life was, of course, much harder than it looked on television, but step-by-step she built a life for herself in the city, and a successful career as a fashion writer. A decade later, she'd done it. She'd found her lobster, too (even if he preferred *Seinfeld*). Having grappled with real adulthood in *real* New York, *Friends* remained her old, familiar favorite—a mental salve she applied during times of stress. "A little Xanax for my eyes," she joked.

Now, weeks away from her wedding, I assumed she was popping an episode of *Friends* every night. Right? "No," Connie told me. "Actually, I've been watching it less and less these days." It wasn't that she loved the show any less—the woman had just tattooed her future husband with a *Friends* reference—but that she didn't *need* it anymore. "Maybe it's because I'm now technically older than they were on the show?" Connie wasn't sure what made her drift away from *Friends*, only that it had become something different to her now. "But," she quickly added, "I won't say no if it's on."

It startled me, at first, to hear this from such a devoted fan. But as I look back on the middle years of *Friends* itself, it all makes perfect sense. That night in her apartment, Connie was at the start of a new chapter, forming a family with her husband. And so was I. The time in our lives when our friends were our family was, on some level, coming to an end.

The beginning of the end happened on *Friends* in the middle of its fifth year, when Chandler and Monica became a couple. It progressed further in the sixth season when they moved in together and got engaged. And it reached the final phase in Season Seven when they married. Though the series carried on for three more, it was no longer a show about six young, unsettled, unattached adults. In truth, Seasons Five through Seven were the years when *Friends* reached the peak of its premise, and then began the journey toward its natural end.

The all-time greatest episode of *Friends* is Season Five's "The One Where Everybody Finds Out." That's just my opinion, but it's right.[64] It takes everything that worked in "The One with the Embryos" and does it again, but even better. If "The One with the Embryos" is *The Godfather*, then this is *The Godfather Part II*.

Once again, the cast is brought together in a ridiculous game of their own making. By this point in the season, Rachel and Joey know about Monica and Chandler's relationship but, for some reason, it still has to be kept a secret. Why? It's not super-clear anymore, but it makes for good TV. For Joey, maintaining the ruse has been a nightmare, and when Phoebe finally finds out, he makes the completely rational argument that they should all just stop this endless game of make-believe. "Or," Phoebe suggests, "we could *not* tell them we know, and have a little fun of our own." Obviously.

What begins with a little teasing (Phoebe flirts with Chandler to make him squirm) quickly evolves into an inter-apartmental war of wills and wit and sexual chicken. It only takes a few minutes before everybody finds out what's actually going on, but at that point it doesn't matter. (Ross is the exception; he's busy with a competition of his own, trying to woo Ugly Naked Guy into subletting him his apartment by outwitting other potential renters.[65]) By the time they know that they know that they know, *we're* completely confused—but who cares?!

As with "The One with the Embryos," this episode (written

---

64   It's actually not just my opinion. This episode was nominated for numerous awards, and is widely cited as *Friends'* peak, both by cultural critics and internet polls. And if the internet says so, it must be right.

65   Ross's situation may seem just as ridiculous as the one happening across the street, but as anyone who's navigated the New York rental market will tell you, this is fairly standard mania.

by Alexa Junge and directed by Michael Lembeck) had the audience in hysterics, even after a dozen takes. The actors, too, had a hard time getting through the shoot with straight faces. "Lisa was always the first to break," Lembeck recalled. And Perry—notorious for cracking up his costars—was barely keeping it together himself. Some scenes they never even got through during rehearsal, they got so giggly. While staging Kudrow's "seductive" dance scene, the rest of the cast urged her to go further, make it even weirder. "And you can see Matthew's little grin," said Lembeck, even in the finished product. "If you keep your eye on him, you can see the twinkle. You can see Matthew—while Chandler is curious, Matthew is enjoying."

That's the fairy dust sprinkled on top: Kudrow and Perry are *right* on the edge of laughter the entire time. It's a perfectly executed scene, but it's almost a blooper. And everyone loves a blooper—the gag reel at the end of the movie, or the *SNL* sketch where an actor breaks. It's a moment when the audience get to see that, yes, they're having fun, too. A blurring of the line between fantasy and reality. On *Friends* in particular, these gag-reel moments are vital. Watching Perry and Kudrow—*and* Chandler and Phoebe—acting out this scene within a scene, both doing their damnedest to make the other break—it's overwhelming. That's what makes this episode—this scene, really—the peak of a show with so many extraordinary high points. It underscores the wish we have that these fictional friendships aren't fictional at all.

"One of the selling points of *Friends* is that we believed they *were* friends, off camera," Elaine Lui told me. Lui (best known as Lainey, to her readers) is an entertainment journalist who specializes in the sociology of gossip media. *Friends*, she points out, had a number of selling points, the first simply being its high caliber. But the highly publicized bond between the cast members was another major asset—one that they recognized and actively promoted in the press. "There were all kinds of stories about how they would always eat lunch together, the three women," said Lui. "I distinctly remember some of those storylines—that Jennifer and Courteney always ate the same thing from craft services. I think it was a turkey salad. That's how specific it got."

A Cobb salad with chickpeas and turkey—sometimes reported as turkey bacon. I remembered it, too. Indeed there have been hundreds of articles (and recipes and diet plans) published in the past twenty years, based on this legendary tidbit from behind the scenes.[66] In terms of gossip it seems so benign, but it demonstrates the incredibly successful symbiotic relationship that *Friends* had with the media. Items like the salad story were an undeniable element to the show's popularity. "When you give details like this—that you always spend lunch together, and that you eat the same thing—you're giving people a sense of intimacy," Lui said. "You're feeding the illusion that what we're watching every Thursday night is *actually* how they are in real life. That's compelling."

Friends had come of age during a period of rapid growth in celebrity and entertainment journalism. Outlets like *Premiere* and *Entertainment Weekly* reported industry news for a mainstream readership, and now behind-the-scenes drama was as watchable as a show itself. Meanwhile, monthly magazine *Us* became *Us Weekly*, and shifted its lens to the personal lives of celebrities—and zoomed in, hard. It was the beginning of the "Stars Are Just Like Us" era, when consumers were less interested in seeing actors at their most glamorous and untouchable, and more eager to see them taking out the garbage. "The distance between celebrity and civilian began to close," explained Lui. But not *all* the way. No one actually wanted the stars to be just like us. Here, too, it was all about aspirational normalcy. The stars are just like us, but slightly better.

---

66   As recently as 2016, Cox mentioned the famous "Jennifer Salad" that Aniston made for them, when the group appeared on a tribute to James Burrows. Aniston waved it off, saying, "Oh, stop. I tossed it."

From the beginning, *Friends* had played well with the press, embracing this blurry line between celebrity and character. Lui cited Julia Roberts's Season Two appearance as a prime example. Roberts had turned up as a love interest for Chandler at the precise moment that tabloids were reporting she and Perry were an item. "That blurred the lines even more, between reality and art," Lui explained. "Because [as a viewer] you're like, 'Oh, my God, they're dating in real life, so let me watch their chemistry during this half hour. Let me see how they look at each other, and how she bats her eyelashes at him, and if he grabs her hand.'" Fans were always looking for a glimpse behind the curtain—and sometimes *Friends* seemed to deliberately open it, both on-screen and in print. The more famous the actors grew, the more their own individual lives became part of the draw.

Shortly after the fifth season ended (with Monica and Chandler almost getting married in Vegas, only to be derailed by Ross and Rachel's drunken wedding), Courteney Cox got married herself, to actor David Arquette. *People* published a detailed recap of the event, under the headline "Friends and Lovers." *People*, too, had amped up its celebrity coverage, to stay competitive with outlets like *Us*—though it made great efforts to maintain an air of respectability. *People* used what one staffer called a "publicist-friendly strategy" (or, as others put it, "sucking up to celebs"), generally choosing stories that seemed positive or wholesome. The bad boy turned family man; the starlet who finally finds true love. *Us* reported the nasty breakups and infidelity, but in *People*, every new couple was made for each other, and every marriage was happy, right up until the amicable divorce.

People's stars-are-just-like-you-want-them-to-be strategy was a perfect fit for *Friends*, and vice versa. The magazine gobbled up items like the salad anecdote, and blitzed the public with cover stories about the cast. As Lui pointed out, most popular shows and movies offered only one or two stars, but with

Friends "they had six people to build narratives around." And all of them came with a built-in angle that matched the magazine's feel-good ethos: The Friends are friends! This was the through line in every story. When Lisa Kudrow was pregnant, her castmates "rallied 'round" her, according to *People*, throwing her a shower and offering to babysit. When Aniston had boyfriend problems, Matthew Perry was her "shoulder to cry on." Even when reporting on Perry's struggle with alcoholism and prescription-drug addiction, *People* reminded readers that his costars would be there for him, every step of the way. He was, as the headline read, "A Friend in Need."

Friendship was a great narrative for the magazine, and it sure didn't hurt the show. In the article on Cox's marriage, the primary focus was not so much the wedding but the fact that Cox's five castmates were in attendance. And one of them brought Brad Pitt as her date.

It had been over a year since Aniston and Pitt were first photographed together, though neither had acknowledged the relationship publicly. By the time they did make an official appearance together, attending the Emmy Awards in September 1999, *People* had already claimed (under another winky headline: "Brad and Friend") that they were engaged and had even found a wedding planner. Both had gone through publicized breakups shortly before getting together—she from Tate Donovan (who played Joshua), and he from fiancée Gwyneth Paltrow (who was Gwyneth Paltrow).

When Paltrow and Pitt were together, they'd been written up as a golden couple; they were like the Kennedys plus Liz and Dick, but blond. In the press, Paltrow was a princess, a beacon of elegance and old-Hollywood glamour. Aniston, on the other hand, was the girl next door—and just what Pitt needed. The *People* piece quoted an anonymous "*Friends* insider" as saying: "Jennifer is the anti-Gwyneth. Gwyneth was into going out and being glamorous. Jennifer is not. She's very nonglam."

Paltrow was movies and Aniston was TV. Paltrow was blond and Aniston was a little less blond. It didn't matter that Aniston was a star on one of the most popular shows in history, or that she'd become a style and beauty icon the world over. When the press compared the two (as it forever would, until *another* movie star entered the picture), Aniston came off as the cutie-pie in jeans. This guileless image had been there from the start, and it had a powerful effect. David Wild noticed it as far back as 1995 after her interviewed her: "*Every* guy I knew wanted to ask, 'Oh, what's her deal? Is she single?' Everyone thought she was, like, the Really Pretty Girl in High School Who Didn't Know How Beautiful She Was. And *they* got it."

Enter: Brad Pitt, the Hollywood Prom King who came along and noticed her, at last. At least, that's how the press would tell it, regardless of the truth. Soon, they really were engaged (and Pitt would eventually make his own legendary cameo on *Friends*). After five years playing the literal girl next door, Aniston's identity was unshakable. She was inextricably bound with Rachel. And all of them were bound to the show.

"We all made movies and realized, no no no no—this is where home is," Perry was quoted (in *People*) during the production of Season Six. Paula Chin, an editor from the magazine, had come for a set visit the week they shot "The One Where Chandler Can't Cry." Chin observed how, after all these years, the cast seemed closer than ever. The women played with each other's hair between setups, and as ever, "the actors can't help cracking each other up during the take." It was a bittersweet (but mostly sweet) picture that Chin painted. The cast contracts were set to expire soon, meaning this could theoretically be *Friends'* last season. They seemed to be growing up and moving on in their personal and professional lives. Cox was married, LeBlanc and Aniston were both engaged, and Kudrow was actually making traction in her film career. They no longer hung out on Thursday nights to watch the show together, and as Schwimmer told

Chin, things had changed, naturally: "As we all get older, we spend more time with our significant others, so of course the dynamic changes." They were in their thirties, and entering a new stage—the time in your life when your friends aren't around as much. But when they were together on the set, they still had that same old chemistry. And no one appeared to be saying goodbye.

On-screen, too, the dynamic had shifted. "Monica and Chandler are really moving in here, and I have to move out, and everything is changing," Rachel cries to Ross in "The One Where Ross Hugs Rachel." It's a sad, all-too-relatable moment—which is quickly smoothed over by a season of funny, not-at-all-sad episodes that insist that absolutely *nothing* is changing. Rachel first moves in with Phoebe, enabling fun setups for the two of them (like "The One with the Apothecary Table"[67]). After that, she moves into Chandler's old room at Joey's (meaning, she's basically living with Monica again, and things are pretty much back to normal).

This season puts more of the comedic responsibility on the four single characters, and while there are no great group games anymore, there are still plenty of classic *Friends* moments: Rachel puts beef in the trifle; Ross and Monica perform The Routine on *Dick Clark's New Year's Rockin' Eve*; Joey…well, Joey gets a new roommate, Janine—and then immediately gets rid of her, and we never have to talk about that again. Joey also gets a new TV show called *Mac and C.H.E.E.S.E.*, which we also do not have to talk about. It's maybe a few too many high jinks for six full-fledged adults, but it's a necessary distraction from the fact that Monica and Chandler are heading deeper into serious cou-

---

67 Aka the greatest product-placement device in television history. In 2004, Patrick Connolly (the chief marketing officer of parent company Williams-Sonoma) called the episode "the gift that keeps on giving. The phones light up with catalog requests every time it airs." Congrats, Pottery Barn. Hope you're enjoying that *Friends* money.

pledom. The show is still good, but nothing will ever be as simple or as fun as it was before. It will be harder and harder to get
the group together, and eventually, it will break apart for good.

Smack-dab in the middle of the season comes "The One That
Could Have Been," aka the what-if episode. What would it be
like if Rachel had married Barry, if Ross and Carol never got
divorced, if Joey was still a soap star, if Chandler had become
a writer, if Phoebe worked in finance, and if Monica was still
Fat Monica?

To be clear, this isn't Monica, but fat. Fat Monica is an entirely different character. The other five wear different clothes
in the what-if, but essentially remain the same people (and that's
kind of the point of the episode). Fat Monica, however, is a car-
toon who bears no resemblance to the confident, mature, mul-
tidimensional Monica. Fat Monica has one dimension: fat. She
speaks in a goofy, nasal voice and jumps at the mention of candy.
She's never had a serious or sexual relationship, and her entire
life revolves around food. And not in the same way that Monica's
does, as a chef who makes the best duck confit and broccoli
rabe. Fat Monica screams (with her mouth full) about mayon-
naise, and keeps Kit Kats on her person at all times. Fat Monica
doesn't even seem related to the earlier versions of herself. The
first time we see her, in the prom video during Season Two—
that's not Fat Monica. That's Monica, when she was fat. Her fat-
ness is still used as a punch line in that episode, but no more so
than Rachel's old nose or Ross's '80s hair. The real Fat Monica
first appears in Season Five's Thanksgiving flashback episode,
during which we learn that Monica lost the weight out of hu-
miliation, after overhearing Chandler make fun of her. Then,
once she's thin, he likes her! Aww?

Fat Monica is a polarizing character today, in an era when
body positivity is a popular concept—if not a sincerely popular
practice. As with gay jokes, old-school fat jokes are considered
impolite or juvenile, but people still laugh at them. Like ho-

mophobia, antifat bias is still deeply ingrained in the American psyche. If it weren't, then Fat Monica would just be Monica.

In all her appearances, Fat Monica is shoved through the same filter of acceptability as Carol and Susan, the married women who never kiss.[68] Fat Monica is tolerable, as long as she's a joke, just like the only other fat character on the show: Ugly Naked Guy.

Still, not everyone sees it like this. A lot of people really like Fat Monica, including many real-life fat women. Writer and performer Mathilda Gregory published an essay on how the character became a role model for her, in terms of self-acceptance. "Fat Monica laughed, and Fat Monica desired. Oh, the lust of Fat Monica! Yes, she ate all the time, but on the other hand, SHE ATE ALL THE TIME," Gregory wrote. "Fat Monica ate publicly and unashamedly because she wanted to, and food is delicious." It's true, this character flouted the expectations set on fat people to spend their lives trying to whittle themselves down, and until then remain invisible—and certainly never eat doughnuts in public. Fat Monica ate doughnuts in public *while dancing*. On one hand, she seemed completely free and comfortable in her body. On the other, it wasn't her body. There was a thin woman under that fat suit,[69] and everyone knew it.

Indeed, Cox's (and Aniston's) weight was the subject of constant media attention. Celebrity thinness in general was a particularly hot topic, and tabloids openly speculated about eating disorders and drug addictions. Meanwhile, fat celebrities (or just not thin ones) who lost weight were championed as success sto-

---

68   Even in this episode, where Ross and Carol invite her over for a threesome, in an effort to spice up their nonexistent sex life. Susan comes in, rips off her jacket, and gives Carol a great, big hug. Apparently, a group-sex storyline is A-okay at this point, but not two women kissing.

69   This was not a scripted scene, either. While shooting the what-if episode, Cox was waiting for the rest of the cast to come onto the stage. "Kevin Bright put on 'Shake Your Groove Thing' and I just grabbed a doughnut and started dancing like crazy in front of the audience," she later said. "God, playing Fat Monica was so freeing!…I could do anything because I was hidden under all that prosthetic makeup."

ries by the very same outlets. The message was clear: thin was aspirational, "too thin" was cause for hand wringing. And fat? Fat didn't go on the cover. The only place you'd see it was in a "before" picture. Even Gregory acknowledged that part of the reason she'd been drawn to Fat Monica was the fact that she was a "before"—a precursor to thin, "normal" Monica. The character only existed only in flashbacks, or in this alternate universe. As ridiculous and theoretical as Stockbroker Phoebe, Fat Monica (fat anyone) had no place in *Friends*' reality.

The what-if episode was a temporary detour out of that reality. When the show came back to its normal timeline, it still seemed to be in a holding pattern. There wasn't a whole lot of plot going on in the second half of Season Six, and a number of stories had clear expiration dates: Ross dating a student; the Bruce Willis episodes; the infamous *Mac and C.H.E.E.S.E.* debacle (now we're really done talking about it, promise). The story wasn't completely stuck, but it did seem to be hitting the snooze button. Perhaps it was a deliberate lull, to make the ending pop. Or maybe they were stalling because they had to.

No one really thought that this season would be the last, and nobody really wanted it to be—certainly not NBC or Warner Bros., both of which were bringing in enormous profits from *Friends*. Warner would earn a reported $1 billion off the first syndication cycle. In 1999, the producers renegotiated their own contract with NBC, signing a new deal that would keep the show on the network for two more years, at $5 million per episode—as long as Warner Bros. delivered the cast, of course. But as production inched closer to the finale, none of the actors had signed anything. No one had even made an offer. "None of us have heard anything," Schwimmer told *People*. And then he said one more thing: "I can't imagine showing up for work and about to rehearse a scene at the coffee shop with one of the cast gone. I just wouldn't want to be here."

They were really going to do it, again. The network and the studio realized that once more the cast was sticking together and negotiating as a team. This time around, they were savvier, and even more famous. One telling comment in *People*, and the message was sent: *Your move.*

Finally, on April 21, 2000, *Entertainment Weekly* announced that negotiations had begun. The actors were reportedly asking for $1 million per episode, plus a larger percentage of the back-end profits. (It would have been an enormous raise, but not an unprecedented sum. In 1998, Paul Reiser and Helen Hunt had gotten million-dollar deals for the final season of *Mad About You*. That same year Tim Allen got $1.25 million per episode of *Home Improvement*. And, lest we forget, Jerry Seinfeld had recently turned *down* an offer of $5 million per episode for a tenth season of *Seinfeld*.)

The cast got a counteroffer of $700,000. No dice. "We want *Friends* to come back and are hopeful it will happen," an NBC spokesperson told the magazine. "It would be a true shame if this can't be resolved," she added ominously. In situations like this, the network itself would be expected to pitch in, and potentially share the cost of cast salaries with the production company. By now, Littlefield had left his position at NBC,[70] and Garth Ancier was the president of NBC Entertainment. It was on him to help sweeten the deal for the *Friends* cast—and to let them know that he could yank it off the table, if it came to that. It did, and quickly.

On Thursday, May 11, the penultimate episode ("The One with the Ring") aired, concluding with Chandler preparing to propose to Monica. By Friday, May 12, they still hadn't reached an agreement. It was three days before the NBC up-front presentation, when the network would announce its fall schedule—

---

70   Or been fired or forced out. That's a whole other story, and if you'd like to read it, I suggest you pick up both Littlefield's own book, *Top of the Rock*, as well as Bill Carter's *Desperate Networks*.

and less than a week before the show's season and/or series finale. On Saturday, May 13, at 4:00 p.m., Warner Bros. delivered a final offer of $750,000. The cast had until Sunday at noon to decide. NBC had set the deadline, but Ancier knew it would take more than a ticking clock. The cast had proven unshakable in their all-for-one stance, and so he had to make it clear that NBC was willing to lose them all.

First, Ancier drew up two potential fall schedules for the upfronts: one with *Friends* in its usual spot at 8:00 p.m., and one with *Just Shoot Me* in the time slot—and no *Friends* at all. Next, he ordered some new promo spots for the season finale—declaring it the *series* finale—and scheduled them to air on Sunday, during NBC's coverage of the NBA playoffs. "I asked the promotion department to cut promos saying, 'You've loved them for seven years. See how it all ends, with the series finale of *Friends*, this Thursday at 8:00.'" Ancier explained the bold move years later, adding that, "People around me felt that was a little on the mean side, but I didn't see any other way to make the threat real."

True, this kind of story didn't jibe with the warm and fuzzy media narrative about this show. Readers didn't want to hear about their Friends using hardball tactics, or being threatened by the big, bad executives. Agents had put their two cents in the press throughout the negotiations, clearly trying to paint a more sympathetic picture of their clients. "They haven't been treated fairly up to this point," one anonymous rep told *EW.* "They are so underpaid it's ridiculous." Perhaps it was true, in the context of all the other million-dollar salaries that other actors were making (on shows that weren't nearly as lucrative as theirs). But it was a bit much, asking the public to feel bad for these TV stars, just because they were making millions every year instead of every week.

Someone had to do something drastic, or NBC would wind up as the network that killed everyone's favorite comedy, and the Friends would become the Friends who bailed. Hardball or not, it worked. NBC got the call around midnight, and the deal was done by sunrise. Ancier yanked the new promos, and on Monday, NBC announced *Friends* would be back for two more years. "This is our Mother's Day gift to America," he told the press. (That was a bit much, too.)

Everybody won. Chandler proposed, Monica said yes, and Season Six ended with no cliffhangers, on-screen or off. They would be back. The cast didn't have million-dollar deals (yet), but they had $750,000 an episode, a bigger stake in back-end profits, and a job that none of them took for granted. It was home, as Perry had said, and they had it good there. A job like this was as close to a 9-to-5 as actors ever got. By now, they'd persuaded the producers to start shoots in the afternoon instead of the evening, and there were no more 2:00 a.m. wraps. They had more time for their families and personal lives, and they had the financial stability to take risks on outside projects—or not! As long as *Friends* endured, no one really had to take on other work. On the other hand, the longer it lasted, the more enmeshed they would become with their sitcom roles, and the harder it would be to succeed in others.

For now, though, everyone was comfortably settled. Unfortunately, it showed. "I think everybody, after Season Six, thought, 'Okay, we had a good season, but the show's starting to get tired,'" recalled Kevin Bright. Well, sure, they weren't kids anymore. Adults get tired. That buzzy, overcaffeinated energy had mellowed into a cozy cup of tea. With two more seasons tacked on to the new contracts, they needed something powerful to perk things up again. And there's nothing like a wedding to make adults act like overstimulated children.

Season Seven rides high on the buildup to Monica and Chandler's wedding. It's different from every other season in the series because everyone knows how it's going to end. And, to a

certain extent, everyone knows what's going to come before the
big day: there will be arguments over the floral arrangements
and dress-buying antics, and *ooph*, just wait 'til Monica's doing
the seating chart. Wedding planning is both completely predictable and constant chaos. It is a period of high-stakes emotional
drama, friend-bonding activities, and wearing clothes that no
one can actually afford in real life. In short, it is the ideal structure for a season of *Friends*. The fun comes from knowing all
the milestones to come, and wondering how they're going to
navigate them. Above all, the wedding gives the show plenty
of organic scenarios to bring the group together. For once, it
makes complete sense that all they do is hang out together and
solve ridiculous problems with irrational solutions. A wedding
is *nothing* but ridiculous problems and irrational solutions. Planning a surprise bridal shower with two days' notice because you
didn't realize the bride was expecting one? Yeah, sounds about
right. Sending a last-minute invite to your idiot friend's parents
because he told them they were invited and now there's no way
out of it? Totally. Weddings bring out the wacky and illogical
side of everyone. It's tradition.

And Monica is nothing if not a traditional bride. She wants
that princess gown and something blue. Despite the fact that
she and Chandler are living together, she even wants to abstain
from sex before the wedding. She's old-school. Which is why
it's a little bit strange that she and Chandler spend an entire episode looking for a minister to marry them—and not a rabbi.

Early on, *Friends* establishes that Monica and Ross Geller are
Jewish. Their background comes up occasionally—Ross buys
Monica a Hanukkah present, and Monica once mentions her
bat mitzvah—but it's typically bypassed, or even contradicted.
The fact that Monica goes all-out for Christmas is conceivable;
it's not unheard of for Jews to get a Christmas tree, particularly
in America, where Christmas is so heavily marketed and secu-
larized. But the fact that she has a copy of the Bible in her liv-

ing room (which comes up in a joke in Season Four) is—well, it's like hunting for a minister. It's weird. If there'd been an episode titled "The One Where Monica Converts to Christianity," then this would all make more sense. Instead, the show simply ignored her Judaism 90% of the time, and assumed the audience would, as well.

It was a fair assumption in this era, when virtually all American sitcoms defaulted to white, straight, and vaguely Christian. There were significant exceptions, like *Seinfeld*, and…*Seinfeld*.[71] But *Seinfeld* was the exception to a lot of sitcom rules; it succeeded by openly flouting them. It went hyper-specific, daring the audience not to get the joke. *Friends* worked its ass off to make sure everyone, everywhere, got it, and liked it. Both shows included culturally Jewish reference points, but *Friends* (which, like *Seinfeld*, was created by Jewish people and written by a largely Jewish staff) almost never identified them as such. It took a show-but-don't-tell approach, which might have gone unnoticed had the show been set somewhere other than New York. But *Friends* did so much showing-not-telling when it came to Judaism that the subject remains a topic of debate among critics and fans. Rachel is usually at the center of these conversations, with many people arguing that she's clearly a Jewish character, but deliberately not identified as one. In 2014, critics Emily Nussbaum and Molly Lambert got into a lengthy Twitter discussion on the subject, Nussbaum saying there was no question. "[The name] 'Rachel' is not ambiguous," she wrote. "It's like naming her Shoshannah Lowenstein, in TV terms." Nussbaum pointed out the show used obvious clues (like Rachel calling her grandmother "bubbe") as well as glaring stereotypes (her nose job, her engagement to a Jewish orthodontist). Lambert argued that these could also just be "ethnic suburban tropes" and not

---

71   Though this show, too, was criticized for not explicitly identifying characters as Jewish. *Seinfeldia* author Jennifer Keishin Armstrong wrote that, "as the series gained more viewers, the criticisms mounted: too Jewish. Not Jewish enough. Even 'too self-hatingly Jewish,'" according to some critics.

necessarily Jewish ones. "Anyway," she added, "I just think it's dangerous to decide that someone 'looks' or 'feels' Jewish, because that's not actually how it works." Nussbaum agreed, but added that she felt just as uncomfortable with those who adamantly argued *against* Rachel being Jewish. "[*Friends* used] so many cues...that it kind of rankles me to insist, 'Hey, she could be anything.'"

Kauffman and Crane have both stated (in interviews after the series ended) that Rachel was Jewish. In fact, Kauffman said she was the only "real" Jew in the group, according to halachic law, because she had a Jewish mother. As for Ross and Monica, she said only their father, Jack (Elliott Gould), was Jewish, though they were clearly raised in the faith. Given details like this, it's evident that the writers did have this in mind—regardless of Monica's minister moment. Like the characters, they were used to being Jews in a vaguely Christian culture, and never was that more obvious than when it came time to write episodes for December (aka Christmastime).

Holiday episodes were always a favorite in the writers' room (hence, the annual Thanksgiving shows). In the seventh season, they took the opportunity to do a Hanukkah episode for the first time: "The One with the Holiday Armadillo." Over the years, Ross had become the character who most strongly identified as Jewish, and they felt it made sense that he would want to share that with his son. The story emerged from a very real conflict that a lot of Jewish or interfaith parents have around Christmas: How do you get your kids psyched about Hanukkah, without coming off like the jerk who took away Santa? "I'm sure *any* non-Christians go through that," Kauffman said, commenting on the episode. "Kids are so aware of Christmas, and so much less aware of any other holiday." She called her own rabbi and asked how she handled the issue. "[She said] it's about identity. It's about saying, during a very Christian time, 'I'm Jewish. I'm *not* that—and that's okay.'"

In dressing up like an armadillo, Ross doesn't exactly succeed in conveying a sense of Jewish identity. But he does manage to teach Ben the story of Hanukkah, along with some help from Chandler as Santa, and Joey as Superman—who flew all the Jews out of Egypt! The hilarity of the scene (Schwimmer's physical humor alone is pure gold) overshadows the compromise beneath. In the end, Ben will only listen to the Hanukkah story while sitting on Santa's lap. It's the kind of compromise that many Jewish parents are probably used to making. For a lot of people, this episode exemplifies the show's handling of Judaism in general: it's clunky, but it's better than nothing.

"Better than nothing" came up a lot in the interviews I conducted for this book. I spoke with a number of people about the representational issues, lack of diversity, and all those elements that make the show dated (as we politely put it). To be honest, I expected more outrage. The internet is packed to the gills with hot-take opinion pieces, as well as thoroughly researched academic papers about how problematic *Friends* is—how quickly it went for the cheap jokes, how rarely it featured minority characters, and on the rare occasions that it did, how poorly those characters were treated. But when I spoke to people one-on-one, there was very little vitriol. For obvious reasons, I made a point to seek out commentators from within those minority groups. Some were fans and others told me up front that they didn't like the show. But those who disliked it told me they thought it was corny, or just not their kind of humor (some folks were in the *Seinfeld* camp). No one cited lack of diversity or homophobia as the primary reason they were turned off by it, because, of course, those problems were not unique to *Friends*. And *Friends* was clearly not a show that wanted to cause controversy or tackle touchy social issues. The general consensus was that TV in that time was not a sophisticated or inclusive landscape, and in some ways *Friends* was better than its peers. By Season Seven, Carol

and Susan had pretty much disappeared from the show, but the
fact that they'd been there at all was *something*. Okay, the Hanukkah episode was a little bit silly and Santa-fied, but you know
what? Better than nothing.

Then there's Chandler's dad. Of all the so-called dated storylines on *Friends*, this one most clearly marks it as a product of its
era. That era being one in which *transgender* was not a word most
people knew. Transphobia was not a touchy social issue because
most people hadn't even heard of it. Today, the trans community
remains one of the most at-risk populations in the world, but in
2001, it was virtually invisible. The fact that *Friends* made such
a big, flashy, nonstop joke of it was hardly controversial at the
time. It was nothing like the lesbian wedding, which had been
handled with such enormous caution. When Chandler's dad
appeared, there were no press conferences or subtle nods to the
political climate. If the show had made a statement about trans
rights or visibility, most of the audience wouldn't have known
what the hell it was talking about.

Chandler's dad[72] is never identified as a trans woman in the
show, but again, Kauffman and Crane both acknowledged the
character as such in interviews after *Friends* ended. (Had they
done so during the run of the series, they probably would have
used the word *transsexual*, a term that predates *transgender* but
is not typically used today.) Throughout the series, Chandler's
dad is alternately referred to as a gay man, a drag queen, or a
cross-dresser. If *Friends* were a contemporary series, this might
be seen as a deliberate commentary on the complex phases of
identity development. But given the time and place, I think it's
safe to say that no one was thinking about those things. They
were just looking for new ways to point out that Chandler's dad
wore dresses.

---

72 For clarity's sake, I'm referring to her as "Chandler's dad" or her stage name,
Helena Handbasket. That's how the character was identified in the show, and
how she was referred to in research materials and by my interview subjects.
I'm using "she" as a pronoun.

As Chandler and Monica's wedding approached, the writers had to make a decision about the groom's parents. Crane said there was much debate over whether or not Chandler's dad should ever be seen on the show. Some said she should remain an off-screen recurring character (like Ugly Naked Guy), but eventually it was decided that she should be at her son's wedding. But who could possibly play her? After seven years of Chandler's-dad jokes, the audience had a pretty vivid (if not clear) picture of who she was. And, of course, *Friends* didn't just do guest stars—it did guest *celebrities*. How many big-name celebs could play a singing, dancing, man-eating Las Vegas headliner with an ambiguous gender identity?

"We went to see if we could get Liza Minnelli," Crane later explained. The first idea was to make Chandler's dad "the best female impersonator ever," and then cast the actual iconic performer in the role. But neither Minnelli nor the others they approached felt comfortable playing an impersonator playing *them*. So they instead looked for a big-name actress to fill the role of Charles Bing—aka Helena Handbasket.

Kathleen Turner was starring in a touring production of *Tallulah*, a one-woman play about Hollywood legend Tallulah Bankhead. Crane saw the show one night and went backstage to speak with Turner afterward. Might she consider taking the part? Turner thought, *I haven't done* that *yet. Why not?* In the years since, Turner has often been asked about her work on *Friends*, and she's readily acknowledged how bizarre the whole thing looks now. "How they approached me with it was, 'Would you like to be the first woman playing a man playing a woman?'" she told *Gay Times* in 2018. "I said yes, because there weren't many drag/trans people on television at the time." She added, "I don't think it's aged well…but no one ever took it seriously as a social comment."

That may be true. And there are many people, even in the trans community, who argue it's ridiculous to critique *Friends* for doing a lousy job with a trans character—because at least it *had* one. Kind of. But while Helena Handbasket was not meant to be taken as social commentary, there were indeed people who took her seriously.

I spoke with Mey Rude, former trans editor of the online magazine *Autostraddle*. She clearly remembers the first time she saw "The One with Chandler's Dad." It was her freshman year of college in 2005, a complicated period in Rude's life. She was trans herself, but still years away from coming out. Like everyone else in the world, she'd grown up without really knowing what it meant to be transgender. "So, when I moved away for college, it was the first time I had internet access by myself, and I could watch TV without my parents seeing," Rude told me. She began to seek out every show or movie that featured a trans character. "I would go online and watch the preview for *Transamerica* over and over again." Other than that, there wasn't much. Sometimes *Law & Order* had trans characters, but they always wound up murder victims. Rude was finally learning what it meant to be trans, at least according to pop culture. It meant being ostracized by society, estranged from your family, and probably killed. There were no stories out there to which she could relate, and no characters she could look to for even a hint of hope or positivity. "Then I found out about this episode of *Friends*."

Chandler's dad first appears in the penultimate episode of Season Seven. It's two weeks before the wedding, and Monica realizes that they haven't gotten an RSVP. "Maybe that's because I didn't send him an invitation," Chandler tells her. As it turns out, he's been deliberately avoiding his dad, who's been trying in vain to reconnect with him for years (even flying to New York). Chandler rattles off a list of reasons, which are both understandable and completely absurd: his dad showed up at his high-school swim meets dressed in drag, and once had sex with Mr. Garibaldi. "Who's Mr. Garibaldi?" Monica asks.

"Does it matter?!" No, fair point. Chandler has plenty of reasons to resent both his parents, and he's not the first child to carry those resentments into adulthood. His character is so obviously shaped by childhood trauma that it would be tragic if it weren't so funny (See: "The One Where Chandler Can't Cry"). But, Monica points out, Chandler's been shit-talking his dad for a long time now. The jokes are getting old, and so is he. Maybe it's time he grew up and got on a plane.

The two of them fly to Vegas and go see Helena Handbasket's cabaret act. The scene opens with a great cameo by an actual trans actress (and Courteney Cox's then sister-in-law), the late Alexis Arquette. She's the waitress who asks if anyone's taken their order yet, causing Monica to go into a pronoun meltdown: "Oh, yeah, she did. Uh, *he* did. *She?* I'm sorry, I'm new!" It's a prescient moment, and one that shows the writers were at least a little conscious of the sensitive area in which they were treading. Helena's reveal is obviously played for big laughs ("And there's *Daddy*," Chandler grumbles) and much of the scene is devoted to Turner making puns and flirting with the crowd in her huskiest tones. But at the center of it is a poignant moment of reckoning between parent and child. She notices Monica's engagement ring, realizing she hasn't been invited to her son's wedding. Finally, Chandler stands up and says he'd love it if she would be there. "Really?" Helena asks. Chandler smiles. "I know it would make me happy—ma'am."

It's a touching moment of sadness, acceptance, hurt, and love, all rolled into one brief exchange. It's doubly heartbreaking to see how badly this woman wants to be in her child's life, and to know she probably never will be. Chandler has made a genuine gesture, but I don't see him going to PFLAG meetings, or forging a new bond with his estranged parent. By the next episode, when she arrives at the wedding, she's a walking punch line again.

"But they *do* invite her to the wedding," Rude pointed out.

"Even though her family makes fun of her, she *is* invited to her son's wedding. You know? It's so sad that that's the kind of representation that, for so long, counted as *good* representation." But, for Rude, it was better than nothing. It let her imagine a future in which she might one day be a parent, and might even be invited to her child's wedding. "I don't know if I would call it 'progressive' or anything like that. But I do think if you're a closeted trans teenager or young adult watching *Friends* [in that era], and you see that episode, you *do* see yourself, in that [character]," Rude said. "There's a pang of familiarity there. And since she's happy—she has a career, she has a boyfriend—that is much better than when you're watching *Law & Order* and every trans character is murdered."

Rude acknowledged the obvious gaffes, some of which are even more confusing than they are offensive. "They have a cisgender woman playing the character—who's very clearly a cis woman. But everyone treats her like she's very *obviously* a man in a wig." There's a storyline in the wedding episode where Monica asks Rachel to keep an eye on Chandler's dad, "the man in the black cocktail dress." Rude pointed out that no one would look at Kathleen Turner and automatically think, *Man in a dress.* "It just comes across as extremely sloppy and extremely confusing and extremely *weird*." But setting aside that heaping pile of missteps, she said, "the character isn't so bad. She's talented and funny and seems to be living a very happy life. Just the way everyone else treats her is terrible." The bottom line was that she was there—at the wedding, on the television. She was evidence that trans people existed, in an era when they were hardly even recognized. "Trans women were starving to see themselves on screen," said Rude. "So, when we saw ourselves in a way that wasn't absolutely terrible, it seemed like a great thing."

It would be many more years before television began, in earnest, to consider things like diverse, responsible representation.

Even now, the envelope only gets pushed a millimeter at a time, and TV is still dominated by white, straight, thin, cisgendered, vaguely Christian characters. But in 2001, *Friends* was already beginning to seem a little dated. Something was changing on television. HBO had introduced series like *The Sopranos* and *Sex and the City*, shattering the molds of TV drama and comedy. The cable revolution was beginning, but an even greater paradigm shift was happening on network television—and not on NBC. In the summer of 2000 (just two weeks after the *Friends* cast signed new contracts), CBS debuted a show about sixteen people— not characters, but "castaways"—forced to compete against each other on an uninhabited island. *Survivor* had exploded into the ratings, blowing everyone else out of the water. For the first time in years, *Friends* and all the other reliable hits were losing their comfortable lead, their viewership flocking in droves toward the next great phenomenon: reality TV.

It was the end of an era, no mistaking it now. NBC was no longer America's number-one network. Jeff Zucker—who had recently succeeded Garth Ancier as the president of NBC Entertainment in December of that year—was frantically trying to right the ship. He'd created the concept of "Supersized Thursday," extending the network's most popular half-hour shows to forty minutes. That would buy him some time while he hunted for a new *Survivor*-sized hit. The strategy worked, but it was only a temporary fix. The Must-See TV years were over. The sitcom wasn't dead yet, but everyone could see its time was fast approaching. And maybe that was okay. Life changes, media evolves, and stories have to end sometime. *Friends* still loomed incredibly large in the TV landscape, but in the months leading up to the seventh season finale, viewership steadily dwindled. The show was due to return in the fall for one last season, but now it was painfully clear that it wouldn't go out on a high note.

It wasn't backlash this time. Season Seven was solid (maybe not spectacular) in terms of quality. There were no Diet Coke debacles or over-the-top stunts that alienated viewers. Many of those who had drifted away came back for the finale. Numbers jumped from 16 million to 30 million, making it the most-watched episode of the year, by far. Would those viewers return in the fall? Probably not. In all likelihood, this was a fond farewell.

And what better send-off than a big, beautiful wedding? What could be more fitting a farewell to a show about the time in your life when your friends are your family? In getting married, Monica and Chandler were closing that chapter and beginning a new one. Like all weddings, it was exciting and sweet and a little bit sad. Of course they would always have their friends, but it wouldn't be the same within the group. It wouldn't be the same show. This was the end of *Friends* as we knew it. What began in Season Five had come full circle. "Everything is changing," Rachel had cried, and two years later, it had changed for good. Everyone was moving on. The bride and groom kissed and the audience cheered. It was the perfect time to say goodbye, and let the Friends head off into the sunset. By then, the spring of 2001, some were already wondering if they'd overstayed their welcome. Then came the fall.

9

The One Where Nobody Died

When people talk about September 11, they usually start with where they were. "I was driving to work, listening to the radio, when the song cut off and the news came on." "I was in algebra class, and I remember that the girl in front of me was wearing a bright pink T-shirt." It's called a flashbulb memory. When we hear of or witness an event so stunning our brains take a mental snapshot of the moment: the smell of burned coffee, the pinch of your new shoes, the sudden silence in the empty sky above. Unlike other recollections, which tend to fade with time, flashbulb memories remain in vivid detail. People start with where they were when it happened, because it's the last thing they remember before everything went hazy. One minute you were at school or work or the grocery store, and the next you were in front of the television, watching.

Lisa Kudrow had just woken up and was in the middle of her usual morning routine, wrangling her three-year-old son and getting ready to head to the studio. Tuesdays were rehearsal days, and this week they had another celebrity guest star. Sean Penn had been cast as an ex-boyfriend of Ursula's who has a brief fling with Phoebe. On top of that, it was the Halloween episode, so there would be tricky, cumbersome costumes to deal with, as well as a big-shot movie star (who was known to be somewhat tricky and cumbersome himself). It was going to be a busy week and Kudrow was trying to get out the door when her phone rang. It was Carlos Piñero, the second AD.

"So, obviously, we're not coming in," he said.

"Obviously? What do you mean?"

"Well, New York's being attacked. Or...we don't even—I don't know. The *country's* being attacked? We don't know." Piñero told her to turn on her TV.

Shortly after American Airlines Flight 11 hit the North Tower, all the networks preempted their normal programming, and switched to uninterrupted news reporting. By the time the South Tower was hit, virtually every American television station was broadcasting live coverage of the attack. Untold millions around the world were watching when it fell.

For days after the attack, all commercials and regular programs were suspended, and viewers remained glued to the news. On that day alone, American adults watched an estimated eight hours of television. Children watched approximately three. On September 15, the *New York Times* reported that the attack had, among other things, set a TV record: it received more consecutive news coverage than any other event in US television history, surpassing the assassination of President John F. Kennedy. In the days and weeks that followed, the country stumbled back to work, then came home every night to watch and listen for any updates, any details or new information that might somehow make sense of this. The *Times* reported that between 30 and 50 million Americans were tuning in during prime time—to network news specifically.

It was noteworthy, the paper added, because traditional network news (like all network shows) had been on a steep decline. In recent years, more and more viewers preferred to get their news online, or from cable outlets like CNN. Old-school nightly programs, with anchors like Tom Brokaw, Dan Rather, and Peter Jennings, seemed increasingly stodgy and slow-paced compared with the high-speed, rapid-fire style of twenty-first century news. The *Times* piece continued: "But during an event of maximum national attention, accompanied by the most acute national distress, television viewers have returned to the place where they had always gone before in such times: their living rooms, to watch and listen to network anchors." In the wake of such unprecedented terror, no one wanted new and flashy. They wanted the familiarity of Jennings and Brokaw, sitting behind the same desks, relaying the day's updates in those same, steady voices. But it was more than that. As Pulitzer Prize–winning journalist Alex S. Jones explained to the *Times*: "It's not just that they're familiar. It's also that they're trusted."

Weeks passed. The news sunk in. Slowly, Americans began to inch back into their normal routines, all the while knowing that normalcy as they knew it was gone for good. We were on the other side of something, treading on uncertain territory and flinching at every loud noise. We still consumed the news en masse, everyone watching like hawks for the next great horror to come crashing into frame. But eventually, everyone wanted—just for a minute—to watch something else.

But everything else was on hold. In Los Angeles, film and television studios had been shut down (as had much of the country's theme parks, shopping hubs, tourist destinations—virtually any place that might draw a crowd). Late-night shows on both coasts stayed off the air for a week, no one knowing if or when it would be safe to return to work. And anyway, what business did they have doing comedy? Would it ever be appropriate or welcome again? David Letterman broke the silence, coming back on the air on September 17 with an emotional monologue and a crowd-pleasing lineup of guests ("Thank God Regis is here, so we have something to make fun of."). Soon after, others followed suit, if only because there was nothing else to do. "They said to get back to work," Jon Stewart said the night *The Daily Show* returned. "And there were no jobs available for a man in the fetal position under his desk crying, which I would have gladly taken. So, I came back here."

It wasn't easy for anyone. Back at Warner Bros., Kauffman, Bright, and Crane had an exceptional challenge on their hands: What do you do with a sitcom set in downtown Manhattan, when downtown Manhattan is now Ground Zero? Not just any sitcom, but one that deliberately avoided certain realities— specifically, death. "We didn't do death well," Crane later explained. It was something they realized early on, particularly after the Season Three storyline where Rachel's boss, Joanna, offers her a promotion, but gets hit by a cab and killed before she can file the paperwork. They'd written it as a moment of dark comedy, but when Joanna's death was revealed, the studio audience barely made a sound. "They could have done it on *Seinfeld* with George," recalled Crane. "We couldn't do it on *Friends*."

In September 2001, nobody wanted black comedy, and least of all from *Friends*. It remained unclear if sitcoms even had a place in this new reality. Would these unscathed characters with their tidy, twenty-two-minute problems come off like a great insult to this injured nation? Shutting down indefinitely was not a solution. But how could they return to a fictionalized Manhattan and just pretend that nothing had happened?

The obvious option was to do a Very Special Episode. Some sort of departure from the canon where they addressed the attacks openly and—no, no, never mind, terrible idea. As a rule, the creators had consciously avoided Very Special Episodes from the beginning, knowing that drama just wasn't their strong suit.

"The dramatic moments that we dealt with mostly had to do with babies or weddings," explained Bright. "No woman ever lost a baby on *Friends*." Some other shows would choose the Very Special Episode route, with middling success. *The West Wing*'s post-9/11 episode "Isaac and Ishmael" played like an educational special, trying to address the topics of both international terrorism *and* American bigotry, but without getting too political about it. It was neither offensive nor very effective. It came off as weird more than anything, but it would have been much weirder if a show like *The West Wing* (taking place in the White House) had ignored the attack entirely. On *Friends*, though, it just wouldn't work. No one wanted to see "The One with the Terrorist Attack."

After talking it through, the producers came to an agreement. Yes, they decided, 9/11 did happen in the world of *Friends*, but it would only be acknowledged in visual cues. American flags went up in Central Perk and in Joey's apartment. The actors would occasionally wear shirts reading "United We Stand" or "FDNY" (as many people did in the months after the attack). They wouldn't show the characters watching Tom Brokaw, but they would leave newspapers out on the coffee table, as if to indicate that yes, they, too, were glued to the news. The Magna Doodle on the back of Joey's door became the most direct signal to the audience, incorporating symbolic phrases or images (like flag doodles, or the Statue of Liberty) throughout Season Eight. The first one appeared in "The One with the Videotape," with an old familiar emblem that was turning up on posters and T-shirts and bumper stickers across the country: I ♥ NY.

These visual gestures seemed the most respectful option. They were a consistent reminder that no one had forgotten what had happened—what was still happening—but they were subtle enough to sustain the show's light tone. That way, hopefully, *Friends* could still be an escape from a dreadful new reality.

The studios reopened and production resumed on "The One

with the Halloween Party," though audiences wouldn't be allowed back in for several weeks. Instead, Warner Bros. employees came in to fill as many seats as possible. Now Kudrow and
her castmates were relieved to be in their Halloween getups (she
was Supergirl, and Chandler was dressed in a giant pink bunny
suit). "Thank *God* [it was] the silliest it could possibly be," she
remembered. It was a strange shoot but a good one. Everyone
cracked up during the scene where Chandler and Ross arm wres-
tle, and Monica notices that Chandler (again, in a bunny costume) is "making his sex face." After sitting at home all week,
watching the relentless stream of agony and fear on the news,
the cast felt relieved to laugh again.

Kudrow began to realize that was their job—providing relief.
She remembered going home one night and turning on the TV
herself. *Will & Grace* was on, and her first thought was: *I wonder
who they knew, in the towers.* Then she remembered that no, this
episode would have been shot before the attack. *Oh, good, I'm
in a world where it hasn't happened yet.* Finally, it dawned on her:
Oh, wait. This is a world where it's not ever going to happen. "And I
almost started crying, from just relief. Okay, oh, my God, thank
God. I can be in a world where there's no such thing as 9/11.
That's great. That's where I wanna be. That's exactly where I
wanna be," she recalled. "And the penny dropped."

She thought of all those fans over the years—before the
attack—who would stop her on the street and gush about what a
fun little escape it was. Only now did she understand the mag-
nitude of that. In the months after it happened, Kudrow would
find herself sitting at a red light in her car, look out the window, and notice someone in the next lane, looking back at her.
Not gawking or waving, just making eye contact. No one said
anything but "Thank you."

Throughout her years on *Friends*, Kudrow had always tried
not to take it all too seriously: "We're not curing cancer. It's
not a big deal. But you know what? It is a big deal when you

can offer people a break from such a devastating reality." Aniston later echoed Kudrow's sentiments, saying, "It was hard to come back to work and do a sitcom when the world was falling apart. I remember feeling very helpless and not knowing what our place was anymore." But when the audience returned, it became immediately clear. Far from subdued, the energy was through the roof. Laughter burst from the crowd, louder than ever. It was tension release, Aniston realized. This was one place in the world where it was still okay to laugh. "We looked at each other and we went, 'Okay, I guess *this* is what we're doing.'"

There was one more thing they had to do, and fast. The first five episodes had already been shot before the attack, including "The One Where Rachel Tells Ross." This episode included a story where Monica and Chandler leave for their honeymoon and get stuck at the airport. In the original version, Chandler sees a sign while going through security: "Hey, look at that. 'Federal law prohibits any joking regarding aircraft hijacking or bombing.'" He turns to the TSA agent and says exactly what you'd expect Chandler to say: "You don't have to worry about me, ma'am. I take my bombs *very* seriously." He and Monica wind up in a detention room getting interrogated by federal agents—a scene in which Chandler says the word *bomb* again, about two hundred times. "Look, this is ridiculous. I was just making a joke. I mean, I know the sign says 'no jokes about bombs,' but shouldn't the sign really say 'no bombs'?! I mean, isn't that the guy we really have to worry about here? The guy *with* the bombs? Not the guy who *jokes* about his bombs. Not that I have bombs!"

For obvious reasons, the story had to go. The writers quickly scripted a new airport scenario, in which Chandler and Monica wind up competing with another pair of newlyweds to get the honeymoon upgrades. They reshot the scenes and recut the episode, making no mention of the change.[73] It was a relatively minor tweak, given what was happening throughout the entertainment industry. Dozens of series and films were being reedited or put on hold, and most live events (including every award show) were either rescheduled or canceled. It wasn't just a matter of poor taste; it was a matter of public safety. An auditorium full of high-profile people was considered a security risk. September 11 changed the way we watched television, and not just the news. Viewers were hyperaware of any mention of the Pentagon or shots of the Twin Towers (many of which were digitally removed). No one needed to see big action-movie explosions, nor did they want to watch a bunch of celebrities walking down the red carpet. And they *really* didn't need Chandler Bing making cracks about being a terrorist.

What they needed was Chandler making cracks about being a newlywed. They needed Monica to be her same old neurotic self, worrying about keeping her apartment clean (not worrying about anthrax like the rest of us). They needed Ross and Rachel to keep up this whole will-they-won't-they thing—even if it was getting slightly ridiculous after eight years *and* an accidental pregnancy. That didn't matter right now. What mattered was that they were there, a constant. Like those anchors who had ushered us through the attack and its aftermath, they, too, were familiar and trusted faces we could turn to for solace.

"I think *Friends* was like comfort food for people at that time," Kauffman reflected years later. "And I was really honored to be comfort food." For some, *Friends* presented a hopeful future— the possibility of normalcy restored. For others, it was a relic of a time before the attack. Ninety-nine percent of the show remained unchanged, and even the few subtle changes felt like a creative risk. Seeing Joey in a T-shirt printed with the name "Capt. Billy Burke" (an FDNY captain who was killed trying

---

73   The original scenes were eventually added as a special feature on the DVD
      collection.

to rescue others in the North Tower) could trigger a cascade of associated memories and mental images that had no place in the world of *Friends*. But to deny those memories and images entirely would be a cruel disservice to a grieving audience. It would be disrespectful to New York, the city that so many viewers had come to know through *Friends*' lens, and had overnight become a place that people feared. It was now more clear than ever that *Friends*' version of Manhattan was a fantasy. But underneath the surface, the show conveyed a very real message shared by New Yorkers and Americans everywhere: *It happened, and we're still here.*

Weeks passed and on set it was back to business as usual. When it came time shoot the holiday show, the producers had an idea. Bright called Warner Bros. to ask if they would foot the bill to fly out four hundred people for the taping. In October, they shot "The One with the Creepy Holiday Card" for an audience of surviving family members of the first responders and victims who had perished in the attack. "That was an amazing night," he recalled. "Can't even really put it to words. Great feeling of giving these people, who had just gone through the worst possible thing, a little break and a little smile again."

In the long term, TV comedy would struggle to reshape itself in a post-9/11 world. "There's going to be a seismic change," predicted *Vanity Fair* editor-in-chief Graydon Carter. "I think it's the end of the age of irony. Things that were considered fringe and frivolous are going to disappear." But in the immediate aftermath, when the wound was still wide open, shows like *Friends* became more relevant than ever. It was an entertaining diversion, and for the moment, diversion was important. Matt LeBlanc remembered opening the *Los Angeles Times* and reading that *Friends* was no longer America's favorite comedy, but America's favorite comfort-food show. "I don't know how that happened," he recalled. But he and the others took it to heart.

"We all said, 'Wow, that's a lot of responsibility. So, let's try to be our best.'"

On September 27, *Friends* debuted its eighth season to an enormous audience—its largest since the Super Bowl episode five years prior. "The One After 'I Do'" reached almost 32 million people, and concluded with a dedication: "To the people of New York City." The same viewers who'd been moving on at the end of Season Seven returned in droves and stayed put. It became the highest-ranked season of the series' run, and for the first time, *Friends* was not only the top comedy, but the number-one show on television. The eighth season would also earn *Friends* its first Emmy for Outstanding Comedy Series.

It's hard to imagine any of that happening had 9/11 not happened first. In any other year, the season would have been either over-the-top or simply tired—and certainly the last. The truth is Season Eight was not *Friends'* finest, though it was the most successful. It had the vigor of a much younger series, and that renewed creative energy overshadowed some of the fundamental flaws. The driving storyline was needlessly complicated: Ross and Rachel are having a baby, but still aren't together for some reason. The Joey-loves-Rachel arc made everyone uncomfortable (including the actors). Above all, the show had aged out of its premise, and its audience had matured, too. If the attack hadn't happened, then *Friends* likely would have continued its gentle decline. Instead, it was revived by the tens of millions who turned to it for comfort, distraction, escape, hope. Suddenly, the show had a reason to go on.

The problem was, it was supposed to be ending.

"Now, uh—are you guys coming back next year?" Jay Leno asked Matt LeBlanc. It was January 30, 2002, and LeBlanc was there to promote *Friends* as it headed into another sweeps period. The interview was going fine; they talked about cars and showed a clip from an upcoming episode. Leno congratulated LeBlanc on the show's big rebound, and LeBlanc gave a polite if subdued thank-you. (Naturally soft-spoken, LeBlanc often came off as subdued in comparison to Joey.) He'd just accepted the People's Choice Award for Favorite TV Comedy on behalf of the whole cast, dedicating the award to the people of New York. "To be a part of something that, right now, takes place in New York, is a special honor," he said. At another point in the interview, Leno made a crack about why the Hollywood Foreign Press Association hadn't given *Friends* a Golden Globe: "Oh, it's foreigners. They don't know! They're all in that 'jihad' crap.'" *Yikes*. No more compassionate monologues or stirring reminders to stand united. The Very Special stage of public mourning had passed, and now came the jihad jokes.

LeBlanc, thank God, didn't laugh or add a comment, but just looked down vaguely into his lap for a moment, then moved on: "But the People's Choice, that's what counts..." He'd been doing this for eight years, and knew how to sidestep an awkward moment and keep the conversation going. He surely also knew that the American public did not want to see one of its Friends engaging in terrorism humor or political commentary, correct or incorrect. US troops were departing for Afghanistan by the thousands, and now, a potent mix of fear and anger was welling up inside the country. Americans were still glued to the news every day, and still rushing back every night to their favorite comedies to soothe themselves to sleep. *That* was LeBlanc's job, and he knew it. The question was, would he keep doing it.

"Are you guys coming back next year? Have you decided?" Leno asked. For the first time, LeBlanc seemed to freeze up. He shifted in his seat, clasped his hands tightly, and then shifted in his seat again.

"Uhhhh, we're—y'know. We're kinda right in the middle of talking about all that." LeBlanc shrugged. "Y'know, we'll see what happens, I dunno."

"Fifty-fifty odds?" Leno pressed. LeBlanc nodded his head and made some noncommittal noises.

"I don't know. We'll see…" Leno quickly launched into another question, talking over the end of LeBlanc's answer. Low-talker that he was, it was hard to hear LeBlanc add: "We'd *like* to come back."

The good news was that everyone wanted that. The network, the studio, the audience, and even the critics had welcomed *Friends* back with open arms, and no one was ready to let go again. Not right this minute, anyway. *Survivor* and its peers were still a powerful presence on the television landscape, but for now, people had had enough of reality as well as reality TV. "I'd rather try to lose myself in a sitcom than another soul-numbing reality show," wrote critic Bruce Fretts. Even lackluster shows were preferable, he added. "The one-hour premieres of *Frasier* and *Spin City*, for example, were so predictable they felt like repeats. Normally, I would mean that as a criticism, but right now, it's just what the doctor ordered."

Friends was now beating *Survivor* every week, and it was not having a lackluster season. It wasn't a return to the pure, frenetic fun of Seasons Five and Six, but there was something new and compelling to the show now. It seemed to have a sense of purpose, and an awareness of the specific job it had to do: be funny. Be *not* reality. For NBC, *Friends* played another crucial role. It was the network's comedy ballast, and if the show did end with Season Eight, Jeff Zucker would have nothing on deck to replace it. Among other things, this was not a good time to lose such a vital source of revenue.

On set, things progressed as planned, though no one was quite sure anymore what the plan was. In the writers' room, it was just as unclear. "We didn't know *what* we were going to do with Ross and Rachel as a couple," Crane recalled. They knew she was going to have the baby, and that it would be his, but that was it. If this was really the last year, the characters could finally get together. But if they were going to come back for one more, then they'd have to make it seem plausible that these two people who loved each other and had a baby *and* lived together were not a couple. For months, said Crane, "we were really walking a line and leaving open the possibility that they could end up together in this season."

No one had any idea how Season Eight was going to end, least of all the audience. The press was tossing out bizarre rumors about the finale plot. The *Star* quoted "well-placed sources" as saying that Rachel was going to die in childbirth, leaving her baby to Monica and Chandler. That seemed even less plausible than Ross and Rachel not being a couple, but who the hell knew? The season wasn't heading in an obvious direction, because nobody knew how things would end off-screen.

There were the usual rumors about the cast, too. Depending on the magazine, it was either Kudrow or Schwimmer, or both, who were ready to leave, while the others were happy to stay for another season. It might have been true, or it might have been the media repeating the same old *Friends* folklore. Kudrow and Schwimmer had long been pegged as the difficult ones or the leaders when it came to negotiations.[74] In public, no one said anything other than that they were talking about it, and like everything else, it would come down to a vote. "The neat thing about being a part of this cast is it's six people, so the majority rules—on just about everything," LeBlanc had explained on Leno. "On where we go for lunch, right up to whether we're coming back."

There are only six people who know the truth about how those votes went, and thus far they've managed to keep it between themselves. But if I had to, I would guess that in 2002 it was either unanimous or close. It wouldn't make sense to leave now. Going out on top had always been the goal—and they were

---

74 Three guesses which one they called "difficult" and which one they called "a leader." I'll wait.

number one, for the first time. But the show had gotten a second wind, and the audience was more devoted then ever. Why leave? For all those movies that were doing so well?

This time, no one waited until the last minute. There were no high-stakes games of chicken or threats from the network. It was just the opposite. The cast indicated they'd be willing to discuss another year, and Zucker tripped over himself to make an offer. On February 11, less than two weeks after LeBlanc's ambiguous answer on Leno, *Variety* reported that, "They'll be there for another year: The cast of *Friends* has agreed to return for the ninth—and final—season."

For one more year of *Friends*, NBC would pay Warner Bros. $7 million per episode, enabling a raise to $1 million apiece for the cast. It was a landmark deal—which made the show the most expensive half hour on television—though Zucker said it was the easiest deal he'd ever made. He'd bought himself another year to find something to fill in the enormous gap the show would leave on the network. "It's no secret how important *Friends* is to NBC," Zucker told the press. "We are obviously thrilled and relieved."

With this renewal, the cast got the deal they'd asked for in 2000. They were now among the highest-paid casts in TV history, if not the highest-paid individuals (Kelsey Grammer had just signed a deal for $1.6 million per episode of *Frasier*). The deal came together with an unprecedented lack of haggling, but the salaries still raised a few eyebrows. Even the actor-friendly *People* couldn't resist the headline: "Friends Not in Need." In the long term, this deal would become part of the show's legacy—the moment when "*Friends* money" became a thing. People would cite it as example of either bloated star salaries or the power of a unified front. But in the short term, the big news was that *Friends* was coming back—for *one* more year.

For the first time, the cast released a joint statement to the public, along with Warner Bros. and NBC. "We are enormously pleased and excited to be returning for a ninth season," the actors said. "We could not ignore the outpouring of public support for the show, and we are looking forward to creating one more season with the best writers, producers, directors, and production people in television." Across the board, the message was clear: no more high-profile contract negotiations or jockeying in the press. Those days were over, and this was it. The actors, the network, and the studio all stated in no uncertain terms how glad they were that the show would be back for another year, and that it would be the last. Bright, Kauffman, and Crane chimed in, expressing gratitude for the chance to give *Friends* a proper farewell: "We will devote the entire twenty-four episodes of the final season to wrap up storylines and send our characters off into the world."

No cliffhangers this time. *Friends* would return once more, to say goodbye.

10

The One Where It Ended, Twice

When a series has been on the air for nearly a decade, two things generally happen. With so much story already told, the show is forced to push past its own boundaries and find new elements to keep things interesting. Sometimes this yields innovative twists that feel organic and energizing. Other times, you're just jumping the shark. In its ninth year, both things happened on *Friends*.

Let's start with the latter, because I can already hear the sound of a thousand fists banging together, giving me the Geller Finger. There remains a heated debate over if and when this time-honored television tradition[75] actually happened on *Friends*. Some say it jumped the shark when Ross said "Rachel" at the altar, instead of "Emily." Others cite the Vegas episode, when the two of them got drunk and married. But those were fairly standard plot twists in the soap opera of Ross and Rachel. The truth is, when compared with other shows, *Friends* never really jumped

---

75 Which began with the infamous fifth-season episode of *Happy Days*, wherein Fonzie quite literally jumps over a shark on water skis.

the shark—but it came pretty close. It put on the water skis and got in the ocean. It had nothing to do with Rachel and Ross, though. The *Friends* shark was Rachel and Joey.

When Kauffman and Crane first approached the cast in Season Eight with the idea of Joey falling in love with Rachel, everybody balked. LeBlanc said it felt incestuous (especially uncomfortable after so many years of cultivating a brotherly bond with the female characters). Plus, LeBlanc later explained, "everyone knows that Ross and Rachel are supposed to be together, and we've spent ten years keeping them apart." The cast felt it would come off as a desperate move, and one that would disturb the audience. Crane insisted that no, it was "like playing with fire." It was a risky move that would pay off in story dividends, like Rachel's pregnancy.

In one way, the twist did succeed, giving the show's most juvenile character a much greater sense of depth and maturity. Now Joey had feelings beyond horny and hungry, and LeBlanc had the considerable challenge of playing those things without losing the dim-witted comedy that was the very basis of his character. He'd pulled it off beautifully in Season Eight (earning his first Emmy nomination), and the performance was so wrenching that it *almost* distracted from the ickiness of the story itself.

Not so much in Season Nine. The tables turned and now Rachel liked Joey, and it was all just too much. Once again, the actors hesitated, and the producers assured them it would be fine—and it would be brief. "We knew that we weren't going to take Joey and Rachel the distance," Crane later explained. Aniston wanted it to be made clear that Rachel was *not* in love with Joey, but was just attracted to him. It had to be a crush, and it had to be more funny than emotional; otherwise, this arc would go from risky to unwatchable.

Kauffman and Crane got it. They knew that, nine years in, they were in prime shark-jumping territory. They'd given an obvious wink to the audience acknowledging as much in the fourth episode: "The One with the Sharks," in which Monica mistakenly believes that Chandler has a fetish for marine life. *Friends* was nothing if not mindful of its viewership. With the end of the series approaching, they had to be vigilant. But they needed *something* to keep Ross and Rachel apart just a bit longer, and at this point it would take a *big* something. Kauffman and Crane understood that the Joey-Rachel relationship would end before it really began. They would never have sex or say the L-word; that would be too much to recover from. Once they actually hooked up, the characters (like the audience) would be too weirded out, and preoccupied with Ross.

In the meantime, they kept Ross preoccupied with Charlie. Charlie was the antishark; she was one of those successful twists that can bring new energy into an older series. Played by comic and actress Aisha Tyler, Charlie became one of *Friends'* most popular guest characters, and the only black woman to appear in multiple episodes. "I don't think anyone is trying to redress issues of diversity here," Tyler said at the time. "There wasn't a sense of 'We're bringing on a black character to change something.' Hopefully, I was cast on the merits." It's hard to imagine she wasn't, given how seamlessly she fit into the series. Unlike many other guest performers, Tyler's comedic prowess and style meshed perfectly with the main cast's. It was clear that Charlie was a temporary character, but she didn't seem like an interloper, throwing off the chemistry, like so many outside love interests did.[76] She fit right in.

But it's also pretty hard to imagine that nobody even realized Charlie was the first and only significant black character on *Friends*. Her appearance was given unusual advance publicity, and NBC put out a series of promotional images featuring Tyler posed with Schwimmer and LeBlanc. That didn't change the fact that she was the right actress for the role. Tyler—who was herself a vocal advocate for diversifying television—pointed out

---

76   Cough, Janine, cough.

that there was nothing in the script or character description about Charlie's race. But the heavy-handed promotion did seem—well, heavy-handed. In the beginning, *Friends'* uniform whiteness was merely raised as pointed comment (i.e., Oprah's "I'd like for y'all to get a black friend. Maybe I could stop by."). But after nine years, more than two hundred episodes, and dozens of guest stars, critics were beginning to wonder how they'd managed to avoid virtually all people of color for so long. Really, hadn't they run out of Caucasians yet?

The viewers were a different story. While television content had changed a great deal since the mid-'90s, it remained a largely segregated landscape. There were black shows targeted toward black audiences, though some of them became popular across many demographics (like *Family Matters*, *Moesha*, and *The Fresh Prince of Bel-Air*). And then there were the so-called mainstream series, like *Friends*, which were almost entirely white and yet were supposed to appeal to everyone. For the most part, they did.

I spoke with writer, producer, and comedian Akilah Hughes, who grew up watching the show with her whole family. Hughes, who is black, sometimes comments on issues like racism and intersectionality in her work, often to hilarious effect (many people know her from her 2014 video short, *Meet Your First Black Girlfriend*). But growing up, she told me, she wasn't bothered by *Friends'* whiteness. No one in her household was. "It wasn't like a hate-watch. That didn't even exist back then," she said. "It was like this is the best show on television, and we're watching it. We don't need to have a cultural conversation. This is it."

If TV hadn't been so resolutely segregated, then yes, she probably would have noticed and it probably would have bothered her. But, like hate-watching, diverse casting didn't really exist back then, either. "Any popular show that wasn't specifically marketed to black people, or on UPN or BET, *was* a white show[77]…black people have always watched shows and movies about white people, because that's what was getting made," Hughes said. "And," she was quick to remind me, "it wasn't that deep back then." Even as a child, she knew better than to have high expectations for TV. The fact that *Friends* was funny, and something she could enjoy with her whole family—that's what made it a good show. If it had been funny, family-friendly, *and* diverse, it would have been groundbreaking. And until recently, TV was not in the business of breaking ground.

I heard the same argument from several other people of color (as well as white people[78]). When I sent an email to author and journalist Keah Brown requesting an interview, she politely declined, because she hated *Friends*. I assumed (classic white-lady move on my part!) that she took issue with the show's representation issues, and I wrote back to Brown saying I'd welcome her thoughts on that, if she'd like to offer any. Brown replied again, saying no, that had nothing to do with it. "I just never found it funny. It's glaringly white, yes, but so is *Will & Grace*, which I happen to love, because it's funny."

Hughes, on the other hand, does find *Friends* funny, even now. Like most people, she enjoys watching the soothing reruns. It's still not a hate-watch, but it is a different viewing experience than it was when she was a kid. "This may be harsh, but it's the way that I watch *Gone with the Wind*. I can enjoy these things even though I know that they could have done a *lot* bet-

---

77   Connie Wang, who is Chinese-American, echoed this sentiment. In addition to *Friends*, she said, "I was also watching shows, like *Moesha*. So, it was all black families, or all black friends." Because she was watching these shows as a child in an all-white community, she got the message: "Black people only hang out with black people. White people hang out with white people." Aside from the short-lived *All-American Girl*, "there was nothing like that for Asians," Wang said. "But if there was one, Asian people would only hang out with Asian people, and that's how I thought it was."

78   "One of the biggest changes in media, in my life, is this shift toward taking television as seriously as we take it now," Chuck Klosterman told me. "Things like 'appointment TV'—no one would have ever said that in 1994. It would have seemed insane. Television was what you watched when there was nothing else to do."

ter by people of color, and women. There's so many problematic things about it. But also, that's just what it was back then. We can't just delete the media that came before, because it *does* inform why we like shows now." Hughes also enjoys the thoughtful critique happening around *Friends* these days. "It's not to its detriment. I think it's given it a lot *more* value," she told me. "I think, maybe even *because* of the hindsight watching now, people are more aware of the fact that there was no diversity. And so they're course-correcting. So, I think that it does serve a historical purpose, in the grand scheme of things." It's become a reference point to hold up against today's programming, much of which is still lagging far behind. "You'll look at [a show] and say, 'Well, at least it's got more diversity than *Friends!*'"

But when the Charlie episodes first aired, Hughes recognized her for what she was: temporary. "It wasn't even in the realm of possibility that they would have a new black friend that would have as much agency and weight in the story," she said. Back then, a sitcom might sometimes feature "one really beautiful black girl, for one story arc, where *maybe* she's dateable—but then we'll go back to just the six white friends." *Friends* had done that in Season Seven, when Gabrielle Union did a one-story guest spot, as a woman who, like Charlie, dated both Joey and Ross.[79] The fact that Tyler appeared in nine whole episodes was unheard of, but still—nobody thought this was the beginning of a new era on *Friends*. How could it be? This was the show's last year.

Right?

---

79 Sherri Shepherd also had a small (nonromantic) role in a Joey-Ross storyline, in Season Four's "The One with Phoebe's Uterus." Joey becomes a tour guide at the museum where Ross works. Shepherd, another guide, explains to him that the "white coats" (scientists) and "blue blazers" (tour guides) can't sit together in the cafeteria. It's an unspoken rule. The story culminates with Ross whipping off his white coat and calling for integration at last: "I say we shed these coats that separate us and get to know the people underneath!" It is a spot-on example of mainstream attitudes about diversity in the '90s: it's brief, it's all about "color blindness," and it's explained by white people. Thankfully, Shepherd steals the show so hard that the storyline is not nearly as memorable as her cameo. "I GAVE YOU MY SNACK PACK!"

* * *

Not six months after the ninth season was announced, with great ceremony, as the final, farewell, definitively *last* season of *Friends*, the rumors began to surface. Maybe it wasn't the end, after all. Despite the fact that every party involved—NBC, Warner Bros., Bright/Kauffman/Crane, and the cast—had publicly declared this year the last, it seemed that someone had changed their mind. In the spring and summer of 2002, trade publications speculated on whether or not it would even be possible to renew a series as expensive as *Friends*. At the time, Warner Bros. was producing the show at a deficit, knowing that syndication fees would more than make up for the expense in the long run. But the current syndication contracts maxed out at nine seasons. (This was a typical cap applied in syndication deals, simply because nine seasons worth of episodes was more than enough for the stations to run throughout the year.) If they did a tenth season, no one would be obligated to buy those reruns, and there was no guarantee they'd be able to sell them. *Friends'* enormous popularity was matched only by its enormous price tag, and while the show was back on top for now, the TV tide was still turning toward reality. If there was even a chance they wouldn't sell the remaining episodes (at a very high price), then a tenth season would be too great a financial risk. As crazy as it sounds, Warner Bros. had little incentive to keep making *Friends*.

Everyone knew that the cast didn't, either. They'd gotten those million-dollar deals—plus their not-inconsiderable salaries from the eight other seasons they'd shot. And they would always have those hard-won cuts of back-end profits. Money was no longer the reason to take a job. At least for a while, they could go off and do plays or indie films or absolutely nothing— as many of them seemed eager to do. Schwimmer had always kept one foot in his Chicago theater community, and was trying to develop his career as a director. Cox was open about wanting to focus on having children, and just as open about the fact that she and her husband were struggling with conception (a struggle that was not made any easier by playing a character who was also dealing with infertility). Kudrow had all kinds of irons in the fire, as an actress and a producer (including a comedy she'd soon pitch with Aisha Tyler). Above all, they'd all come on board for the ninth season knowing it would be the last. They'd already made plans and signed other contracts for the following year. The whole point of Season Nine was to give the show a big, beautiful ending. They had said so, in print.

Bright, Kauffman, and Crane were ready, too. In their position, they always had to be ready for the show to end, either in cancellation or in a contract dispute. With every cast negotiation, they had to consider the possibility that Season Two, or Six, or Eight, might be it. At a certain point, they had to know. "You can't keep writing the last season," Crane later put it. They, too, were planning to start their post-*Friends* lives. After the finale, they decided, Bright/Kauffman/Crane Productions would end, as well. Kauffman and Crane had gone from a barn at Brandeis to off-off-Broadway cabarets, to writing pitches on airplanes, to *Dream On*, to that Norman Lear fiasco, and, finally, to this: the show that had changed their lives and so many others. They'd been writing partners for more than twenty-five years. Now, they could just be *friends*.

They had the show right on track, heading toward its end, when Jeff Zucker screamed, "PIVOT!"

What he actually said was, "I don't want to ever believe that it's absolutely going to be the end." This was July 2002, during a Television Critics Association press tour. Zucker conceded that it probably was the end, regardless, as no one could imagine a deal that would override the one they'd just made. But, he added, "I wouldn't 100% put nails in the coffin yet." This was a pivot indeed, given the declarative final-season announcement just a few months prior. The next day, the executive producers made their own statements to the press (and, by proxy, to Zucker),

reaffirming that they *were* 100% sure this was it. Fine, maybe
99%. "We have the feeling that creatively we're there," said
Kauffman. "Not that we couldn't come up with another season
if that were in front of us. But it does feel a bit like things are
coming full circle... We don't want to overstay our welcome."
Crane added: "If this was not going to be the last season, we'd
have to know that right now." The signal-sending had begun.

A few weeks later, Kudrow dropped some telling comments
indicating the cast, too, was 99%—well, more like 75%—ready
to go. "You know, we all get along, and we still have fun, and
the writers are still working really hard and they do good stories," she said in an interview. Okay, but hadn't they just told
the world that Season Nine was goodbye? Yes, but: "Now, I
hope not."

Zucker was well beyond hopeful. He was desperate. He still
didn't have a *Survivor*—nor did he have a new *Friends*. For years,
he'd been hunting for something to tighten NBC's slippery hold
on Thursday nights, and fill the gap that *Friends* would leave.
Will & Grace was strong at 9:00 p.m., holding steady in the top
20, but surely it would take a hit without its powerful lead-in.
Scrubs was popular with critics, but audiences remained unsure
about it. If anything, *Scrubs* seemed to be growing into a cult hit,
à la *My So-Called Life*, and that was not the kind of hit he needed.
He needed another *Friends*, and until he found it, he would shell
out record-breaking sums to keep the old one. Again.

At this point NBC was paying Warner Bros. $7 million per
episode for the ninth and final season of *Friends*. While negotiating that deal, Zucker had asked the studio what it would
take for him to get just one more—theoretically. Ten million
dollars an episode, they told him. $240 million in total. That's
what it would cost to pay for production, and to keep the cast
and showrunners' lucrative contracts in place without Warner
Bros. losing money on the show. And that was assuming the
creators were up for it, and that all six cast members could be

convinced to stay. All of that seemed extremely unlikely, but it didn't matter, anyway, because this was all a ridiculous hypothetical, and no way would NBC agree to pay the unheard of sum of $10 million for thirty minutes of television. At that rate, it would be the network losing money on the (hypothetical, never-gonna-happen) tenth season of *Friends*, and Warner Bros. had no plans to ask them for it. Then, out of the blue, Jeff Zucker showed up and offered it.

I asked media executive Lauren Zalaznick about this decision. What might drive a network that already had the most expensive half hour in television history to throw additional millions on the pile and make it even *more* expensive? Her answer: "Nothing's as cheap as a hit. Nothing." Again, Zalaznick was well aware that the sitcom genre was dying, and that the shift toward reality TV was unstoppable. Indeed, she was one of the people leading and shaping this new genre (she would soon become the chairman of entertainment networks & digital at Bravo). Still, she said, the old adage applies. Even a fading hit in a dying genre was worth it from a business perspective. In 2002, *Friends* still commanded enormous ad rates, and drew in tens of millions of reliable viewers. It had slipped just a bit from its Season Eight rebound, going from number one to number two. Slippage or not, you didn't let go of a number-two show. You held on for dear life.

As for Warner Bros. and their nine-season syndication cap, Zalaznick said, "Look at it the other way. With such an enormous hit, it actually sucks to be in a prenegotiated deal. You want to be able to take it out and leverage it to the highest bidder, literally, for *any* amount of money." In fact, she added, if their current syndication partners didn't buy the new episodes, it would've been even better for Warner. "People would have been desperate to get those late seasons of *Friends* on their air—especially if they didn't have the first nine." It was a show of incalculable value to the network and the studio, no matter what the up-front costs. In situations like this, Zalaznick said, the business decision is a no-brainer. The creative decision is the hard part.

Even with the reality-TV takeover progressing by the day, a show like *Friends* would always have fans. Reality programs were new and mean and modern, and viewers flocked to them, enthralled. But *Friends* was the old, loyal love they kept returning to—despite the fact that it was past its peak. "It's like any relationship," Zalaznick explained to me. "If you really look back on it, and you force yourself to think about the apex of the relationship—and this can be for work, for personal, etc.—it was usually excellent to good to fair for the exact same amount of time as it was fair to poor to *over*. But because you have so much invested in that relationship, and because it was so good for so long, you kinda don't realize it, at that midpoint. At that peak."

That, I think, explains the other decision—the creative one. There were several factors, surely, including the unexpected pile of cash Zucker had just dumped on the table. But again, that kind of money becomes less enticing when you already *have* that kind of money. (Just ask Jerry Seinfeld, the man who turned down $110 million for his own hypothetical tenth season.) Rather, I think, when you're forced to confront the end of something—be it a job, a relationship, or a phase of your life—you simply appreciate it more. You look around and notice everything and everyone you're going to miss. Any bad memories give way to a flood of nostalgia, and suddenly you realize how good you've had it.

"And this is the last season for *sure*?" Jay Leno asked Jennifer Aniston. "Or you think there's a chance?" It was August 2002, just before the start of the ninth season, and once again Leno had one of the cast members on his couch, answering the same question he'd asked a year ago. As an NBC star himself, he seemed to have been delegated the role of network inquisitor; actors weren't the only ones who could negotiate via the media. A week prior, he'd had LeBlanc on again, given him a puppy on the air (a chihuahua, like LeBlanc's childhood dog), and then leaned in to ask if he and his castmates might stick around and help the network out: "We got nothin'." LeBlanc—again, holding a puppy against his chest—mumbled something about conversations, and then hurriedly suggested they change the subject.

Aniston was only slightly less vague in her answer. Was it really the end? "Well, look, y'know. I say that today. It seems like it's our last season, and it's in our minds that it's our last season." At this, the audience moaned and Aniston made a sad face in agreement. "I know." Leno, undaunted, chimed in again: "Well, you got an *Emmy* nomination.[80] Congratulations on that." Except it didn't sound like congratulatory salute so much as a gentle scolding to remember the show and the network on which she got that very nice nomination. And that it was, in fact, the only work for which she'd ever been nominated—for an Emmy or anything else.

By this point, Aniston had appeared in more than a dozen feature films, many of them well received (though none of them box-office successes). In addition to traditional rom-coms like *Picture Perfect*, she'd played the female lead in the cult-hit comedy *Office Space*, and voiced a character in the animated sci-fi film *The Iron Giant*. While her film work was often praised by critics, she'd yet to find a role big or distinct enough to make audiences forget about Rachel. The night she appeared on Leno in 2002, she was promoting the one that might just do it.

The Good Girl was one of the year's most acclaimed independent films, starring Aniston as a depressed Texan woman stuck in a lousy marriage and a meaningless job. Justine, the titular good girl, has a messy affair with a younger guy (played by Jake Gyllenhaal), gets blackmailed into sleeping with another man, gets pregnant, lies to her abusive husband, and in the end winds

---

80   That year, the cast decided (as a group, naturally) to submit themselves in the Lead Actor and Actress categories. Until then, they'd submitted as Supporting performers, but, as Matthew Perry joked at the ceremony, "It didn't work out too well for us." Kudrow was the only one who'd won.

up in the exact same place she started: stuck and unhappy, but now, with a baby. Aside from the baby, this character was the polar opposite of Rachel, and Aniston nailed it. As with her other film roles, the critics pointed out, she was clearly trying to diversify and avoid a lifetime of typecasting. But this time, she'd actually done it. Justine was so remarkably *not* Rachel, that it was all anyone could talk about. "Jennifer Aniston has, at last, decisively broken with her *Friends* image in an independent film of satiric fire and emotional turmoil," raved Roger Ebert. "It will no longer be possible to consider her in the same way." *New York Times* critic Elvis Mitchell noted the flat, sodden voice and "morose physicality" with which she embodied the role, so different from the high-energy, hand-waving comedy she did on television. It was impossible to avoid comparing and contrasting Justine, Rachel, and Aniston herself. Mitchell wrote: "It's Ms. Aniston who surprises in *The Good Girl*. In some ways she may feel as trapped as Justine by playing Rachel Green, the poor little rich daddy's girl of television's *Friends*."

It was an apt choice of words. That poor little rich girl she'd played for so long had made Aniston a poor little (extremely) rich star. Had she played any other character on any other show, then *The Good Girl* might have been Aniston's breakout film role and the start of a new career for her. She had the range, and she was certainly willing to make the effort. But that's the trap of television stardom: the bigger you are on the small screen, the harder it is to get out of it.

"A lot of movie stars have a defining role," Anne Helen Petersen told me. Petersen is a culture writer and reporter, with a PhD in media studies, who specializes in the history of celebrity. She argued there are many major film actors who are forever linked to certain parts. Anne Bancroft had Mrs. Robinson, Anthony Hopkins has Hannibal Lecter. "But that's still only two hours on the screen." With television, its hundreds of hours. "Jennifer Aniston was Rachel Green for so many nights, for so long…and didn't have a developed screen persona or a star image before that point. So, of course it's going to be the foundation of her star image." Movie actors can have iconic roles, but with television actors it's the other way around. The roles own *them*.

There are exceptions, naturally. Petersen cited George Clooney, who was able to transition to film and build an enormous career there, but only because he left *ER* early, in its fifth season. "He got out of Doug Ross as soon as he saw the writing on the wall," she said. *ER* ran for fifteen years, and was the number-one show for many of them. Clooney could have stayed there for as long as he liked, and earned a fortune as well as a comfortable career in the television industry. But had he stayed a minute longer, he would have been Doug Ross forever.

In part, it's just simple math. People spend so much more time with TV characters, and they do so in the comfort of their own homes. Even today, as TV has grown prestigious and virtually all media is consumed via the internet, there's a different sense of occasion in watching a movie—if only because it has a definitive end. With TV, there's always the promise of more—one more episode, another season, or maybe a reunion special. Even when characters die on-screen, we're never fully convinced they're dead.

Then there's the issue of star image that Petersen referred to. In the public eye, all celebrities get somewhat conflated with the parts they play, including movie actors. It's not always a bad thing. Director Cameron Crowe once told a story about going to a bar with John Cusack, star of his film *Say Anything…* Cusack had played many other roles in popular films, though *Say Anything…* was a fan-favorite. Someone at the bar approached Cusack, asking, "Are you Lloyd Dobler?" Cusack replied: "On my better days, yes, I am Lloyd Dobler." It became a legendary anecdote about Cusack—one that showed how silly we are to think of actors as their characters, *and* gave us reason to believe that maybe we're a little bit right. Maybe John Cusack is Lloyd Dobler, sometimes.

Dobler was an indelible part of Cusack's star image, but for the actors on *Friends*, character was the image, full stop. There weren't just one or two anecdotes floating around, but scores of detailed stories about what great pals they were, what they ate for lunch (together!), and rumors about Aniston getting pregnant (just like Rachel!). The cast never pushed back against the public's desire to think of them as the parts they played, and often seemed to welcome it. Why not? They *were* real-life friends, and they did each lunch together, and people liked knowing that when they watched the show. But after nine years, the narrative of *Friends* had taken on a life of its own and swallowed them whole.

Aniston in particular was subsumed by Rachel. On-screen and in the media, her image was still that of a sweet, relatable, uncomplicated gal who just wanted to be a mommy. "She really tried to counter that with *The Good Girl*," Petersen told me. "That was this role that was like, 'Oh, what if she's kind of a dirtbag?'" In the years that followed, Aniston would choose many unlikable, unglamorous, or otherwise anti-Rachel roles: a low-income housekeeper who steals from her employers; a traumatized, disabled pill addict; a horrible boss. "I've been fascinated by the way that she has chosen a bunch of these dirtbag roles, but people still insist that actually she's America's Sweetheart—and keep trying to map this desire to have a baby onto her," said Petersen. "I think the ideological forces that have coalesced around 'Jennifer Aniston' are much larger than whatever Jennifer Aniston actually is."

She and her castmates would always have careers, and some of them would even have more iconic roles. Kudrow already had *Romy and Michele's High School Reunion* (her character was a spacey blonde, but somehow nothing like Phoebe). In 2005, she would cocreate and star in *The Comeback*, as Valerie Cherish (here, her character was a former sitcom star, but somehow nothing like Kudrow).

LeBlanc's trajectory was perhaps the most fascinating. He leaned into the legacy rather than fighting it. First, there was *Joey*, the infamous and brief *Friends* spin-off, in which he continued playing the character until the series was canceled in 2006. After that, he took a four-year sabbatical, turning down all work and vanishing from public. In 2011, he reappeared with *Episodes*, a series cocreated by David Crane and Jeffrey Klarik, in which he starred as "Matt LeBlanc." It was a satirical version of himself that deliberately played on the star image of a washed-up, womanizing, drunken has-been—and it was great. A pitch-black comedy that delightfully skewered LeBlanc and Joey, allowing the actor to embody a whole new role. "Matt LeBlanc" became Matt LeBlanc's most critically acclaimed role, earning him his first Emmy Award and a second chapter in his career. Still, there was no escaping *Friends*. It loomed too large in public consciousness. LeBlanc had stopped trying to break out of the legacy, and just built a life inside it. And why the hell not? It was a pretty comfortable life in there. Yes, he'd have to put up with people asking him how he was doin' every time he left the house. But there were worse fates than having had a hit sitcom, working with people you loved, getting rich, and getting typecast forever as a Friend.

That was one of the factors the cast discussed when they met to vote on Season Ten in the fall of 2002. Kauffman and Crane had already decided that, yes, they could extend the show for another year—but no further. It was time to start aiming for the definitive ending, either this year or next. Now it was up to the cast to decide which. LeBlanc recalled weighing the pros and cons with the group: Should they do more, or was it time to get out before they all got pigeonholed? He replied, laughing, "I think the damage is done there." This time it was Aniston who raised concerns. The show had just won an Emmy (as had she). The numbers were good but probably not going to get any better. Didn't they want to go out on a high? In an interview a year later, shortly before the series finale, Aniston would acknowledge it was true, she was the holdout: "I was also feeling like, 'How much more of Rachel do I have in me? How many more stories are there to tell, for all of us, before we're just pathetic, still living across from each other?'"

Aniston reportedly suggested a compromise. She would return, but only for twelve episodes, instead of the usual twenty-four. As ever, it was all for one and one for all. The other cast members (many of whom were vocal about wanting to return for a full season) stuck by her. There would be no Rachel-free episodes. If Aniston did only twelve, so would the rest of them. That wouldn't work for Jeff Zucker. Half a season of *Friends* would only save half of his bacon. Zucker pressed, getting on the phone with the cast himself to try to persuade them. He made a counteroffer of eighteen episodes. Still, they hedged and the stalemate continued.

It was Friday, December 20—the last shoot night of the calendar year, and the last chance to make a deal. No one could come to terms on the scheduling issues, and the agencies were about to shut down for the holidays. On the business end, nothing could get done between now and the new year—and by then, it would be too late in the season for a change this big. (For the writers, it was already going to be an extremely tight squeeze. In July, Crane had said they'd need to know "now" if Season Ten was happening. They were five months past that deadline and none the wiser.) By Friday, the likelihood of a tenth season was rapidly dwindling, and still the phones kept ringing. Even for a *Friends* negotiation, this one was getting ridiculous.

Kevin Bright, who was directing that week, had stepped in as a de facto negotiator between the cast and the network. "So what was happening was we'd go out and shoot a scene, and then I'd get on the phone with NBC, and then I'd meet with the cast." All day and into the night, Bright ran back and forth between the phone and the dressing room where the cast waited together. He'd relay a new number or proposition, wait for an answer, run back to the phone, and then get everyone back on-stage for the next scene. It was a long day and everyone was tense. At one point, the network threatened to walk away. The negotiations weren't going anywhere, so maybe it was time to let *Friends* die, after all. For the first time, no one knew for sure if they were bluffing.

Of *course* they were bluffing. Shortly before midnight, the cast came back with one last offer, and NBC grabbed it. The actors agreed to eighteen episodes, provided that one of them be a clip show.[81] Done. Bright and the cast finished taping and went home. Zucker had his tenth season, and a little more time to find his next Thursday night hit.

A few months later, he did. In May 2003, NBC announced a new reality competition program starring Donald Trump. Many would cite *The Apprentice* as the true end of the Must-See TV years, when NBC gave up on comedy and joined the other side. It was winning, after all.

As for the *Friends* team, they now had another year to reconcile their mixed feelings about leaving the show behind and going off into the unknown. (And when they did, the cast would have another $18 million to take with them, which sure didn't hurt.) "I think, as far as everybody was concerned, it was yet one more way to procrastinate the end coming," Bright recalled. "I think that was a little bit of a relief for all of us."

That's what Season Ten feels like: an elongated version of Season Nine. It's a bit like watching the extended cut of a great movie, and realizing that maybe those extra scenes and bits of dialogue were edited out for a reason. But still, it's a really great movie.

Season Ten demonstrates just how strong *Friends* really was.

---

81   Hence, "The One Where Chandler Gets Caught."

It stumbles into some of the pitfalls of a long-running show, and a lot of its stories just seem like ways to keep the characters occupied before the end (which, of course, they were). Exhibit A: Phoebe changes her name to Princess Consuela Banana-Hammock. I somehow doubt that pitch would have flown in Season Four, but ridiculous though it may be, it's so well executed that it still makes you laugh. Season Ten soundly disproves the critics who for years claimed the show relied on its good looks and youthful marketability, rather than creative fortitude. Step-by-step, the characters' storylines are wrapped up, and while everyone gets their own perfect ending, they don't then vanish off into the sunset. The pacing slows, giving the show a sense of realism that wasn't there before. Monica and Chandler buy a house, but it still takes months of paperwork and packing before they can actually move in. Phoebe gets her fairy-tale wedding, but once she's home from the honeymoon, she still goes to work and gets coffee with her friends. The writing does an excellent of reminding us that stories end, but life goes on, without hitting us over the head with goodbyes. Even with the obvious foot-dragging toward the finale, there are still a number of classic *Friends* moments, and jokes so simple and solid you can't believe they haven't made them already. Phoebe tries to teach Joey French. Ross gets a spray tan. "JOEY DOESN'T SHARE FOOD." For my money, that line alone makes Season Ten worth watching.

Ultimately, these moments are mere distractions from the overall tension building in the background. The tenth season, like the first, has an anxious energy to it. This time, it's not the fear of a fledgling pilot, but the deep desire of an iconic hit that does not want to let its audience down.

It was a very real possibility. Series finales are notoriously messy or polarizing. You can't please everyone, and finales that try to do so inevitably turn out too sweet and *way* too self-aggrandizing. On the other hand, if you go too simple or, God forbid, ambiguous, then audiences rage. There are people in this world who are still mad about *The Sopranos* finale. *Friends* was in a unique predicament, because it had built such a close bond with its audience. It had succeeded for this long by paying close attention to what viewers wanted, and never betraying their trust. In one way, that gave them a leg up, because the creators knew exactly what needed to happen in the finale. In another way, they were screwed, because everyone could see what was coming from a mile away.

The *what* and *when* were obvious: Ross and Rachel would wind up together in the end. The only surprise would be *how*. And after ten years, a brief marriage, and a baby, it was hard to imagine what *could* unite this couple in a permanent way. "[The series finale] was probably the toughest episode that David and I ever wrote," recalled Kauffman. It had to create a sense of closure, and allow for plenty of tears, but it still had to be funny. "It was very important to us that it not feel like some strange anomaly. It should *feel* like the show," said Crane. They didn't want to do "The One That Takes Place in the Future," or attempt some gigantic twist and reveal it was all Phoebe's drug-induced hallucination or Rachel's dream.[82] They'd seen what happened with *Seinfeld*'s finale, which—in the grand tradition of *Seinfeld*—was neither sweet nor emotional. That was in keeping with the show's tone, but it was still deemed a huge disappointment. Kauffman and Crane were determined not to let that happen. This was not the time to go rogue. Their finale had to meet everyone's expectations without being predictable. It had to feel special, but not different. "So there was just a *little* bit of pressure on us," said Kauffman.

After months in the writers' room breaking the story, Kauffman and Crane wound up writing the script over the holiday break. She was in Hawaii with her family, and he in Vermont. Via long-distance phone calls, the two of them wrote. Crane

---

82 Both of those concepts would later emerge among the many *Friends* conspiracy theories online.

took long walks in the snow, mulling jokes and dialogue, then headed back inside to get on the phone with Kauffman. It was strange and difficult, to finish the show they'd been writing together for a decade, and even harder to do it over the phone, five thousand miles apart from one another. But writing the last one, said Crane, "was not as difficult as *shooting* the last one."

LeBlanc was the one who started it. On January 16, 2004, he and the others were clustered around the orange couch on the Central Perk set between takes. It was the first day of filming "The Last One" (because it was an hour long, the second half would be filmed the following week, on January 23). Everyone had been weepy and struggling all day—all season, really. But again, it was just another show night and they had to keep it together if only to stay on schedule. Already the makeup touch-ups were taking forever, what with all the welling eyes and nose-blowing. That's when LeBlanc realized something. He turned to his castmates and said: "Do you realize this is the last coffee shop scene?" And everyone just lost it.

Bright, who was directing the episode, gave up and stepped off the set. "It's a total breakdown," he told other producers, explaining what LeBlanc had done. "Now they're all just *gone*." The actors sat there, crying it out and taking turns comforting each other. (Imagine the last day of high school, if high school had lasted for ten years.) On set were dozens of friends and family members who'd been invited to watch or be extras, including Crane's life partner, Kudrow's husband, and Nancy Josephson—the agent who'd first met Kauffman and Crane back at that off-Broadway theater in 1985, and suggested they give TV a shot. The background of Central Perk was filled with so many lawyers and agents that Kauffman joked it had suddenly become the world's oldest coffee-shop crowd. Her own children, who'd been coming to the set since infancy, would later appear as extras in the airport scene, as would Bright's. Cousins, nieces, assistants, spouses, Pilates instructors—"everybody found their way into this last episode somehow," said Bright. In part, they were there for moral support. "But also, it made it feel like the extended family was there with us. Everybody who had been a part of the show for ten years was there for the ending."

David Wild was there, too. Over the years, he'd become part of that extended family, having written that first iconic *Rolling Stone* feature, and then a companion book for Season One. He'd interviewed them so frequently that he'd once joked about being "the seventh ugly Friend," he told me. "But I knew that was never true." He'd seen how they'd huddled together in those crazy early days, and grown into one of the most powerful teams in the television industry. Now, when he saw them at an industry party or in the Warner Bros. dining room, he might say hello but would never ask to join them. "I didn't overstep... I don't even know if they *liked* me. But they trusted me as someone who knew who they were, got their sensibility, and probably knew when to give them space." No, there were only six members of that club, but Wild had become a trustworthy outsider.

As the finale approached, Warner Bros. approached him to write another authorized book about the series—offering the same fee he'd gotten for the first. Wild turned it down. The studio quickly came back to him, saying the cast would only agree to the book if he was the author. Wild said okay, then he would write it if they did this deal *Friends*-style. Whatever the actors got paid for the book, he'd be paid equally. They agreed. Ten years prior, it would have been an absurd request, but with their own contracts, the cast had set a precedent. It wasn't just the raises they got, but the hands-on way they handled their business. "They *audited* everything, to make sure they got paid. And I was a beneficiary of that, very, very much," said Wild. "There was a check, in the middle of the writers' strike, that was the nicest check I ever got. And I think it's only because I, for a brief, shining moment in time, was like a seventh Friend. And paid as such."

Wild was on set for the finale shoot, taking notes for the book and grabbing interviews whenever he could. It was no easy task, what with the entire cast and crew trying to stop crying long enough to finish the final Central Perk scene. "We almost didn't get through," said Kauffman. Around 10:30 that night, they finally wrapped. Once the stage was clear, the crew began tearing down Central Perk, for good. In the delirium of the day, it hadn't occurred to anyone that this was coming. Realizing what was happening, the cast came down from their dressing rooms. The producers, the office staff—everyone drifted to the stage. "And we just watched it go down," said Kauffman. "And it was like losing a little piece of yourself." Afterward, they sat on the bare floor where Central Perk had been and had a little impromptu party. They signed the walls with sentimental notes and called dibs on souvenirs. Someone passed around shots from a bottle of Patrón and set decorator Greg Grande made a toast: "The memories we made on Stage 24 are better than any dreams we ever had."

When they came back to shoot the rest on January 23, everyone was a mess before the cameras even started rolling. From the beginning, Aniston had been designated Most Likely to Cry, and this season she'd been in tears since the first table-read. Cox was the stalwart professional—the one who rarely flubbed a line and almost never broke when the rest of them got the giggles. But on that day, even she knew it was just a matter of time. Her husband, David Arquette, came to the set with a video camera to document the big event. Aniston's dad and Schwimmer's parents were in the audience, too. One of the producers had put together a *Friends* "yearbook" and now it was even more like high school. A handful of guest stars returned to watch the final taping, including Hank Azaria, Aisha Tyler, Paul Rudd, and

Maggie Wheeler. Wheeler was coaxed into doing a little Janice ("Oh. My. God.") to help warm up the crowd. "Lots of people ask me if I worried about playing a character that distinct—especially that distinct in *voice*—and whether or not I'd get type-cast," Wheeler reflected later. "I wasn't concerned about that at all, and I never worried about the aftermath. I just wanted to enjoy myself and bring that character to life. I am so proud and so happy to have participated in something that has given people so much joy." Years later, people would still approach her at the grocery store, and ask for a Janice laugh. And she'd oblige, unbothered. "Being recognized for that is an honor."

That day, the audience went wild for the Janice bit. There wasn't much need for warming up; the crowd was so alight with tension and excitement. With other season finales, they had pretaped certain scenes without an audience, to keep cliff-hangers or big reveals from leaking before the episode aired. For the last episode, the producers debated whether or not to pretape—or perhaps to fill the audience only with friends and colleagues. How else would they keep the media from reporting every detail? But, more importantly, they wanted every inch of the show to be good—and it was *always* better with a real audience. "The hell with it," they decided. "It'll get out or it won't get out." There was so much hype around the finale, and already a number of stories had surfaced, most of which were way off base (including a rumor that they'd shot several different possible endings). And again, there weren't that many twists to conceal. Everyone knew that Monica and Chandler's baby would be born. The only surprise was the fact that they had twins.[83] Most viewers also knew that Cox herself was now

---

83 Which is, to be fair, a pretty absurd scenario. Here, I'd like to point out that the writers did know when they were pushing the boundaries of reality. "There's a lot of debate that goes on as to how much can you credibly believe," Crane explained. "And you have a lot of leeway…within the conventions and the tone of the show, and sitcoms." They knew it was unrealistic, but they also knew audience did not expect grounded reality from *Friends*. "We're not making a documentary here."

pregnant (another story that had been heavily covered in the press), and it didn't seem worth it to try to hide her body completely with weird camera angles and giant bags. No one wanted a *Friends* finale where Monica only appeared from the neck up. So again, *to hell with it.* They decided to shoot it all in front of the audience, put Cox in an oversize shirt, and just not worry about keeping secrets. Really, what was the point?

There were no alternate endings. It was always going to be Ross and Rachel, and an empty apartment. Kauffman and Crane had once toyed with an ambiguous reunion for the couple—or a scenario in which they didn't get back together, but it seemed like *maybe* they could someday. But they soon realized that no, that would only leave everyone painfully unsatisfied (themselves included). "We had dicked the audience around for ten years," as Crane delicately put it. "And we didn't see any advantage in frustrating them."

The only problem, in fact, was that they'd put so much creative effort into keeping Ross and Rachel apart. Going into Season Ten, they realized maybe they'd done too good a job. Ross and Rachel really did seem like platonic friends, and amicable coparents. They didn't even seem to hang out much without the rest of the group. So, Kauffman and Crane began to tiptoe their way back into the romance, bringing up little reminders of the past, both the good parts and the lousy parts. Ross goes home to Long Island with Rachel when her father has a heart attack, reminding us of how he loved her as a teenager. Later, they run into her old work friend Mark, and Ross's maniacal jealousy comes out all over again. Rachel gets a job in Paris, and only then does the truth become obvious (to Ross, that is). It's actually been easy for the two of them to stay apart for so long, because they've been in close proximity. The enticing possibility of them has always been there—and Ross and Rachel are all about the drama of potential romance rather than the stability of a relationship. Or at least they were, back when they got together. But that was a long time ago.

Initially, Kauffman and Crane planned a story (slated to run two episodes before the finale) where they go to Paris together, and Ross begins to fall for her again. They cut it. It wasn't necessary, and actually seemed like *too* much justification. Ultimately, neither the characters nor the audience needed a grand romantic adventure to bring Ross and Rachel back together. In the end, there is no big reason for them to fall in love again. It's simply that they *are* in love, and they're finally grown-up enough to admit it. It's time to stop, well, dicking each other around.

Rachel got off the plane. Monica and Chandler came home with twins. Everyone thought the last tape night would take forever, but it seemed to fly by. "Can't something go wrong?!" Crane thought. "Can't something slow us down? It's happening too quickly." But there they were, in the empty apartment, setting up for the final scene. Now, Cox seemed to crack. During one of the last sections of dialogue, she forgot one of her lines. They stopped, she checked the line, and they started again. And again, she flubbed it. Over and over, Cox stumbled through words, unable to get the line out. Watching her, their ballast, struggling with the ending, the weight of this moment sunk in deeper. The purple walls were stripped bare, ready to be taken down. A sunset-tinted light shone through the window. It was over, and it was just so sad. Cox missed the line again, as a brutal tension filled the room. Once more, Matthew Perry stepped in to shatter it: "Somebody is gonna get fired."

A familiar trick, but it still worked like new. Cox said her line, then they said the rest of them, and then there was nothing left on the page. Bright had them do the scene again, just to be safe, but only the first take was used. Repeating the ending took too much out of the actors as well as the audience. Anyway, he said, "it all came out perfect, the first time."

11

The Comeback

On the evening of August 11, 2015, Comedy Central UK put out a vague but tantalizing message on its Twitter feed: "We're throwing a Friends party!" The tweet linked to an announcement on the company's website for something called Friends-Fest: a five-day "experiential event" in east London, where fans could browse memorabilia and take photos on replica sets of Monica's apartment and Central Perk. That same week, Comedy Central UK had renewed its license with Warner Bros. to broadcast reruns of the series through 2019. The licensing fee was not disclosed, though reports estimated it to be somewhere in the neighborhood of "colossal." Comedy Central would only say the deal was a significant investment.

Maybe a little too significant, in fact. *Friends* had been on the air virtually nonstop for the last twenty years. And so much had changed in those last two decades. For starters, there was a whole hell of a lot more to watch on television, and much of it was of equal or higher quality than this throwback sitcom.

Comedy hadn't died at the hands of reality, after all. It had rebounded and diversified, taking on new forms: satires like *The Daily Show* and *The Office*; mockumentary-style series like *Modern Family* and *Arrested Development*; surrealistic, hyperspecific worlds like *30 Rock*; barely fictionalized improvisational comedies like *Curb Your Enthusiasm*. Even the traditional multicamera sitcom returned with new creative fortitude, in shows like *How I Met Your Mother* and *The Big Bang Theory*—both of which were often touted *Friends 2.0*. In this new golden age of television, audiences expected shows to be smart rather than snappy. They wanted nuance and surprise, in addition to sparkling comedy.

Furthermore, fewer and fewer people were watching those shows *on* television itself, preferring to get their entertainment the same way they got everything else: via the internet. Comedy Central had just paid untold millions to air a show that everyone had already watched a hundred times, on a platform that was going out of style. If this rerun investment was going to pay off (or simply break even), then they had to do something to generate fan interest. An event like this might be a fun, fresh way to remind viewers of their old favorite show. They could take selfies on the orange couch and sip coffee from giant mugs, and then (fingers crossed) go home and watch a few episodes (knock wood) on their channel. At the very least, FriendsFest would be a good barometer to gauge how many people still cared about *Friends*. If enough were willing to buy a ticket and come to an event, then maybe they'd be up for turning on the television.

The next day, August 12, at noon, @ComedyCentralUK put out another tweet, announcing that tickets for FriendsFest were now on sale. Thirteen minutes later, they were sold out.

It's hard to pinpoint the moment it started, but around ten years after *Friends* ended, it had its biggest resurgence yet. I remember the first time I noticed it, sitting at my desk at Refinery29, a popular women's media site where I worked as a writer. It was

2014, and I was scrolling through a list of our most popular recent stories. Every other headline seemed to have the word *Friends* in it: fun *Friends* fashion stories, behind-the-scenes anecdotes, thoughtful opinion pieces about the dated, problematic characters. By the time Netflix announced its own acquisition of the show, the internet was bubbling over with breaking-news stories about *Friends*—a show that had been off the air for ten years. And, I realized, I had written plenty of those stories myself! Like everyone else, I was having some sort of relapse of *Friends* fever.

Strange, considering we all should have been inoculated by then. Comebacks happen all the time, but the curious thing about this one was that *Friends* had never really gone away. In the US, too, it had been running in ceaseless syndication on multiple channels. It was so omnipresent that it should have been mere background noise—the kind of show you only watch in dentists' waiting rooms—but instead, it was the hottest thing on TV. Or on your phone.

Years later, the revival continues. Offline, too, devotion to the series has only grown. *Friends* was always a symbol of '90s style, but over the years it evolved into its own distinct subgenre of fashion. Urban Outfitters began stocking little white T-shirts, like the ones they wore on *Friends*—as well as little white T-shirts with the *Friends* logo printed on them. *Friends! The Musical Parody* debuted off-Broadway in 2017, and was such a success that its eight-week run was extended by almost a year. Long before FriendsFest, Central Perk–esque cafés opened all over the world, in Beijing, Singapore, Dubai, Saint Petersburg, Egypt, and Bulgaria, to name a few.

The show has now reached viewers in more than one hundred and thirty countries (and that's not including those who've gotten it online) in approximately forty languages. It's become a popular tool for learning English. YouTube is now full of tutorials featuring clips from the show, but people have been using reruns to study the language since before YouTube even existed. During a recent US tour, members of the K-Pop group BTS talked about how their parents made them watch the DVDs growing up, crediting their ease with the language to the show. In 2017, the *New York Times* interviewed several Spanish-speaking Major League Baseball players who became bilingual thanks to *Friends*. Mets player Wilmer Flores, who is from Venezuela, pointed out that the show was far more helpful than traditional classes when it came to learning American English because it gave him a sense of how people really spoke. It did not, however, give him an accurate picture of the country, nor the city for which he played. "In photos, it all looks the same, but the traffic and driving around is way different," he told the *Times*. Indeed, traffic is one of many real-life elements of New York that *Friends* omitted entirely—including, the *Times* noted, people who look like Flores.

Today's television comedy paints a much more diverse image (though it still doesn't come close to a realistic depiction of America's population, let alone New York's). In light of shows like *Jane the Virgin*, *Grey's Anatomy*, *Orange Is the New Black*, and...well, pretty much everything, *Friends'* flaws are all the more noticeable. They've added a complicated undertone to the current wave of *Friends* nostalgia, especially for the many young people who are only just discovering the series. Today's city-dwelling twentysomethings have even less in common with the ones on *Friends*, and yet they are the show's biggest fan base.

My cousin, Dizzy Dalton, is one of them. She was born in 1992 and first saw *Friends* as a six-year-old. Back then, she was too young to pick up on most of the cultural references or incongruities, and it didn't matter. "It was a kind of *humor* I could understand," she told me. She got hooked on the show the way little kids do, bugging her parents and three older siblings to come watch it with her. Soon, the whole family capitulated and became fans. Now, *Friends* quotes have become a kind of family shorthand, and the show is a nostalgic pastime. When they're together over the holidays, unwinding on the sofa, it's one of the few things everyone can agree on—though Dizzy remains the die-hard fan. She puts it on in the background when she's cooking, so familiar with every episode that she doesn't even need to look at the screen to watch it. "It's like wrapping yourself up in a warm blanket," she told me. But now, she does notice things about the show that shock her: the gay jokes, the overwhelming whiteness, etc. She still takes comfort in it, but at the same time, "it very much offends the sensibility."

More than anything, she's put off by its treatment of women. "There's a fair amount of slut shaming in it, as well," she pointed out, citing storylines like the one where Rachel tells Ross how many guys she's slept with (and he flips out). "There's a lot of shaming of the girls for sleeping with people, and then Joey can go out and sleep with everyone," she says. To her, though, this highlights the progress that's been made. *Friends* is an old show with old problems. Some are problems we're still dealing with, sure, but many of these storylines would just never happen now. She lives in a world where terms like *slut shaming* exist. When *Friends* was created, it was just *slut*, full stop. "I mean, clearly things must have changed so much in the last twenty, twenty-five years."

Some things, yes. But others had only begun to change in recent months. I had that conversation with Dizzy in October 2017. That same week, the *New York Times* and the *New Yorker* published in-depth reports exposing decades of alleged sex crimes perpetrated by film producer Harvey Weinstein. It was both a shocking exposé, and not all that surprising. It seemed like the reckoning that Hollywood had coming for a century. As more women in the industry came forward to share their stories of abuse, coercion, and assault, the experiences revealed a broad spectrum of behaviors afflicting women in the entertainment business. Some shared stunning assault allegations, like those leveled at Weinstein, while others had been harassed or threatened or pushed out of the industry. The open secrets about Hollywood were, at long last, being dragged into the spotlight. The #MeToo movement bloomed. Many people assumed that phrase began with Weinstein. But the Me Too campaign had been around for over a decade. It was originated by black civil rights activist Tarana Burke, in 2006. None of this was new. It was just that nobody paid much attention, until now.

That same year, in April 2006, Amaani Lyle lost her case. Lyle had been hired as a writers' assistant on *Friends* in 1999, and was terminated four months later. She'd been interviewed for the job by Adam Chase and Gregory Malins, the writer/executive producers she'd later work under, in addition to Andrew Reich (another writer/supervising producer on the show). During the interview, they'd told her it was crucial she be able to type very fast, because her primary job was to sit in the room and record what the writers said while brainstorming. They'd also told her that "the humor could get a little lowbrow in the writers' room." This was a comedy show about young, sexually active adults, after all. It was just part of the process.

That much Lyle understood (it was early in her career, but she'd been in writers' rooms before). What was never made clear, though, was what distinguished "the process" from just a bunch of guys sitting around telling blow-job stories. Was it part of the process to recount stories about women gagging and vomiting on your dick? Pretending to jerk off constantly, bringing in a pornographic coloring book, and make racist jokes about black women and tampons—that was brainstorming? Was it necessary to gossip about one of the cast members' alleged fertility problems, and speculate about her "dried-up pussy"?

These are a few of the alleged comments and incidents that Lyle later detailed in court documents. According to her legal declarations, this kind of behavior was common and accepted (or even encouraged) in the writers' room. But it was her supervisors—Chase, Malins, and Reich—who were the worst, she claimed. None of these alleged statements were directed at Lyle herself. But it was, quite literally, her job to listen to them.

During her tenure, Lyle said, "I was constantly being exposed to writers and producers making statements and comments that had nothing to do with the *Friends* television show, that were offensive because they were racist, sexist, and obscene." Often, when recounting personal stories about their sex lives, she said her supervisors told her not to include them in her notes. So, it seemed there was a line somewhere, between the creative process and so-called locker-room talk. Though, even when talking about the characters, it wasn't always clear what constituted work. Lyle claimed that one of the writers frequently fantasized about an episode where Joey would sneak up on Rachel in the shower, then rape her. As she explained in a 2018 interview, "It was very hard to distinguish, 'Okay, is this something that they want to put in a script eventually? Or are they just bored, and it's two o'clock in the morning, and they're tired?'" Lyle did understand that she was not in a position to rock the boat. Apparently, this was how hit TV shows got made. "It's something where [I] wouldn't have questioned the process if I hadn't been accused of not doing my job."

Chase and Malins terminated Lyle after four months, on the basis of poor job performance. They claimed her typing was too slow to keep up with the conversation. It came as a shock because, up until that point, Lyle thought she was doing fine. She had been urged to work on her speed, but she'd also been told not to worry about it. Indeed, according to court records, Chase had told her she was "doing a good job" the night before her termination. There was another writers' assistant on staff, who (as two *Friends* producers later testified) often missed jokes, made errors when typing, and "spaced out" during meetings. He wasn't fired. In fact, he was soon promoted.

He was also white and male, like most of people in the writers' room. Lyle didn't believe her typing was the problem. She thought it was more to do with the fact that she was a black woman working on a famously undiverse show—and that she had pointed it out. During her time on the job, Lyle testified, she protested *Friends'* persistent lack of diversity on more than one occasion. She urged Chase and Malins to hire black actors (or extras, at least) and pitched stories involving black characters. Pitching and critiquing weren't part of her job as an assistant— but neither were they firing offenses. She believed that Chase, Malins, and Reich just didn't want her around.

Lyle immediately filed complaints with the Department of Fair Employment and Housing, alleging that she'd been fired out of retaliation and on the basis of gender and race discrimination, and that during her time on *Friends*, she was subject to both racial and sexual harassment. She was soon granted a right to sue. This began a six-year-long legal process that brought Lyle up against not only those three writers, but NBC, Warner Bros., and Bright/Kauffman/Crane Productions. Early on, the court ruled that Lyle had been an employee only of Warner Bros. (not NBC or Bright/Kauffman/Crane), but the creators were still forced to address Lyle's allegations. They were the top of the creative food chain—the ones who (supposedly) had the most control over what got written, and therefore *how* it got written. Kauffman indicated as much in her own testimony: "There is a word that I find offensive. I don't allow it in the room... It's one of those words that people use for the female genital area, that is never used when I'm in the room." Lyle herself said this was true. Chase, Malins, and Reich never said that word when Kauffman was around. But they used it regularly when she wasn't. As Lyle further testified, one of them had called Kauffman herself a cunt.

Lyle's case was initially dismissed in 2002, when an LA county judge ruled that she had not provided sufficient evidence. In 2004, an appeals court partially reinstated the case, excluding the claims about her termination. Apparently, there still wasn't enough evidence to support Lyle's allegation that she'd been fired for reasons other than poor performance. But, the court ruled, the harassment claim seemed potentially valid. For that, Lyle was entitled to a trial. Warner Bros., in turn, appealed that decision, and soon the case was headed for the California Supreme Court.

Lyle's case was reinstated on April 21, 2004, two weeks before the series finale of *Friends*. The press remained remarkably quiet on the matter, and the few reports that did appear were brief, with all the dirty details scrubbed as clean as could be: "Lyle says she was offended by off-color banter among the writers," reported *Entertainment Weekly*, in one of the three sentences it devoted to the case. The finale was coming, and that was supposed to be the big news. Ross and Rachel united at last, Monica and Chandler's baby, millions of Americans tuning in for a bittersweet farewell. No one wanted to spoil *Friends* now.

They succeeded. The general public heard little about *Lyle v. Warner Bros.*, even when it made it to the state's Supreme Court. It was growing into a landmark case: freedom of speech v. sexual harassment law. Stories like Lyle's were, of course, incredibly common. Writers' rooms were notoriously raucous and raunchy (to put it politely), and typically hostile to women—if there even were any in the room. The Writers Guild of America reported that, in 1999, more than 75% of television employees were male, and almost 93% of them were white ("and there is little evidence to suggest that this pattern is changing"). Depending on the show, the environment in those rooms fell somewhere between *Lord of the Flies* and *Porky's*. Harassment claims were nothing new in Hollywood. Allegations like Lyle's were so commonplace that they usually never even made it out of the building, let alone all the way to court. What made Lyle's case so unusual was that she pursued it at all.

But the biggest surprise was the defense. In their own testimonies, the defendants corroborated many of Lyle's claims about their behavior. But, they argued, it was all part of the writing process. The blow-job stories, the demeaning language and masturbation simulations—things that might be considered harassment in other contexts were fine in the writers' room. In fact, the defense argued, they were job requirements: "Because 'Friends deals with sexual matters, intimate body parts and ris-qué humor, the writers of the show are required to have frank sexual discussions and tell colorful jokes and stories (and even make expressive gestures)...'" What Lyle called "harassment" they argued was "creative necessity."

This was a first. The "creative necessity" defense was (as the appellate court had noted) "unique in the annals of sexual harass-ment litigation." But hundreds of leaders in the entertainment industry—as well as publishing, advertising, education, and jour-nalism—stepped in to support it. Numerous amicus briefs were submitted to the court, insisting that if Lyle succeeded, it would be an unconscionable assault on freedom of speech. It would destroy creative expression and lead to censorship on a massive scale. Journalists would stop reporting on sensitive subjects, and the entire news industry would come under threat. Teachers would be compelled to censor themselves and unable to prop-erly educate. Activist and advocacy groups joined in to support Warner Bros., too, including Feminists for Free Expression and the Foundation for Individual Rights in Education (FIRE). Greg Lukianoff, a director at FIRE, said that this case could "destroy the free and open exchange of ideas...it would transform 'harass-ment' into the exception that swallowed the First Amendment."

The WGA, DGA, and SAG also filed a brief on the defense's behalf, signed by more than a hundred film and television writ-ers, including Norman Lear, Larry David, James L. Brooks, and David Milch. "Group writing requires an atmosphere of com-plete trust," the brief stated. "Writers must feel not only that it's all right to fail, but also that they can share their most private and darkest thoughts without concern for ridicule or embarrassment or legal accountability."

Far fewer spoke up on Lyle's side, but she did have a handful of vocal supporters. UCLA law professor Russell K. Robinson wrote a brief on her behalf, signed by several other legal scholars and professionals. They called bullshit: "There is ample record evidence of gender-denigrating sexual talk and conduct with no discernable connection to the writing process," the brief stated. The facts of the case made it obvious (to them) that the defendants were manipulating the concept of creative freedom to justify plain old sexual harassment, "which should enjoy no protection from the First Amendment." If the court sided with Warner Bros., it wouldn't protect free speech as much as it would strip protection from people who were already at a massive disadvantage in this environment. "This repeated sexual conduct not only failed to advance the creative process," Robinson wrote. "It also perpetuated an exclusionary culture that marginalizes female writers and writers' assistants in an industry where women are substantially underrepresented. This Court must reject Respondents' sweeping First Amendment argument because it would eviscerate antidiscrimination law in all 'creative industries' and leave women, as well as people of color and others, without legal protection."

In the end, though, the defendants won. On April 20, 2006, the California Supreme Court ruled unanimously in their favor and dismissed Lyle's case, declaring that what she experienced was not harassment, nor a hostile work environment. Most of the "sexual antics" and comments she alleged were "nondirected" and did not prove "sufficiently severe or pervasive," according to the court. But the primary factor here was context. The ruling stated that "the *Friends* production was a creative workplace focused on generating scripts for an adult-oriented comedy show featuring sexual themes." The creative necessity defense had worked.

One of the judges, Justice Ming Chin, wrote an additional opinion, underscoring his support for this ruling. "The writers here did go at times to extremes in the creative process. Some of what they did might be incomprehensible to people unfamiliar with the creative process. But that is what creative people sometimes have to do," he wrote. It was critically important to protect free expression in the writing process—and the importance of protecting employees from what might happen in that process was "in comparison, minimal." Justice Chin added that no one was forced to join a creative team, and those who *choose* to "should not be allowed to complain that some of the creativity was offensive."

The entertainment industry cheered en masse. To them, this was a resounding victory for freedom of expression—for freedom itself. The threat of censorship was lifted, and now writers could once again feel safe to do their jobs. *Lyle v. Warner Bros.* had given them even greater liberty than they'd had before. Now, there was a legal precedent; the California Supreme Court had made it absolutely clear that they could say and do pretty much anything in the name of creativity, without fear of consequences.

They argued that this was a win for all Americans, really. "Audiences want something fresh. They want something surprising and they want something that rings true. None of that was going to happen if writers had to start pulling punches," WGA representative Marshall Goldberg told the *Los Angeles Times*. This ruling "tells [writers] they can continue to create as freely as they want, and I think that is huge."

Lyle herself did not comment. She'd already left television, joined the air force, and was living in Germany at the time. But once again, the small minority on her side spoke up in dissent. From their perspective, the court had squandered an opportunity to give this business a necessary wake-up call—to make it a more inclusive, sophisticated industry that would invite so many *more* artists to join in that creative process. Instead, it had just made Hollywood an even safer haven for the people already in power to do with it what they would—be it a TV writer drawing pornographic doodles, or a legendary film producer setting up auditions in hotel rooms. Employment lawyer Jeffrey Winikow was also quoted in the paper. The ruling, he said, "will continue to create this atmosphere where a woman really has to desensitize herself to all forms of misogyny to succeed in that business." Lyle's own lawyer, Mark Weidmann, made only one comment: "This sets way back the rights of women to be free from sexual harassment."

Ten years passed. The *Friends* revival began, riding high on a wave of '90s nostalgia. *Lyle v. Warner Bros.* did not resurface with it—but like the show, it had never really gone away. It did indeed become a landmark ruling, which set a legal precedent for all Americans. Lyle's case quietly lived on in HR materials all over the country, as a reminder to employees of what does *not* constitute harassment or hostility, and what they may not complain about.

Then one more year passed. In 2017, Hollywood's reckoning finally began. Now everyone could see just how "minimally" the industry protected its own. Women (and a number of men) spoke up about the abuses they had suffered, be it an incident of sexual violence or a persistent barrage of grotesque verbal harassment. Scores of other alleged predators were outed after Weinstein, many of whom openly admitted their behavior. A few even outed themselves before someone else could do it, so clear was the writing on the wall: time was up. It started in Hollywood, and now women all over the world were saying it. It was the end of another era—hopefully.

Only then did Lyle's name reemerge. TV writers and journalists began to wonder aloud, on social media, how the *Friends* harassment case might have played out if it had happened now. Another question hovered over the discussion: If the court had found in her favor back then, would change have come much sooner?

Eventually, Lyle herself came forward to address the case for the first time in many years. She'd spent much of the last two decades as a journalist covering military topics, and was now working as a communications strategist for the Pentagon. Speaking with WNYC host Jami Floyd in January 2018, she said, "I'd pretty much tried to put [the case] behind me and go on with my life. I didn't want to be defined as the woman who lost a case against one of the biggest shows in the history of television. I knew there was a lot more to *me*, and my journey, than that." Lyle said the renewed interest in her story was heartening, though it did force her to relive the whole experience. Still, she added, she had no regrets about the past and was resolutely (if cautiously) optimistic about the future: "The dialogue has to be sustained, and it has to continue. And it has to equate into action, instead of just legal briefs and sound bites. It has to be a very deliberate process to be inclusive to everyone, and make people feel like they belong there."

Otherwise, it would be all too easy for everyone to fall back into the same old routines and everything to resume, shitty business as usual. Lyle herself said that if she hadn't been fired, if she'd had chance to become a fully fledged *Friends* writer, then she probably would have kept her head down and gone with the flow. In another 2018 interview, with the *New Yorker*'s Dana Goodyear, Lyle explained: "Looking back, if I had kept on with that trajectory in my career and they didn't criticize my work, I wouldn't have scrutinized the process... I wouldn't have cared how the sausage was made."

If we're honest, most of us would probably say the same, especially when it comes to *Friends*. This series has come to represent everything beloved from the good old days—all *kinds* of good old days: the heady 1990s, the world before 9/11, the years before smartphones took over our lives. To some, it is a reminder of their youth, and their own friendship-families. To younger generations watching it now, it is a throwback to a simpler time, and all that that implies.

Friends is not the only old-school show to experience both a comeback and controversy in its later years. *Seinfeld* has weathered similar criticisms on diversity and sexism in the series, as well as major off-screen drama. In recent years, Jerry Seinfeld has made insensitive or offensive comments on so many hot-button topics (Bill Cosby, Black Lives Matter, autism) that it almost seems like he's *trying* to become less popular. In 2006, a few months after the Lyle case was dismissed, Michael Richards (who played Kramer) was captured on video at a comedy club in the midst of a stunning racist tirade, screaming about lynching and hurling slurs at people in the crowd. Unlike *Lyle v. Warner Bros.*, this incident got enormous press attention. Richards was booted out of the business for years (though not forever), and the infamous rant became an indelible part of his legacy—as it should've been. In terms of *Seinfeld*, though, it didn't leave much of a mark. Fans seemed capable of denouncing Richards while still enjoying Kramer, just as they were able to recognize the problematic elements of *Seinfeld* and still laugh at the jokes. For the most part, it didn't stop them from loving the show, and it sure as hell didn't stop them from begging for a reunion.

Friends is different. Like *Seinfeld*, it, too, has become a period piece, but all its dated flaws have been covered in thick layers of buttercream nostalgia. The problems are in there somewhere, but if you're not looking you could easily miss them. Even stories like Lyle's have been buried deep beneath the overwhelming adoration. In part, I think it is because the show holds up so well in other ways. The comedy still works. The magic between the actors is still palpable. Even with fewer phones and more gay jokes, it still feels absolutely relevant and relatable. That time in your life when your friends are your family still exists. Some things don't change. *Friends* is a reminder of that, and that's why so many of us reach for it in times of grief or fear, when catastrophe strikes or when life seems suddenly unrecognizable. Even more than a relic of the past, it is a symbol of what is constant—the things and the people who will always be there for you.

Some things do change, though. Some things change for the better. *Friends* is a reminder of that, too. After all, this is a show that began with a woman running out on a loveless marriage, abandoning tradition, and starting a new life on her own terms. Today, would Rachel even have a wedding to run out on? Or would she already be living in the city, juggling a fashion internship while waiting tables to make rent? Would Ross and Carol be getting divorced, or would they have split in college and become friends after she came out freshman year? Would Chandler be taking his dad's phone calls?

There are no definitive yeses or nos to these hypothetical questions about fictional people. The point is that now there are many more possible answers than there were when *Friends* premiered in 1994. Or even when it ended in 2004. Even since its comeback circa 2014, some things have changed dramatically. We like to think of the past as simple, but simple isn't always better.

The fact that people are even revisiting Amaani Lyle's case now, after a decade of silence on the matter, is evidence of progress. Were the case tried today, it's possible the court would rule in the exact same way. But it's difficult to imagine that quite so many people would see that as a victory. The way the public responded to her story back then is very different from the way it treated the avalanche of stories that came later. Had Lyle stood up and made her case today, she would not have been standing alone. That's all we know for sure. It's cold comfort, but as Lyle said herself, it's a good reason to be optimistic.

In one way, *Friends* is just like *Seinfeld*: ever since it ended, people have been calling for a comeback. Rumors began even as they were shooting the finale. "A reunion?" Jennifer Aniston replied to an AP reporter who was visiting the set during rehearsal. Was it true there was a reunion movie in the works? Flummoxed, Aniston answered: "We haven't even left yet."

It was the last time she'd ever be surprised by that question. She and the others had spent ten years sitting on talk-show couches, getting grilled by Leno about whether or not *Friends* would be renewed. Now, they'd spend the rest of their professional lives fielding a similar query: *Would they ever consider rebooting the show? How about an anniversary special? Congrats on the wedding/the baby/the Broadway play you're starring in! So, any news on that* Friends *reunion?*

All of the cast members went on to have successful careers, objectively speaking. There was no talk of a *Seinfeld* curse, dooming the actors to a future of failed shows.[84] Courteney Cox built on her TV career, both on and off camera. In 2009, she had another hit with *Cougar Town*, a single-camera comedy that ran for six seasons on ABC. The show was coproduced by Coquette Productions—the company she'd formed with then-husband David Arquette in 2003. (The couple separated in 2010, but remained producing partners.) Cox was both the lead actress and an EP on *Cougar Town*, and soon began directing, as well. Aniston and Lisa Kudrow both appeared in guest roles, as did Matthew Perry, who played a love interest for Cox's character. Not quite a reunion, but close.

Cox later returned the favor, doing a guest role on Perry's show *Go On*. And this time it was almost certainly a favor. *Go On* was one of a handful of Perry's post-*Friends* series that didn't stick: *Mr. Sunshine, Studio 60 on the Sunset Strip*. Perry himself was always praised for his performance and capability as a lead. But none of the series made it past two seasons. Still, Perry continued to pop up on television with relative frequency, doing guest spots or recurring roles on shows like *The Good Wife* and *Children's Hospital*. After *17 Again*, Perry drifted out of the film world, despite having had more success there than some of his old costars. He'd

---

84   Nor did this "curse" seem to work on the cast of *Seinfeld*. Just ask Julia Louis-Dreyfus, if you can find her under that pile of Emmys.

had his share of big-screen disasters, as well, some of which had coincided with the lowest points in his addiction (Perry got sober in 2001). Having grappled with it so publicly, Perry became an advocate for recovery services. He lobbied for judicial reform to better serve nonviolent drug addicts caught up in the system, and he opened a sober living home in 2013. Addiction became a theme in Perry's first play, *The End of Longing*, which he wrote and eventually starred in, both off-Broadway and in London's West End. The character was an alcoholic—a highly exaggerated version of himself during his darkest days. In other words, it was the kind of role no one would ever offer him. "People still see me as Chandler, the goofy, sarcastic guy, and this is not that," he told *Variety*. "I don't think that anybody's out there thinking, 'I'll write this for Perry,' other than me. So, I did that, and I think probably the next thing I do will be written by me, too."

Schwimmer, too, returned to theater, just as he'd intended to do. His original plan—to spend a year in Hollywood and make some quick cash for Lookingglass—had taken a little longer than expected, but at least the cash part had worked out pretty well. Schwimmer threw himself into directing, onstage as well as for television and film. He'd spent years honing his skills under the exceptional guidance of *Friends'* directors, and during his time on the show he directed ten episodes himself. After *Friends*, directing became a refuge. Schwimmer was a gifted actor but an uneasy celebrity, and he hadn't adapted to fame as well as the others. "It was pretty jarring and it messed with my relationship to other people in a way that took years, I think, for me to adjust to and become comfortable with," he told the *Hollywood Reporter* in 2016. "As an actor, the way I was trained, my job was to observe life and to observe other people. So, I used to walk around with my head up, really engaged and watching people. The effect of celebrity was the absolute opposite. It made me want to hide under a baseball cap and not be seen." After *Friends*, he said, "I was trying to figure out: How do I be an actor in this new world, in this new situation? How do I do my job?"

Schwimmer eventually found his footing and began doing more on-camera work, including his popular performance as Robert Kardashian in *The People v. O.J. Simpson*. Mostly, though, he remained behind the scenes. In early 2017, he produced a series of short films, written and directed by Sigal Avin, each depicting a typical instance of sexual harassment (all based on real-life accounts). They released the #ThatsHarassment series in April 2017, hoping to revive the dormant conversation around sexual misconduct in the workplace. The films were riveting and well crafted, and full of famous faces (Cynthia Nixon, Emmy Rossum, Schwimmer himself). Still, the series didn't get much attention when it debuted in the spring. That fall, it was a different story. After Weinstein, #ThatsHarassment returned as a massive PSA campaign backed by RAINN, the Ad Council, and the National Women's Law Center. Schwimmer jumped back into the press, promoting not only #ThatsHarassment but #MeToo, #TimesUp, and #AskMoreOfHim—a campaign he cocreated with David Arquette, urging men in the entertainment industry to become more active allies in these movements. Outspoken as he is on these issues, Schwimmer has never commented publicly on Amaani Lyle's case. He did, however, make some telling remarks about one of the #ThatsHarassment films—in which a model gets verbally harassed by a photographer during a photo shoot (on a set full of people, who say nothing). "That scene is something all of us in the entertainment industry can somehow relate to…all the witnesses in the room and how complicit everyone is," he said in an interview with *Cosmopolitan*. "And by the way, the young woman is not the only person being harassed in that scene. Any person in that room that was made to feel uncomfortable, or as if they had no choice but to be subjected to what was happening in that room, was harassed."

★ ★ ★

Kudrow, too, developed an off-camera career, while consistently working as an actress. She launched the comedy *Web Therapy* in 2008, as the star and cowriter. It began as a low-budget web series, and was adapted by Showtime in 2011. Schwimmer, Perry, Cox, and Matt LeBlanc all made several guest appearances (as did Meryl Streep, Billy Crystal, Julia Louis-Dreyfus, and dozens of other people you would never imagine appearing in a low-budget web series). Kudrow's 2005 cult hit *The Comeback* returned for a spectacular follow-up season in 2014. The story had evolved from a spot-on, brutally funny satire, to a gut-wrenching commentary on Hollywood's ageism, sexism, and the hollow promise of fame—that was still, somehow, brutally funny. Both the show and Kudrow's performance were distinct and powerful enough that audiences forgot all about Phoebe. Or they would have, had more viewers actually tuned in. In the grand tradition of cult phenomenons, *The Comeback* never got the audience it deserved.

Still, Kudrow has long been touted as one of (if not *the*) most successful of the *Friends* cast. She's consistently worked in both television and film (including big box-office comedies like *Analyze This* and *Easy A*, dark indies like *Wonderland*, Pixar films, thrillers—you name it). She hasn't become a movie star, nor has she truly shaken off the legacy of *Friends*. But all her professional choices indicate that—like LeBlanc—she's not really worried about those things. Those are losing battles, and why fight them when you've already won so big? Back when she started auditioning, Kudrow's dream was to become a regular on a sitcom. She got her big pie-in-the-sky wish, and then some. And then some more.

Now, Kudrow remains a supporting star, but one who almost always steals the show. She's doesn't sweat the *Friends* questions, and she doesn't waste time trying to convince people she's not Phoebe. She's an improv comic, after all. She just keeps the scene going with a "yes, and."

LeBlanc, like Kudrow, appears utterly unbothered by the

goofy specter of Joey. Unlike her, he didn't try to carve out a new path after *Friends* (and *Joey*). He just seemed to stop trying, period. And it worked. *Episodes* earned him a Golden Globe, and for the first time in his career, people realized that Matt LeBlanc was *good*. "A lot of times people will speak slowly to me because of Joey," he often told the press. With *Episodes*, they played on those assumptions, turning the fictional Matt LeBlanc into a manipulator who let people think he was dumb in order to get what he wanted.

But, after *Episodes*, LeBlanc went back to just going with the flow, taking gigs he liked. He signed a deal to host *Top Gear* (which let him talk cars for a living), and he produces and stars in the CBS comedy *Man with a Plan*. It isn't *Friends* by any stretch of the imagination, but it is a sitcom—familiar territory. LeBlanc has never tried to replicate the success of his first big hit. And, as he's always quick to point out, he doesn't have to. Financially speaking, none of them do, after making what he calls "fuck-you money" (a lot of other people probably say that, too, but not to his face). In fact, it was an even bigger fuck-you than we thought. "Let me just go on the record as saying: a million dollars a week was wrong. It was 1.3," he corrected an *Entertainment Weekly* reporter in 2012. "We clear? I mean, $300,000 a week is not something to shake a stick at."

Aniston remains the show's most visible star. She plays lead roles in big movies (*The Break-Up*, *Marley & Me*, *Horrible Bosses*), lands enormous endorsement deals (everything from skin-care products to "smart" water to prescription eye drops), and hardly an hour passes without her name or her face appearing in the media. She has become the kind of celebrity who will always be famous and always work, if she wants to. But no matter what she does—on-screen or off—she does it hand in hand with Rachel Green. It's not that Aniston herself is incapable of playing other kinds of roles. It's simply that there is no other character, film, or tabloid story big enough to overshadow Rachel. Every day, millions of people in hundreds of countries are going back to watch reruns and laugh at her putting beef in the trifle.

"But she's not a *victim*," David Wild told me. "I think she's had an amazing life. She's had an amazing career. I *don't* feel bad for her." Despite her many undeniable successes, victimhood has become an even larger part of Aniston's image in the years since both *Friends* and her first marriage ended: the wife who got jilted; the woman who was robbed of motherhood; the poor little TV rich girl who just can't win on the big screen. "All of this stuff about her persona—I don't know how much it has to do with her at *all*," said Wild. "I don't think she's fucked up. I think *we're* fucked up, in how we think about people like her." Wild often writes and produces award shows, and he still sees Aniston from time to time. It's always a pleasant encounter— like bumping into an old colleague at a work event. But it's also like bumping into Jennifer Aniston at the Emmy Awards. Even Wild struggles to see past the layers of her celebrity and remember the struggling actress he first interviewed at a coffee shop on Beverly Boulevard. "I did it myself! A couple years ago, I did some show where she was speaking, and I had to write a speech for her." The two of them were chatting, and Wild said, "Oh, let's get a picture." Aniston said sure, they should take a photo together. Reunion! Oh, no, Wild corrected. Aniston had misunderstood. "I didn't want to take the picture *with* her." He was the writer and she the celebrity; the writer doesn't get in the shot. She was thinking two old work friends, but he was thinking Jennifer Aniston. "I had a moment of realizing *she's* not the strange one," Wild recalled. "We're the strange ones, in how we've projected so much onto these people."

Still, Wild has remained a trusted journalist to Aniston and her castmates, and he's interviewed them individually over the years, as they promoted their new shows and movies. So, it's often been his job to bring up the *F*-word. Normally, they're fine with a little *Friends* talk, up to a point. In 2012, Wild interviewed Aniston for *$ellebrity*, a documentary about paparazzi and the celebrity photo industry. "She's never been anything but really, really nice to deal with, in my experience," he said. "But I remember asking one too many *Friends* questions of her." Aniston didn't protest, but her demeanor changed, just so. "I could just tell, she had moved on. She didn't want the third *Friends* question."

So, can you do a reunion already? That one's unavoidable. Over the years, the cast have obliged somewhat, appearing in twos and threes in sketches on *Ellen* and *Jimmy Kimmel Live*. Five out of six showed up for a group interview for NBC's tribute to James Burrows (Matthew Perry was in London, doing *The End of Longing*). They've done numerous cameos on one another's post-*Friends* shows, but never have all six of them appeared together on-screen since the finale. Thanks to the internet, we have a steady stream of rumors that they're planning a grand revival. Every time two or more of them are photographed out together in LA, it stirs up gossip that they're shooting something. Usually, it's Kudrow, Aniston, and Cox (who have remained close), and more often than not, they're just walking to their cars after dinner. In January 2018, a video titled *"Friends* (2018) Movie Teaser Trailer #1" was uploaded to YouTube. It was obviously fake—a very well-edited compilation of clips of the actors in other roles (which anyone who has been to the movies, watched television, or browsed the internet in the last fifteen years would pick up on immediately). Still, it went instantly viral, getting almost 13 million views as of this publication.

If anything, the buzz has only grown in recent years, as other sitcoms from the '80s and '90s have gotten revivals: *Roseanne*, *Will & Grace*, *One Day at a Time*, *Fuller House*. Shortly after the fake trailer popped up, Kudrow appeared on *Conan*, and the inevitable question arose. "I mean, *something* should be done. I don't know what," she said. "They're rebooting everything. How does that work with *Friends*, though? That was about people in their twenties, thirties. The show isn't about people in their forties, fifties. And if we have the same problems, that's just sad."

Some shows reboot well. *Will & Grace* returned in 2017, virtually unchanged in style and tone, with the same punny humor and total disregard for political correctness. But *Will & Grace* always had an inherent social commentary woven into its premise. When it first debuted, it was a show about women and gay people in the '90s—the DOMA and don't-ask-don't-tell years. When it came back, it was a show about women and gay people in the Trump era. *Roseanne*, too, had a place in contemporary culture. Polarizing as it was, *Roseanne*'s themes—class, economic insecurity, politically divided families—were just as relevant (and just as inflammatory) in 2018 as they'd been in 1988.[85]

Friends has no such hook. As a story, it's timeless, but not as a show. It isn't pegged to historical themes, but to the personal histories of these six characters. It's about them *then*. From a storytelling perspective, it would be close to impossible to reunite these characters—for the exact same reasons it's so hard to reunite the actors. They have new jobs and families and they live in different cities. It would take some big life event to bring the characters back together, and now that the weddings and babies have been had, all that's left are funerals—and no one wants to see that. "I just don't know if I want to see all of us with crutches [and] walkers," Schwimmer said in 2018. As everyone knows, the cast members have no financial incentive to reboot the series, and a reunion movie seems implausible for other reasons. When *Sex and the City* went to the big screen, Cox said, "I wish we could do that with *Friends*. The thing is, the characters from *Sex and the City* hopped all over Manhattan. On *Friends*, we were always stuck in the apartment and that coffeehouse... I don't think it's going to happen." If it were, she said, Kauffman and Crane would have to be involved. "Would [they] want to write it?"

For more than a decade, the answer has been a consistent

---

85 Barr herself proved more than "polarizing" in 2018, thanks to her Twitter presence. After a particularly overt racist tweet, the reboot was canceled and the concept retooled into a new show, without her.

and firm *no.* "Someone asks me every day," Kauffman said in 2015. "I don't get upset. I understand that people want to relive that. But you can't relive that. We can't go back to that time in our lives." Furthermore, she added: "Let's be honest, reunions generally suck." As Crane explained it, "We ended *right.* It felt right... I think all the people who say, 'Oh, I want to see them again!' You really don't. And I think they would turn on us on a dime." Crane's advice: the story has been told, from beginning to end. If you want to revisit, it's all right there for you, in reruns. "Watch those! We did it!"

You never know. "Anything is a possibility," Aniston said in 2018. "I mean, George Clooney got married." Logistics and money, all that could be sorted out. As long as everyone is still on good terms, there's always a chance. But with each passing year, the reunion concept seems better off as a daydream. "That show was about a finite period in people's lives," LeBlanc said in 2017. "And once that time's over, that time's over." Trying to recapture it only sours the memory. "I went through that period in my own life. And when I revisit people from that time, it's not the same. It's just not. You can never go back, you can only move forward."

Some things belong to the past. *Friends* is a story from a bygone era. It endures in the universal truths it tells about kinship and love and growing up. It lives on in our collective memory, along with our old roommates and first boyfriends, the inside jokes we used to make, and the cheesy songs we sang in the car, volume up and windows down. There's a tempting bittersweetness in reflecting on those days—laughing at old photos, cringing at our haircuts. But as LeBlanc said, there is no going back to those places and people. They have changed and so have we, and that is as it should be. Best to leave them right where they belong: in that time. Then we'll never lose them. We'll always know where they are.

★ ★ ★ ★ ★

ACKNOWLEDGMENTS

Quick story: back in the winter of 2015, as I was dragging myself through a brutal round of rewrites on my first book, I watched *Friends* every single night. I was a first-time author working on a memoir, and after a day spent sitting alone at Starbucks, sorting through the messy reality of my own life, it was a blissful relief to unwind with my warm, familiar (albeit fake) pals at Central Perk. The show played such a crucial role in getting me to the finish line that I actually planned to mention *Friends* in the acknowledgments. But at the last minute I decided to cut it, worried that thanking a *sitcom* at the end of my first book might somehow damage my authorial reputation and prevent me from getting the chance to write a second book. Two years later, I did. You're holding it.

Thus I must start these acknowledgments by doing what I should have years ago, and thank the creators, cast and entire creative team behind *Friends*. It seems I owe you much of my career. In all sincerity, thank you for creating a show of unparalleled resonance and endurance that altered so many lives—my own included.

I am incredibly grateful to Hanover Square Press, Peter Joseph and the spectacular team who truly championed this book. Above all, I have to thank my editor, John Glynn, who guided me and my book through this journey with patience, vigor, excitement, and a razor-sharp eye. I couldn't have written this book without you (and probably wouldn't have even tried). I'd also like to thank my copy editor, Christine Langone, without whom the words and sentences in this book would make a lot less sense (and have way too many commas).

Endless thanks to my agent and friend, Allison Hunter. You are my literary lobster.

I'm deeply indebted to the many people who offered their time, opinions and perspectives on *Friends*, including Anne Helen Petersen, Elaine Lui, Sarah Beauchamp, Keah Brown, Toby Bruce, Nancy Deihl, Kimberly Chrisman Campbell, Tyler Coates, Dizzy Dalton, Akilah Hughes, Elana Fishman, Ryan O'Connell, Lauren Zalaznick, Tijana Mamula, Mey Rude, Connie Wang, and Chuck Klosterman. Additional thanks to David Wild, who provided invaluable insight into life on the *Friends* set, not only in our interview but in his own books and articles about the series. Thank you to the Television Academy Foundation, and the historians who maintain its interview archive—a tremendous resource.

Thanks as well to authors Warren Littlefield, T. R. Pearson, Bill Carter, Jennifer Armstrong, and Martha Bayles, whose work gave exceptional insight into this period of American television and its impact on the wider world.

Eternal thanks to the teachers who urged me to become a writer (particularly Julie Faulstich and Jack Murnighan), and the editors who made me a better one. I'd especially like to thank those who've helped me grow as a culture writer, including Neha

Gandhi, Anna Maltby, Christene Barberich, Missy Schwartz, Molly Stout, Leila Brillson, and Eric Hynes.

Thank you to The Wing, a place and a community that has truly changed my life (and kept me sane throughout the process of writing a book).

Thank you, thank you, thank you to my husband, Harry Tanielyan, who cheered me on every damn day. Thank you for all the salads, the shoulder squeezes, the pick-me-up notes, and the high-fives. And thanks for letting me take over the TV for about a year. We can watch something else now.

Thank you to my family, who gave me (among other things) the faith and ability to even imagine a career as a writer. Shout-out to my aunt and cousins in the UK, whose collective knowledge on *Friends* is impressive bordering on alarming. Thank you for being my *Friends* think tank. Special thanks to my dad and my grandfather, who both listened to me talk a *lot* about *Friends* in the last year. Neither of them have seen the show, but both of them cheered on this book with the same interest and excitement usually reserved for the Yankees.

Finally, thanks to my own beloved friends, particularly Jonathan Parks-Ramage, Chrissy Angliker, and Deborah Siegel. This book is dedicated to you, because you are—and always have been—there for me.

SOURCE NOTES

Introduction: The Sweet Spot

14 A reported 16 million: Adam Sternberg, "Is 'Friends' Still the Most Popular Show on TV?" Vulture, Mar. 28, 2016, http://www.vulture.com/2016/03/20-somethings-streaming-friends-c-v-r.html.

15 118 million (and counting): Rani Molla, "Netflix now has nearly 118 million streaming subscribers globally," Recode, Jan. 22, 2018, https://www.recode.net/2018/1/22/16920150/netflix-q4-2017-earnings-subscribers.

15 ratings were up by 10%: Lucy Mangan, "Friends is still a hit after 22 years. And I think I know why," *The Guardian*, Mar. 30, 2016, http://www.theguardian.com/commentisfree/2016/mar/30/friends-millennials-gentler-simpler-time.

15 demographic is aged 16–34: Michelle Davies, "Friends for ever: Why we're still loving the hit TV show 20 years on," *Daily Mail*, Oct. 19, 2013, http://www.dailymail.co.uk/home/you/article-2465332/Friends-Why-loving-hit-TV-20-years-on.html.

15 "the sweet spot": Martha Bayles, *Through a Screen Darkly* (New Haven & London: Yale University Press, 2014), 69.

Chapter One: The One That Almost Wasn't

20 "They're 20-something": Bill Carter, "THE ANNOTATED CALENDAR; TELEVISION," *New York Times*, Sep. 11, 1994.

20 "that time of your life": David Crane, interviewed by Beth Cochran, "David Crane and Marta Kauffman Interview," Television Academy Foundation, Oct. 7, 2010, https://interviews.televisionacademy.com.

21 Wednesday afternoon in 1985: Marta Kauffman, interviewed by Beth Cochran, "David Crane and Marta Kauffman Interview," Television Academy Foundation, Oct. 7, 2010, https://interviews.televisionacademy.com.

21 "I kept thinking": Ibid.

22 "really not good": David Crane, interviewed by Beth Cochran.

22 "And he said, 'No'": Marta Kauffman, interviewed by Beth Cochran.

22 "It was one of those": Ibid.

22 "I don't even know which": David Crane, interviewed by Beth Cochran.

22 "We have a barn": Marta Kauffman, interviewed by Beth Cochran.

23 Seth Friedman and Billy Dreskin: Ibid.

23 "An angst-driven": Ibid.

24 landing off-Broadway: Seth Friedman, David Crane, and Marta Kauffman, *Personals* (New York: Samuel French, Inc.), 4.

24 "Entertaining and ingenious": "Personals- A Musical Review," Stageplays. com, https://www.stageplays.com/products/personals_-_a_musical_review.

24 "Unfailingly mirthless": Frank Rich, "STAGE: 'PERSONALS,' MUSI-CAL COMEDY," *New York Times*, Nov. 25, 1985.

24 television agent Nancy Josephson: Ben Grossman, "Josephson Makes Name for Herself," Broadcasting & Cable, Oct. 7, 2005, https://www. broadcastingcable.com/news/josephson-makes-name-herself-108269.

25 "crazy": David Crane, interviewed by Beth Cochran.

25 "Talk about your…lame": Ibid.

25 "We sat in the rental car": Marta Kauffman, interviewed by Beth Cochran.

25 "And then we were able": David Crane, interviewed by Beth Cochran.

25 "I saw the play": Grossman, "Josephson Makes Name for Herself."

26 twenty-four hours to make the call: Marta Kauffman, interviewed by Beth Cochran.

26 "And I sit up": Ibid.

26 "The meeting that…going to happen": David Crane, interviewed by Beth Cochran.

26 John Landis had a bungalow: Kevin Bright, interviewed by Jenni Matz, "Kevin Bright Interview," Television Academy Foundation, Mar. 29, 2016, https://interviews.televisionacademy.com.

27 "thousands": Marta Kauffman, interviewed by Beth Cochran.

27 "We went in": David Crane, interviewed by Beth Cochran.

27 "By the time we got off": Ibid.

27 "And they said": Ibid.

27 "adult": Benjamin Svetkey, "HBO's 'Dream On' is the sauciest show on television," *Entertainment Weekly*, Jun. 19, 1992, http://www.ew.com/article/1992/06/19/hbos-dream-sauciest-show-television.

28 "the bubble burst": Susan King, "Premium Stakes : In the changing and competitive world of pay TV, channels rely on new tactics for viewers," *Los Angeles Times*, Jul. 28, 1991, http://articles.latimes.com/1991-07-28/news/tv-154_1_movie-channel.

28 grew by only 1.8%, with 4.5%: Ibid.

28 "'It needs to be funnier'": David Crane, interviewed by Beth Cochran.

28 "We were actually... I hate you": Ibid.

29 "When we first started": Kevin Bright, interviewed by Jenni Matz.

30 "He's really good...editing room": David Crane, interviewed by Beth Cochran.

30 "We had shorthand": Kevin Bright, interviewed by Jenni Matz.

30 Two years into: Ibid.

30 all that eager: Ibid.

30 "It was one of those": Ibid.

30 "We said to [Moonves]": Ibid.

31 It flowed right out: David Crane, interviewed by Beth Cochran.

31 "We wrote...pulling teeth": Ibid.

31 "white-collar *Roseanne*": Kevin Bright, interviewed by Jenni Matz.

31 "We did everything right": David Crane, interviewed by Beth Cochran.

31 "Around that...disappointment": Kevin Bright, interviewed by Jenni Matz.

31 "It was interesting": Ibid.

32 "We were looking...that feeling": Marta Kauffman, interviewed by Matt Lauer, "A Farewell to Friends," *Dateline NBC*, May 5, 2004.

32 "This show is about...scary": Marta Kauffman and David Crane, "'Insomnia Café' Pitch," republished by Writers Guild Foundation, Jan. 9, 2015, https://www.wgfoundation.org/well-friends-resurgence.

32 "It's about friendship": Ibid.

32 "we were driving...overcaffeinated": Marta Kauffman, interviewed by Beth Cochran.

33 "The pitch was like...theater": Karey Burke, interviewed by authors Warren Littlefield and T.R. Pearson, *Top of the Rock*, 249.

33 "I remember pitching": David Crane, interviewed by Beth Cochran.

33 three days flat: Marta Kauffman, interviewed by author David Wild, *Friends 'til the End* (New York: Time Inc. Home Entertainment, 2004), 215.

33 "At the point where": David Crane, interviewed by Beth Cochran.

33 A suggestion that came: Ibid.

34 "we had absolutely...James Burrows": David Crane, interviewed by authors Warren Littlefield and T.R. Pearson, *Top of the Rock*, 273.

34 "I literally had": Elizabeth Kolbert, "The Conception and Delivery of a Sitcom: Everyone's a Critic," *New York Times*, May 9, 1994.

35 "Pat the Cop": Marta Kauffman, interviewed by Matt Lauer.

35 "You gotta remember": Kevin Bright, interviewed by Jenni Matz.

35 "the coffee shop on": Ibid.

35 "They came to us": Ibid.

35 color of the couch: Marta Kauffman, interviewed by Beth Cochran.

36 "At first, he": David Crane, interviewed by Beth Cochran.

36 "fire came out": Marta Kauffman, interviewed by Ben Blacker, "A Conversation with Marta Kauffman," ATX Festival, YouTube video, Jul. 3, 2015, https://www.youtube.com/watch?v=7o-UTYbez2c.

36 "She got what": Marta Kauffman, interviewed by author Yael Kohen, *We Killed* (New York: Sarah Crichton Books, 2012).

36 "For sleeping with": Marta Kauffman, interviewed by Beth Cochran.

36 erection: Kolbert, "The Conception and Delivery of a Sitcom: Everyone's a Critic."

37 "Kevin worked with": David Crane, interviewed by Beth Cochran.

37 "Pace it up": Ibid.

37 "If you don't": Ibid.

37 "The opening sequence": Kevin Bright, interviewed by Jenni Matz.

38 "I said to the editor": Ibid.

38 "*Kevorkian*": Marta Kauffman, interviewed by William Keck, "Friends: A 20th Anniversary Oral History," Sep. 16, 2014, https://www.emmys. com/news/industry-news/friends-20th-anniversary-oral-history.

38 "the miracle": David Schwimmer, interviewed by authors Warren Littlefield and T.R. Pearson, *Top of the Rock*, 273.

Chapter Two: The One with Six Kids and a Fountain

39 "Give me the plane": James Burrows, interviewed by Peter Hammond, "An Evening Honoring James Burrows," Academy of Television Arts & Sciences, Oct. 7, 2013, https://www.emmys.com/video/evening-honoring-james-burrows-friends.

39 "These kids...for dinner": James Burrows, interviewed by Gary Rutkowski, "James Burrows Interview," Television Academy Foundation, Dec. 17, 2013, https://interviews.televisionacademy.com.

40 "so *fancy*": Jennifer Aniston, interviewed by Peter Hammond, "An Evening Honoring James Burrows," Academy of Television Arts & Sciences, Oct. 7, 2013, https://www.emmys.com/video/evening-honoring-james-burrows-friends.

40 "last shot": James Burrows, interviewed by Peter Hammond.

40 "They loved these characters": James Burrows, interviewed by Peter Hammond.

40 "last fling...over": James Burrows, interviewed by Gary Rutkowski.

40 "Everyone was like": Lisa Kudrow, interviewed by Karen Herman, "Lisa Kudrow Interview," Television Academy Foundation, Dec. 12, 2012, https://interviews.televisionacademy.com.

41 Diet Coke endorsement: Stuart Elliott, "THE MEDIA BUSI-
NESS: Advertising;Marketers see gold in the photogenic cast of a
huge NBC hit," *New York Times*, Feb. 2, 1996, https://www.nytimes.
com/1996/02/02/business/media-business-advertising-marketers-see-
gold-photogenic-cast-huge-nbc-hit.html.

41 "They didn't have": James Burrows, interviewed by Gary Rutkowski.

41 "We were having…cards were": Jennifer Aniston, interviewed by Peter
Hammond.

42 a bully: Tim Cooper, "Friends in high places," *The Guardian*, Nov. 25,
2001, https://www.theguardian.com/film/2001/nov/25/features.magazine.

42 Ian McKellen's one-man show: Claire McCartney, "How One Unbelievable Ian McKellen Performance Inspired David Schwimmer to Become
an Actor," Vulture, May 22, 2016, http://www.vulture.com/2016/05/
david-schwimmer-on-ian-mckellens-influence.html.

42 "I watched this guy": Ibid.

42 Roseanne Barr's first divorce: From Times Wire Services, "Roseanne
Barr's Ex-Husband Files Palimony Suit," *Los Angeles Times*, Aug. 24,
1990, http://articles.latimes.com/1990-08-24/entertainment/ca-1421_1_
roseanne-barr-s-former-husband.

42 childhood household: David Schwimmer, interviewed by Scott Feinberg,
Awards Chatter, podcast audio, Aug. 15, 2016, https://www.hollywood-
reporter.com/race/awards-chatter-podcast-david-schwimmer-919432.

42 Arlene Colman-Schwimmer: "Mergers & Acquisitions: Lawyers in
Love- Alumni Who Met at BLS and Married," Brooklyn Law School,
https://www.brooklaw.edu/newsandevents/blslawnotes/2010-2009/
spring/mergersacquisitions/Page3.

43 "criminal law professor": Arlene Colman-Schwimmer, ed. Barbara J.
Love, *Feminists Who Changed America*, 1963-1975 (University of Illi-
nois Press, 2006).

43 "When I was there": David Schwimmer, interviewed by Tim Cooper, "Friends in high places," *The Guardian*, Nov. 25, 2001, https://www.theguardian.com/film/2001/nov/25/features.magazine.

43 "not going to Broadway": David Schwimmer, interviewed by Laurie Taylor, *In Confidence*, Sky Arts, Jul. 9, 2014.

44 "Mind you": David Schwimmer, interviewed by Scott Feinberg.

44 "This is how naive": Ibid.

45 "I worked at": David Schwimmer, interviewed in The Columbus Dispatch, "Mob violence, fatherhood part of David Schwimmer's new AMC series," Jun. 2, 2016, http://www.dispatch.com/content/stories/life_and_entertainment/2016/06/04/1-mob-violence-fatherhood-part-of-david-schwimmers-new-amc-series.html.

45 "Hey, Schwimmer...Thousand Island": Ibid.

46 "hangdog vulnerability...minds": Marta Kauffman, interviewed by Beth Cochran.

46 "As beautiful...to it": David Schwimmer, interviewed by Laurie Taylor.

47 asked Benson: David Schwimmer, interviewed by authors Warren Littlefield and T.R. Pearson, *Top of the Rock*, 271.

47 It wasn't as if: David Crane, interviewed by Beth Cochran.

47 Matthew Perry was broke: Matthew Perry, interviewed by Kevin Pollak, *Kevin Pollak's Chat Show*, "Kevin Pollak's Chat Show #13," podcast audio, May 3, 2009, http://www.earwolf.com/episode/matthew-perry.

47 beat up Trudeau: Matthew Perry, interviewed by Jimmy Kimmel, *Jimmy Kimmel Live*, YouTube video, Mar. 15, 2017, https://www.youtube.com/watch?v=vWZsF3bUNhs.

47 "I've been giving it": retrieved from @JustinTrudeau Twitter, Apr. 1, 2017, https://twitter.com/JustinTrudeau/status/848157413668790274.

47 "I think I will pass": retrieved from @MatthewPerry Twitter, Apr. 2, 2017, https://twitter.com/MatthewPerry/status/848555381009907713.

48 "he mostly saw him": Matthew Perry, interviewed by Kevin Pollak, *Kevin Pollak's Chat Show*, "Kevin Pollak's Chat Show #232," podcast audio, Mar. 17, 2015, http://www.earwolf.com/episode/matthew-perry-2.

48 "I would never bring a girl": Ibid.

48 "I was a guy who": Dana Kennedy, "FILM; The Fame He Craved Came, but It Wasn't Enough," *New York Times*, Aug. 18, 2002, https://www.nytimes.com/2002/08/18/arts/film-the-fame-he-craved-came-but-it-wasn-t-enough.html.

49 *Second Chance*: "Boys Will Be Boys," IMDb, https://www.imdb.com/title/tt0092447.

49 Gaddafi's death: Nick Carbone, "Short-Lived 1987 Sitcom Foreshadowed Gaddafi's 2011 Death," *Time*, Oct. 23, 2011, http://newsfeed.time.com/2011/10/23/short-lived-1987-sitcom-foreshadowed-gaddafis-2011-death.

49 "head baggage handler": Matthew Perry, interviewed by Kevin Pollak, "Kevin Pollak's Chat Show #13."

50 "It was the script that": Ibid.

50 "There's this guy": Ibid.

51 he had jokes: David Crane, interviewed by Beth Cochran.

51 "Could that teacher be": Matthew Perry, interviewed by Kevin Pollak, "Kevin Pollak's Chat Show #232."

51 Craig Bierko: Marta Kauffman, interviewed by authors Warren Little-field and T.R. Pearson, *Top of the Rock*, 257.

52 Matthew Perry impression: Craig Bierko, interviewed by Tanner Thomason and Heather McDonald, *Hollywood Today Live*, YouTube video, Aug. 3, 2016, https://www.youtube.com/watch?v=tXl3gYmetX8.

52 "I instantly knew": Matthew Perry, interviewed by Kevin Pollak, "Kevin Pollak's Chat Show #13."

52 "He came in": Marta Kauffman, interviewed by Beth Cochran.

53 "the classiest lady": Lisa Kudrow, interviewed by Karen Herman.

53 *Alice in Wonderland*: Jeffrey Zaslow, "Balancing friends and family," *USA Weekend*, Oct. 8, 2000, http://159.54.226.237/00_issues/001008/001008kudrow.html.

53 "What kind of adult": Lisa Kudrow, interviewed by Karen Herman.

53 "That's the kind of mom": Ibid.

54 hemispheric dominance and headache types: LV Kudrow, L Kudrow, MI Messinger, HB Messinger, "Handedness and headache," *Cephalalgia*, Feb. 14, 1994, https://www.ncbi.nlm.nih.gov/pubmed/8200028.

54 "punching that joke": Lisa Kudrow, interviewed by Karen Herman.

54 "remember to do it this way": Ibid.

54 "I just kept trying to": Ibid.

54 "and I realized": Ibid.

55 "Fantastic…drive you": Ibid.

55 "I started with": Ibid.

55 "We've never seen": Ibid.

56 wanted to be on a sitcom: Lisa Kudrow, interviewed by Josh Horow-
   itz, *Happy Sad Confused*, "Lisa Kudrow," podcast audio, Nov. 10, 2014,
   http://www.mtv.com/news/podcasts/happy-sad-confused/lisa-kudrow.

56 "originally wanted": Lisa Kudrow, interviewed by Chris Hardwick,
   Jonah Ray and Matt Mira, *The Nerdist*, "Lisa Kudrow," podcast audio,
   Dec. 13, 2014, https://soundcloud.com/the-nerdist/lisa-kudrow-1.

56 "at the rehearsals": Ibid.

56 Maybe it was a sign: Lisa Kudrow, interviewed by Karen Herman.

57 Robin Schiff, tried: Ibid.

57 "I heard what happened": Ibid.

57 Michel Richard: Ibid.

57 "It literally lightened": Ibid.

57 "I don't think…an hour": Ibid.

58 Cheers & Jeers: Ibid.

58 "It was *exactly*": Marta Kauffman, interviewed by Beth Cochran.

58 "No notes": Lisa Kudrow, interviewed by Karen Herman.

59 "I don't know that": David Crane, interviewed by Beth Cochran.

60 after her freshman year: Gregory Cerio, "Handy Woman," *People*, Nov.

27, 1995, https://people.com/archive/cover-story-handy-woman-vol-44-no-22.

60 "But I loved it…easy": Courteney Cox, interviewed by Sam Jones, *Off Camera with Sam Jones*, "Courteney Cox," podcast audio, Mar. 30, 2017.

60 "I just thought": Ibid.

61 "I'll take this ride": Ibid.

61 fan mail: Courteney Cox, interviewed by Claudia Winkleman, Liquid News, BBC Choice, YouTube video, https://www.youtube.com/watch?v=E_AtPQkxGHY&t=641s.

62 "we wanted her to do": Marta Kauffman, interviewed by Beth Cochran.

63 "I'm Monica": Kevin Bright, interviewed by Jenni Matz.

63 "I remember thinking": Courteney Cox, interviewed by author David Wild, *Friends 'til the End*, 53.

63 "We chatted on the way": Leah Remini, *Troublemaker* (New York: Ballantine Books, 2015).

63 ladies' room: Courteney Cox, interviewed by author David Wild, *Friends 'til the End*, 53.

64 "Courteney had said": Lisa Kudrow, interviewed by Karen Herman.

64 "Normally, there's a": Lisa Kudrow, interviewed by James Rampton, "Friends actress Lisa Kudrow: 'People still see me as Phoebe,'" *Express*, Jan. 11, 2015, https://www.express.co.uk/life-style/life/551174/Friends-actress-Lisa-Kudrow-interview.

64 "She was the one": Ibid.

65 "handsome, smug…women": Elizabeth Kolbert, "Finding the Absolutely

Perfect Actor: The High-Stress Business of Casting," *New York Times*, Apr. 6, 1994, https://www.nytimes.com/1994/04/06/arts/finding-the-absolutely-perfect-actor-the-high-stress-business-of-casting.html.

65 "He wasn't quite": Marta Kauffman, interviewed by Beth Cochran.

65 "Lake Talk": Matt LeBlanc, interviewed by Conan O'Brien, Conan, Jan. 23, 2014, YouTube video, https://www.youtube.com/watch?v=29FO0t6Sp0o.

65 "everybody had some": Matt LeBlanc, interviewed by Katie Couric, "A Farewell to Friends," *Dateline NBC*, May 5, 2004.

65 "LEGO college": Matt LeBlanc, interviewed by Nichole Bernier, "MATT LEBLANC ON PLAYING HIMSELF IN 'EPISODES,'" *Boston Common*, Mar. 1, 2014, https://bostoncommon-magazine.com/matt-leblanc-on-friends-why-joey-was-cancelled-and-playing-himself-on-episodes.

66 "I got ants": Matt LeBlanc, interviewed by Bart Mills, "A Real Bud : Fox sitcom About Working-Class Pals Wears Well On Matt LeBlanc," *Los Angeles Times*, May 24, 1992, http://articles.latimes.com/1992-05-24/news/tv-71_1_matt-leblanc.

66 five hundred bucks: Matt LeBlanc, interviewed by Nichole Bernier, "MATT LEBLANC ON PLAYING HIMSELF IN 'EPISODES.'"

66 a very Joey moment: Matt LeBlanc, interviewed by Katie Couric.

66 "I'd just hoped": Matt LeBlanc, interviewed by Dawn O'Porter, "Matt LeBlanc on life after Friends," *Radio Times*, May 11, 2015, https://www.radiotimes.com/news/2015-05-11/matt-leblanc-on-life-after-friends.

66 "Everybody wanted him": Flo Greenberg, interviewed in Friends - The One In Their Own Words, Ilc Ltd., 1999, YouTube video, https://www.youtube.com/watch?v=-bt5z3pR6D0.

67 "He was sent for": Ibid.

67 eleven dollars: Matt LeBlanc, interviewed by Garth Pearce, "Mum was broke but she always supported me," *The Sun*, Mar. 7, 2011, https://www.thesun.co.uk/archives/news/413040/mum-was-broke-but-she-always-supported-me.

68 This was a show: Matt LeBlanc, interviewed by authors Warren Littlefield and T.R. Pearson, *Top of the Rock*, 261.

68 Just like real: Matt LeBlanc, interviewed by author David Wild, *Friends 'til the End*, 117.

68 "Welcome back": "The One Where Monica Gets a Roommate," *Friends*, Season One, Episode 1.

68 "What happened": Matt LeBlanc, interviewed by authors Warren Littlefield and T.R. Pearson, *Top of the Rock*, 261.

68 "I'll never forget": Marta Kauffman, interviewed by Beth Cochran.

69 Chevron gas station: Warren Littlefield, interviewed by Rob Shuter, "Warren Littlefield Talks Jennifer Aniston's Journey To 'Friends,'" *Huffington Post*, May 3, 2012, https://www.huffingtonpost.com/2012/05/03/warren-littlefield-jennifer-aniston_n_1475363.html.

69 "failed sitcom queen": Jennifer Aniston, interviewed by Jenelle Riley, "Conversations with Jennifer Aniston," SAG-AFTRA Foundation, Dec. 12, 2014, YouTube video, https://www.youtube.com/watch?v=d1GUn2z7MoM&t=992s.

69 "Will it ever happen": Warren Littlefield, *Top of the Rock*, 263.

70 "I wanted to be": Jennifer Aniston, interviewed by Prof. Richard Brown, "Jennifer Aniston," *Movies 101*, Oct. 14, 2015, https://www.imdb.com/title/tt0821330.

70 "I didn't think": Jennifer Aniston, interviewed by Jenelle Riley.

70 perpetually broke: Jennifer Aniston, interviewed by Jenelle Riley.

71 bike messenger: Ibid.

71 "It was quite": Ibid.

71 "I couldn't book": Jennifer Aniston, interviewed by Prof. Richard Brown.

71 borrowed a hundred: Jennifer Aniston, interviewed by Jenelle Riley.

71 "I'd just apologize…weeks": Jennifer Aniston, interviewed by Prof. Richard Brown.

72 "God, I wanted": Warren Littlefield, *Top of the Rock*, 263.

72 "The role is potentially": David Crane, interviewed by Beth Cochran.

72 "thousands": Marta Kauffman, interviewed by Beth Cochran.

73 "She was everything": Jennifer Aniston, interviewed by Prof. Richard Brown.

73 "Sweet'N Low": "The One Where Monica Gets a Roommate," *Friends*, Season One, Episode 1.

73 Upper East Side girls: Jennifer Aniston, interviewed by Jenelle Riley.

74 "We held our breath": David Crane, interviewed by authors Warren Littlefield and T.R. Pearson, *Top of the Rock*, 263.

74 "we saw Jennifer": Kevin Bright, interviewed by Jenni Matz.

74 "the best one": David Crane, interviewed by Beth Cochran.

74 "We asked to see": Kevin Bright, interviewed by Jenni Matz.

74 "We were like six pieces": David Schwimmer, interviewed by Katie Couric, "A Farewell to Friends," *Dateline NBC*, May 5, 2004.

74 a chill ran down: Marta Kauffman, interviewed by Beth Cochran.

75 "fun and exciting": Lisa Kudrow, interviewed by Karen Herman.

75 "We were always": David Crane, interviewed by Beth Cochran.

75 "You know they're...do that": Jennifer Aniston, interviewed by Peter Hammond.

76 "This is the funniest": Lisa Whelchel, "Why Lisa Whelchel Turned Down Rachel Role on 'Friends,'" Where Are They Now, Oprah Winfrey Network, YouTube video, Jan. 14, 2014, https://www.youtube.com/watch?v=yIC_whaNIsk.

76 "This show is going": Jennifer Aniston, interviewed by Jenelle Riley.

76 "I remember a girlfriend": Ibid.

77 pass for New York: Kevin Bright, interviewed by Jenni Matz.

77 "This could be": Ibid.

77 Magritte painting: Ibid.

78 "something with the fountain": Ibid.

78 "we have an idea": Marta Kauffman, interviewed by Beth Cochran.

78 "pruny fingers": Matt LeBlanc, interviewed by Jimmy Kimmel, Jimmy Kimmel Live, YouTube video, Aug. 8, 2017, https://www.youtube.com/watch?v=hKQtufNc-C8&t=243s.

78 "they were very": Marta Kauffman, interviewed by Beth Cochran.

78 "I don't think we": Lisa Kudrow, interviewed in *People*, "Lisa Kudrow and Matt LeBlanc Dish on Why Phoebe and Joey Never Hooked Up," Sep. 11, 2015, https://people.com/tv/friends-matt-leblanc-lisa-kudrow-on-phoebe-and-joey-never-hooking-up.

78 "I don't remember": Ibid.

78 "class clown": Matt LeBlanc, interviewed in *People*, "Lisa Kudrow and Matt LeBlanc Dish on Why Phoebe and Joey Never Hooked Up."

79 "You've got six": Matthew Perry, interviewed by author David Wild, *Friends 'til the End*, 12.

Chapter Three: The One with Marcel and George Clooney

84 "don't even have a pla": "The One with George Stephanopoulos," *Friends*, Season One, Episode 4.

85 "Even if people": "The One on the Last Night," *Friends*, Season Six, Episode 6.

85 den mother: James Burrows, interviewed by Gary Rutkowski.

85 "Monica's kids": Ibid.

85 "It's like all my life...Daddy": "The One Where Monica Gets a Roommate," *Friends*, Season One, Episode 1.

86 "I was scared": Jennifer Aniston, interviewed by Craig Tomashoff, "I'll Be There For You," *People*, Apr. 7, 1995, https://people.com/archive/ill-be-there-for-you-vol-43-no-15.

86 "kind of a dick": David Schwimmer, interviewed by Bruce Fretts, "NBC's newest hit sitcom," *Entertainment Weekly*, Jan. 27, 1995, http://ew.com/article/1995/01/27/nbcs-newest-hit-sitcom.

86 "the brother type": Matt LeBlanc interviewed by Craig Tomashoff, "I'll Be There For You."

86 "Could it be that": Matt LeBlanc, interviewed by author David Wild, *Friends 'til the End*, 117.

86 "Because I'm afraid": Matt LeBlanc, interviewed by authors Warren Littlefield and T.R. Pearson, *Top of the Rock*, 292.

87 "they just seemed like": Marta Kauffman, interviewed by Matt Lauer.

87 "hate fuckers": Taffy Brodesser-Akner, "Ross and Rachel vs. Sam and Diane: Who Is the Better Couple?" Vulture, Oct. 3, 2016, http://www.vulture.com/2016/10/tv-couples-ross-rachel-sam-diane.html.

89 "What is this place": "The One with Two Parts: Part 1," *Friends*, Season One, Episode 16.

89 "a thirty-minute commercial": Tom Shales, "FALL TV PREVIEW," *Washington Post*, Sep. 22, 1994, https://www.washingtonpost.com/archive/lifestyle/1994/09/22/fall-tv-preview/5147e53e-bfd2-4aae-be75-0e95c561cad9.

89 "there's really nothing": Howard Rosenberg, "TV Reviews : NBC's Strongest Evening of the Week Has Its Weak Spot," *Los Angeles Times*, Sep. 22, 1994, http://articles.latimes.com/1994-09-22/entertainment/ca-41409_1_martin-short-show.

89 defaced the signs: David Wild, "'Friends': Six Lives on Videotape," *Rolling Stone*, May 18, 1995, https://www.rollingstone.com/tv/news/friends-six-lives-on-videotape-19950518.

90 "I am so...do that": "The One with Two Parts: Part 2," *Friends*, Season One, Episode 17.

91 "It's such an unrealistic": *All-American Girl*, quoted by David Wild, "'Friends': Six Lives on Videotape."

91 "It was like starting": Matt LeBlanc, interviewed by author David Wild, *Friends 'til the End*, 118.

92 "This show today": Oprah Winfrey, *The Oprah Winfrey Show*, Mar. 29, 1995, YouTube video, https://www.youtube.com/watch?v=RaC57X6RIPc.

92 "Well, if you don't": Ibid.

92 "When you hear": Ibid.

92 "Bad": Matthew Perry, *The Oprah Winfrey Show*.

93 "I'd like for y'all": Oprah Winfrey, *The Oprah Winfrey Show*.

93 "As a matter...the sack": Ibid.

93 "They remind you of": Ibid.

93 "it's real life": unnamed college student, *The Oprah Winfrey Show*.

94 "Didn't know it": Lisa Kudrow, *The Oprah Winfrey Show*.

94 "Did you know": Lisa Kudrow, interviewed by Karen Herman.

94 "Who *were* those": Matthew Perry, interviewed by David Wild, "'Friends': Six Lives on Videotape."

96 "As completely corny": Courteney Cox, interviewed by David Wild, "'Friends': Six Lives on Videotape."

96 "always the hostess": "The One with Rachel's Crush," *Friends*, Season Four, Episode 13

96 "Usually...reruns": Kevin Bright, interviewed by Jenni Matz.

Chapter Four: The One Where Two Women Got Married

98 "Could there BE": Angela Hamilton, "Friends: Could There BE Any More Gay Jokes?" Previously.TV, http://previously.tv/friends/friends-could-there-be-any-more-gay-jokes.

98 "If the homo sapiens": "The One with the Giant Poking Device," *Friends*, Season Three, Episode 8.

99 "how goes the dancing": "The One with the Ballroom Dancing," *Friends*, Season Four, Episode 4.

99 "I now pronounce": "The One with the Lesbian Wedding," *Friends*, Season Two, Episode 11.

100 "We never did it to": Marta Kauffman, interviewed by author David Wild, *Friends 'til the End*, 216.

100 "A family like ours": Ibid.

100 "Who should we call": "The One with the Dozen Lasagnas," *Friends*, Season One, Episode 12.

101 partner is white: Stephen Tropiano, *The Prime Time Closet* (New York: Applause Theatre & Cinema Books, 2002), 210.

101 "comfortable with being": "Can't Help Loving That Man," *Roc*, Season One, Episode 8, quoted by Todd VanDerWerff, "Watch: TV's first gay wedding is a perfect summation of how far America has come," Vox, Jun. 26, 2015, https://www.vox.com/2015/6/26/8852929/gay-wedding-tv-history-roc.

101 "You have somehow managed": "December Bride," *Roseanne*, Season Eight, Episode 11.

101 "I hate to shop": Ibid.

101 "But do you like": Ibid.

102 "I'm not trying to": David Crane, quoted in *The Spokesman-Review*, "Gingrich To Officiate At Lesbian Wedding On 'Friends' - Candace, That Is," Nov. 20, 1995, http://www.spokesman.com/stories/1995/nov/20/gingrich-to-officiate-at-lesbian-wedding-on.

102 "like alcoholism": Newt Gingrich, quoted by *The Associated Press*, "Gingrich opts for gay tolerance," *The Register-Guard*, Nov. 24, 1994, https://news.google.com/newspapers?id=QlBWAAAAIBAJ&sjid=w-sDAAAAIBAJ&pg=6914,5891670&.

102 "that gay people": David Crane, quoted in *The Spokesman-Review*.

102 "sees everything": The One with the Lesbian Wedding," *Friends*, Season Two, Episode 11.

102 "You didn't marry": Ibid.

102 "I went straight from": Ibid.

103 "carefully sensitive…counterpart": Suzanna Danuta Walters, *All The Rage* (Chicago: Chicago University Press, 2001), 183.

103 "We were disappointed": Jane Sibbett, interviewed by *Metro*, "Carol and Susan weren't allowed to kiss when they got married on Friends," Sep. 15, 2017, https://metro.co.uk/2017/09/15/carol-and-susan-werent-allowed-kiss-when-they-got-married-on-friends-6931148.

103 "*Now* I've seen": "The One with the Lesbian Wedding," *Friends*, Season Two, Episode 11.

103 "How lovely": Jane Sibbett, interviewed by Suzanne Corson, "Interview with Jane Sibbett," AfterEllen, Jan. 27, 2008, http://www.afterellen.com/tv/28458-interview-with-jane-sibbett.

103 "pulled back": Jane Sibbett, interviewed by *Metro*, "Carol and Susan weren't allowed to kiss when they got married on Friends."

104 "one in full military": Walters, *All The Rage*, 183.

104 "We took it very seriously": Debra McGuire, interviewed by Elana Fishman, "'Friends' Costume Designer Looks Back on 10 Sea-

sons of Weddings," Racked, Jun. 7, 2017, https://www.racked.com/2017/6/7/15742358/friends-tv-show-weddings.

105 "unacceptable risk": Public Law 103-160, 10 U.S.C. § 654, enacted Feb. 28, 1994

105 "behavior disorders...transvestism": Army Regulation 40–501, enacted May 17, 1963.

105 "Polls indicated that": Eric Schmitt, "THE TRANSITION: News Analysis -- Challenging the Military; In Promising to End Ban on Homosexuals, Clinton Is Confronting a Wall of Tradition," *New York Times*, Nov. 12, 1992.

105 "honorable compromise": Pres. William J. Clinton, quoted by Ann Devroy, "President Opens Military To Gays," *Washington Post*, Jul. 20, 1993.

105 "People I worked with": John McGuire, interviewed by Eric Schmitt, *New York Times*.

105 "She said...lipstick lesbian": Jessica Hecht, interviewed by *Metro*, "Video: Jessica Hecht hired because she 'didn't look like a lesbian,'" https://metro.co.uk/video/jessica-hecht-hired-didn-t-look-like-lesbian-1537313.

106 "They needed at least": Lea DeLaria, quoted by author Suzanna Danuta Walters, *All The Rage*, 183.

107 "We do not believe": Ron Kelly, quoted in *New York Daily News*, "COUPLE OF NBC STATIONS SAID 'I DON'T' TO LESBIAN 'FRIENDS,'" Jan. 19, 1996, http://www.nydailynews.com/archives/entertainment/couple-nbc-stations-don-lesbian-friends-article-1.727123.

107 two calls: Marta Kauffman, interviewed by Lacey Rose, "Comedy Showrunner Roundtable: Reunions You'll Never See (Sorry, 'Friends' Fans!), Diversity and How to Write Sex Scenes," *Hollywood Reporter*,

Jun. 9, 2016, https://www.hollywoodreporter.com/features/comedy-showrunners-discuss-diversity-sex-scenes-900826.

108 "Here's a wacky thought": "The One with the Candy Hearts," *Friends*, Season One, Episode 14.

108 "Because it says so much": Jane Sibbett, interviewed in "Friends of Friends," featurette extra, *Friends* The Complete Series (Warner Home Video, 2006), DVD.

109 "do you love her": "The One with the Lesbian Wedding," *Friends*, Season Two, Episode 11.

109 "you did a good thing": Ibid.

109 only about 6%: GLAAD's Where We Are on TV Report- 2017, https://www.glaad.org/whereweareontv17.

109 "I think for the": Jane Sibbett, interviewed in "Friends of Friends."

Chapter Five: The One Where We All Got the Haircut

110 a UK study: Elisa Roche, "Jennifer Aniston's a cut above for 11 million women," *Express*, May 26, 2010, https://www.express.co.uk/news/uk/177204/Jennifer-Aniston-s-a-cut-above-for-11-million-women.

111 "We learned a lot": Marta Kauffman, interviewed by author David Wild, *Friends 'til the End*, 40.

111 "when she stopped being": "The One with the Princess Leia Fantasy," *Friends*, Season Three, Episode 1.

112 "I've had so many": Lauren Tom, interviewed in "Friends of Friends." featurette extra, *Friends* The Complete Series (Warner Home Video, 2006), DVD.

112 "When she crossed": Marta Kauffman, interviewed in *The Nineties*, "The One About TV," *CNN*, Jul. 9, 2017.

116 the 13th Generation: William Strauss and Neil Howe, "The Third Turning: Culture Wars (1984-2005?)," *The Fourth Turning* (New York: Three Rivers Press, 1997).

116 Nearly half: Susan Gregory Thomas, *In Spite of Everything* (New York: Random House, 2011), xv.

117 "Generation X included significantly more": Jessica R. Sincavage, "The labor force and unemployment," *Monthly Labor Review, Bureau of Labor Statistics*, Jun. 2004, https://www.bls.gov/opub/mlr/2004/06/art2full.pdf.

117 "oldest-marrying": Strauss and Howe, *The Fourth Turning*, 594.

117 "ersatz social arrangements": Ibid.

118 "We really didn't know": Lisa Kudrow, interviewed by Karen Herman.

118 "running on panic": David Crane, interviewed by Beth Cochran.

119 (reportedly $22,500): Brian Lowry, "Cast Gets a Reason to Stay 'Friends' a While Longer," *Los Angeles Times*, Dec. 23, 1996, http://articles.latimes.com/1996-12-23/entertainment/ca-11880_1_warner-bros.

119 salaries varied widely: Bill Carter, "'Friends' Cast Bands Together To Demand a Salary Increase," *New York Times*, Jul. 16, 1996.

119 "favored nations": Courteney Cox, interviewed by Sam Jones.

120 viewing parties: Stuart Elliott, "THE MEDIA BUSINESS: ADVERTISING; The Diet Coke empire strikes back, under the guise of 'Friends,'" New York Times, Jan. 1, 1996. https://www.nytimes.com/1996/01/01/business/media-business-advertising-diet-coke-empire-strikes-back-under-guise-friends.html.

120 calling cards: Stuart Elliott, "THE MEDIA BUSINESS: Advertising;Marketers see gold in the photogenic cast of a huge NBC hit."

120 "The contemporary personality": Frank P. Bifulco Jr., quoted by Stuart Elliott, "THE MEDIA BUSINESS: Advertising;Marketers see gold in the photogenic cast of a huge NBC hit."

121 "the biggest marketing": A.J. Jacobs and Jeff Gordinier, "6 PACT," *Entertainment Weekly*, Jan. 19, 1996, http://ew.com/article/1996/01/19/6-pact.

121 "That's where I give": Lisa Kudrow, quoted in *People*, "Saying Goodbye to *Friends*," Apr. 8, 2004, https://people.com/premium/saying-goodbye-to-friends.

121 "run it they did": Matt LeBlanc, interviewed by Stuart Elliott, "THE MEDIA BUSINESS: Advertising;Marketers see gold in the photogenic cast of a huge NBC hit."

122 Super Bowl lead-out: The Nielsen Company, http://www.nielsen.com/us/en/insisghts/news/2010/on-average-halftime-show-performers-score-500-post-game-sales-bump.html.

122 sales spiked: Mark Gleason, "THE MARKETING 100;DIET COKE/'FRIENDS' FRANK BIFULCO," AdAge, Jun. 24, 1996, http://adage.com/article/news/marketing-100-diet-coke-friends-frank-bifulco/78700.

122 "Crosses the Line": Steve Johnson, "Ad Nauseam," *Chicago Tribune*, Jan. 26, 1996, http://articles.chicagotribune.com/1996-01-26/features/9601260324_1_friends-show-inflatable.

122 "national epidemic": James Endrst, "Have 'Friends' ... You Know ... Gone Too Far?" *Hartford Courant*, Feb. 9, 1996, http://articles.courant.com/1996-02-09/features/9602090047_1_friends-phenomenon-diet-coke-ross-and-rachel.

122 "LET THE BACKLASH": Newsweek Staff, "LET THE BACKLASH BEGIN!" *Newsweek*, Feb. 11, 1996, http://www.newsweek.com/let-backlash-begin-179758.

122 "There is a possibility": Warren Littlefield, quoted by Jessica Shaw, "'Friends' Takes Off," *Entertainment Weekly*, Feb. 9, 1996, http://ew.com/article/1996/02/09/friends-takes.

123 "absolute low point": David Crane, interviewed by William Keck, "Friends: A 20th Anniversary Oral History," Academy of Television Arts & Sciences, Sep. 6, 2014, https://www.emmys.com/news/industry-news/friends-20th-anniversary-oral-history.

123 "Until you have": Kevin Bright, interviewed by Jenni Matz.

123 "If the six": Lisa Kudrow, interviewed by Karen Herman.

123 "I've got to get": Matt LeBlanc, interviewed by authors Warren Littlefield and T.R. Pearson, *Top of the Rock*, 359.

Chapter Six: The One After
"The One After the Super Bowl"

125 "Do not be divided": Interview with David Wild, Feb. 16, 2018.

125 a proposition: David Schwimmer, interviewed by authors Warren Littlefield and T.R. Pearson, *Top of the Rock*, 351.

126 a whopping $3 million: "NBC & 'FRIENDS' TO STAY COZY FOR A COUPLE MORE YEARS," *New York Daily News*, Aug. 4, 1997, http://www.nydailynews.com/archives/entertainment/nbc-amp-friends-stay-cozy-couple-years-article-1.785125.

126 $4 million a pop: Eric Mink and Richard Huff, "'FRIENDS' HOPE TEAMWORK PAYS," *New York Daily News*, Jul. 16, 1996, http://www.nydailynews.com/archives/entertainment/friends-hope-teamwork-pays-article-1.742805.

126 polled outside: Jess Cagle, "'Friends' go on strike for a raise," *Entertainment Weekly*, Jul. 26, 1996, http://ew.com/article/1996/07/26/friends-go-strike-raise.

126 "salary virus": Sharon Waxman, "HARDBALL AT UNDER-COVER," *Washington Post*, Jul. 26, 1996, https://www.washingtonpost.com/archive/lifestyle/1996/07/26/hardball-at-undercover/2f59eeb1-daac-47d2-9043-a15637fe2c9a.

126 casting sessions: Ibid.

127 "What I would have": Dick Wolf, interviewed by authors Warren Littlefield and T.R. Pearson, *Top of the Rock*, 354.

127 "If they come to you": Matt LeBlanc, interviewed by author David Wild, *Friends 'til the End*, 122.

127 "both the production": Eric Mink and Richard Huff, "'FRIENDS' HOPE TEAMWORK PAYS."

127 "I'm not going to say": Kevin Bright, interviewed by Jenni Matz.

128 scaled-up salaries: "NBC & 'FRIENDS' TO STAY COZY FOR A COUPLE MORE YEARS," *New York Daily News*.

128 "And then we decided": Lisa Kudrow, interviewed by Karen Herman.

130 "How do you guys": "The One with Frank Jr.," *Friends*, Season Three, Episode 5.

130 "There's definitely a part": Jennifer Aniston, *How Friends Changed The World*, Channel 4, May 22, 2004.

130 "the lynchpin": David Crane, interviewed by author David Wild, *Friends 'til the End*, 70.

132 "*just* a job": "The One Where Ross and Rachel Take a Break," *Friends*, Season Three, Episode 15.

132 "It's just changed": "The One with the Morning After," *Friends*, Season Three, Episode 16.

Chapter Seven: The One Where They All Go to London (And Everywhere Else in the World)

134 "America rewards": Ricky Gervais, "The Difference Between American and British Humour," *Time*, Nov. 9, 2011, http://time.com/3720218/difference-between-american-british-humour.

135 "15 Yemen Road": "The One with All the Rugby," *Friends*, Season Four, Episode 15.

135 "seven, seven": "The One with Phoebe's Uterus," *Friends*, Season 4, Episode 11.

135 "How you doin'": "The One with Rachel's Crush," *Friends*, Season Four, Episode 13.

135 "We didn't want to": David Crane, interviewed by Joyce Eng, "*Friends*: The One with the Oral History of the Trivia Game Episode," *TV Guide*, Jan. 18, 2018, http://www.tvguide.com/news/friends-oral-history-trivia-game-embryos-episode.

135 "It's really early": Lisa Kudrow, interviewed by Karen Herman.

136 a group of writers: Seth Kurland, interviewed by Joyce Eng, "*Friends*: The One with the Oral History of the Trivia Game Episode."

136 gone overbudget: Kevin Bright, interviewed in "Friends Final Thoughts," featurette extra, *Friends* The Complete Series (Warner Home Video, 2006), DVD.

137 "edge of their seats": Kevin Bright, interviewed by Joyce Eng, "*Friends*: The One with the Oral History of the Trivia Game Episode."

137 "our people-pleasing": David Crane, interviewed by Beth Cochran.

137 "They would sometimes": Marta Kauffman, interviewed by Beth Cochran.

138 "We had to trust": Ibid.

138 numerous variations: David Crane, interviewed by Joyce Eng, "*Friends*: The One with the Oral History of the Trivia Game Episode."

139 "And the ability": Kevin Bright, interviewed by Joyce Eng, "*Friends*: The One with the Oral History of the Trivia Game Episode."

140 same week: Helen Baxendale, interviewed by Cassandra Jardine, "Family or Friends?" *Telegraph*, Dec. 28, 2006, https://www.telegraph.co.uk/culture/tvandradio/3657446/Family-or-Friends.html.

140 "I would not": David Scwhimmer, interviewed by Celia Walden, "David Schwimmer interview," *Telegraph*, Jun. 27, 2011, https://www.telegraph.co.uk/culture/8594277/David-Schwimmer-interview.html.

140 "You couldn't walk...America": Helen Baxendale, interviewed by James Rampton, "When Helen Baxendale was in Friends she got mobbed in the street, but now she reveals: I'm so glad I gave up fame for a family," *Daily Mail*, Feb. 10, 2012, http://www.dailymail.co.uk/tvshowbiz/article-2099082/When-Helen-Baxendale-Friends-got-mobbed-street-reveals-Im-glad-I-gave-fame-family.html.

141 "Beatles in reverse": Kevin Bright, interviewed by Jenni Matz.

141 "all they wanted": Ibid.

141 "At a time when": Sarah Ferguson, Duchess of York, interviewed by author David Wild, *Friends 'til the End*, 109.

142 "We revealed Monica": David Crane, interviewed by Beth Cochran.

143 "would-be-speaking": "The One with Ross's Wedding," *Friends*, Season Four, Episode 23.

144 "People didn't know": Sahar Hashemi, *How Friends Changed The World*.

144 "colonial hangover": Shoaib Daniyal, "'Friends' cured India of its colonial hangover - and made it fall in love with America," Scroll.in, Sep. 26, 2014, https://scroll.in/article/680842/friends-cured-india-of-its-colonial-hangover-and-made-it-fall-in-love-with-america.

145 "I fear that": Paroma Soni, "*Friends* From India," Slate, May 9, 2018, https://slate.com/culture/2018/05/friends-overwhelming-popularity-in-india-makes-me-worry-about-the-shows-gender-stereotypes.html.

145 "dislodge chai": Shoaib Daniyal, "'Friends' cured India of its colonial hangover - and made it fall in love with America."

Chapter Eight: The One Where Everything Changed

151 "we could *not* tell": "The One Where Everybody Finds Out," *Friends*, Season Five, Episode 14.

152 "Lisa was always…enjoying": Michael Lembeck, interviewed by Amy Wilkinson, "Friends: An oral history of 'The One Where Everybody Finds Out,'" *Entertainment Weekly*, Apr. 3, 2017, http://ew.com/tv/2017/04/03/friends-untold-story-phoebe-everybody-finds-out.

153 "Jennifer salad": Courteney Cox, interviewed by Andy Cohen, "Must See TV: A Tribute to James Burrows," NBC, Feb. 21, 2016.

154 "publicist-friendly": Jill Goldsmith, "People who need People," *Variety*, Jul. 9, 2006, https://variety.com/2006/film/news/people-who-need-people-1200340454.

154 "sucking up": Ibid.

155 "rallied 'round": Paula Chin, "The Buddy System," *People*, Jan. 24, 2000, https://people.com/archive/cover-story-the-buddy-system-vol-53-no-3.

155 "shoulder to cry": Ibid.

155 "A Friend in Need": Jill Smolowe, "A Friend in Need," *People*, Jun. 5, 2000, https://people.com/archive/a-friend-in-need-vol-53-no-22.

155 "Brad and Friend": Ann-Marie O'Neill and Kyle Smith, "Brad and Friend," *People*, Mar. 8, 1999, https://people.com/archive/cover-story-brad-and-friend-vol-51-no-9.

155 "anti-Gwyneth": Ibid.

156 "We all made": Matthew Perry, interviewed by Paula Chin, "The Buddy System."

156 "the actors can't": Paula Chin, "The Buddy System."

157 "As we all get": David Schwimmer, interviewed by Paula Chin, "The Buddy System."

157 "really moving in": "The One Where Ross Hugs Rachel," *Friends*, Season Six, Episode 2.

157 "the gift that keeps": Patrick Connolly, quoted in Chief Marketer, "LIVE FROM THE CATALOG CONFERENCE: THE WILLIAMS-SONOMA BRANDS HAVE 'FRIENDS,'" May 4, 2004, http://www.chiefmarketer.com/live-from-the-catalog-conference-the-williams-sonoma-brands-have-friends.

159 "Fat Monica laughed": Mathilda Gregory, "Fat Monica Was The TV Role Model I Never Expected," BuzzFeed, Aug. 16, 2015, https://www.buzzfeed.com/mathildia/why-i-loved-fat-monica.

159 "ate publicly": Ibid.

159 "grabbed a doughnut": Courteney Cox, interviewed by Glenn Whipp, "A look back (and ahead?) at 'Friends,'" *Los Angeles Times*, Jun. 9, 2010, http://articles.latimes.com/2010/jun/09/news/la-en-courteneycox-side-20100609.

160 $5 million: Josef Adalian, "NBC's new best 'Friends,'" *Variety*, Jul. 21, 1999, https://variety.com/1999/tv/news/nbc-s-new-best-friends-1117744041.

160 "None of us have": David Schwimmer, interviewed by Paula Chin, "The Buddy System."

161 $1 million: Variety Staff, Josef Adalian and Michael Schneider, "'Friends' extends," *Variety*, May 14, 2000, https://variety.com/2000/scene/news/friends-extends-1117821605.

161 "We want *Friends*": unnamed NBC spokeswoman, quoted by Lynette Rice, "'Friends' demand a raise," *Entertainment Weekly*, Apr. 21, 2000, http://ew.com/article/2000/04/21/friends-demand-raise.

162 4:00 p.m.: Variety Staff, Josef Adalian and Michael Schneider, "'Friends' extends."

162 potential fall schedules: Bill Carter, *Desperate Networks* (New York: Broadway Books, 2006), 102.

162 "I asked the promotion": Garth Ancier, interviewed by ABC News, "Prime-Time Salary Wars," https://abcnews.go.com/2020/story?id=123651.

162 "haven't been treated": unnamed agent, quoted by Lynette Rice, "'Friends' demand a raise."

163 "Mother's Day gift": Garth Ancier, quoted by Variety Staff, Josef Adalian and Michael Schneider, "'Friends' extends."

163 "I think everybody": Kevin Bright, "Producers Commentary," *Friends*: The Complete Seventh Season (Warner Home Video, 2004), DVD.

165 "as the series gained": Jennifer Keishin Armstrong, *Seinfeldia* (New York: Simon & Schuster Paperbacks, 2016), 159.

165 "not ambiguous": retrieved from @emilynussbaum Twitter, Aug. 13, 2014, https://twitter.com/emilynussbaum/status/499671609649954816.

165 "ethnic suburban tropes": retrieved from @mollylambert Twitter, Aug. 13, 2014, https://twitter.com/mollylambert/status/499670493671067650.

166 "dangerous to decide": retrieved from @mollylambert Twitter, Aug. 13, 2014, https://twitter.com/mollylambert/status/499681202584821760.

166 "so many cues": retrieved from @emilynussbaum Twitter Aug. 13, 2014, https://twitter.com/emilynussbaum/status/499688245697867777.

166 halachic law: Marta Kauffman, interviewed in *Jewish Telegraph*, "Written Off, But She Co-Created Friends," 2011, https://www.jewishtelegraph.com/prof_119.html.

166 identified as Jewish: David Crane, interviewed by Amanda Pazornik, "It's been six years, but they'll always be my Jewish Friends," *Jewish News of Northern California*, Nov. 12, 2010, https://www.jweekly.com/2010/11/12/its-been-six-years-but-theyll-always-be-my-jewish-friends.

166 "I'm sure *any*": Marta Kauffman, "Producers Commentary," *Friends*: The Complete Seventh Season.

166 "it's about identity": Ibid.

167 flew all the Jews out: "The One with the Holiday Armadillo," *Friends*, Season Seven, Episode 10.

168 *transsexual*: GLAAD Media Reference Guide, https://www.glaad.org/reference/transgender.

169   much debate: David Crane, "Producers Commentary," *Friends*: The Complete Seventh Season.

169   "Liza Minnelli...ever": Ibid.

169   *I haven't done* that: Kathleen Turner, interviewed on *Sunday Brunch*, Channel 4, Apr. 8, 2018, retrieved from @SundayBrunchC4 Twitter, https://twitter.com/sundaybrunchc4/status/999660680801406978.

169   "How they approached": Kathleen Turner, interviewed by Sam Damshenas, "Friends actress Kathleen Turner says the show hasn't aged well for LGBTQ rights," *Gay Times*, Feb. 20, 2018, http://www.gaytimes.co.uk/culture/99396/friends-actress-kathleen-turner-says-show-hasnt-aged-well-lgbtq-rights-exclusive.

170   "Maybe that's...matter": "The One with Chandler's Dad," *Friends*, Season Seven, Episode 22.

171   "Oh, yeah...ma'am": Ibid.

172   "the man in the": "The One with Monica and Chandler's Wedding," *Friends*, Season Seven, Episode 23.

Chapter Nine: The One Where Nobody Died

176   "So, obviously...know": Lisa Kudrow, interviewed by Karen Herman.

176   hours of television: Mark A. Schuster, M.D., Ph.D., Bradley D. Stein, M.D., M.P.H., Lisa H. Jaycox, Ph.D., Rebecca L. Collins, Ph.D., Grant N. Marshall, Ph.D., Marc N. Elliott, Ph.D., Annie J. Zhou, M.S., David E. Kanouse, Ph.D., Janina L. Morrison, A.B., and Sandra H. Berry, M.A., "A National Survey of Stress Reactions after the September 11, 2001, Terrorist Attacks," *New England Journal of Medicine*, Nov. 15, 2001, https://www.nejm.org/doi/full/10.1056/NEJM200111153452024.

176   consecutive news coverage: Bill Carter and Jim Rutenberg, "AFTER THE ATTACKS: TELEVISION; Viewers Again Return To Tradi-

tional Networks," *New York Times*, Sep. 15, 2001, https://www.nytimes.com/2001/09/15/us/after-the-attacks-television-viewers-again-return-to-traditional-networks.html.

176 between 30 and 50: Ibid.

177 "But during an event": Ibid.

177 "It's not just that": Alex S. Jones, quoted by Bill Carter and Jim Rutenberg, "AFTER THE ATTACKS: TELEVISION; Viewers Again Return To Traditional Networks."

178 "Regis is here": David Letterman, quoted by Ken Tucker, "How Letterman handled his first post-terror show," *Entertainment Weekly*, Sep. 21, 2001, http://ew.com/article/2001/09/21/how-letterman-handled-his-first-post-terror-show.

178 "They said to get back": Jon Stewart, *The Daily Show with Jon Stewart*, Comedy Central, Sep. 20, 2001, http://www.cc.com/video-clips/1q93jy/the-daily-show-with-jon-stewart-september-11--2001.

178 "didn't do death well": David Crane, interviewed by Beth Cochran.

179 "The dramatic moments": Kevin Bright, interviewed by Jenni Matz.

180 fill as many seats: Brian M. Rafferty, Gillian Flynn, and Allison Hope Weiner, "September 11th: Hollywood on Guard Duty," *Entertainment Weekly*, Oct. 5, 2001, http://ew.com/article/2001/10/05/september-11th-hollywood-guard-duty.

180 "[it was] the silliest": Lisa Kudrow, interviewed by Karen Herman.

180 "making his sex face": "The One with the Halloween Party," *Friends*, Season Eight, Episode 6.

180 *I wonder who*: Lisa Kudrow, interviewed by Karen Herman.

180 "almost started crying": Ibid.

180 "Thank you": Ibid.

180 "not curing cancer": Ibid.

181 "back to work": Jennifer Aniston, interviewed by *People*, "Saying Goodbye to *Friends*," Apr. 8, 2004, https://people.com/premium/saying-goodbye-to-friends.

181 "look at that": "The One Where Rachel Tells Ross," deleted scene, *Friends*: The Complete Eighth Season (Warner Home Video, 2004), DVD.

181 "this is ridiculous": Ibid.

182 "like comfort food": Marta Kauffman, interviewed by author David Wild, *Friends 'til The End*, 226.

183 "an amazing night": Kevin Bright, interviewed by Jenni Matz.

183 "seismic change": Graydon Carter, quoted by Caroline Kepnes, "The After Words," *Entertainment Weekly*, Dec. 21, 2001, http://ew.com/article/2001/12/21/after-words.

183 "how that happened": Matt LeBlanc, interviewed by Stacey Wilson Hunt, "Emmys 2011: Matt LeBlanc on Playing Matt LeBlanc," *Hollywood Reporter*, Aug. 17, 2011, https://www.hollywoodreporter.com/news/emmys-2011-matt-leblanc-playing-223273.

184 "coming back": Jay Leno, *The Tonight Show with Jay Leno*, Jan. 30, 2002, YouTube video.

185 "it's foreigners": Ibid.

185 "To be a part of": Matt LeBlanc, interviewed by Jay Leno, The Tonight Show with Jay Leno, Jan. 30, 2002.

185 "that's what counts": Ibid.

186 "I'd rather try": Bruce Fretts, "Predictable sitcom premieres are a relief," *Entertainment Weekly*, Sep. 28, 2001, http://ew.com/article/2001/09/28/predictable-sitcom-premieres-are-relief.

186 "We didn't know": David Crane, "Producers Commentary," *Friends*: The Complete Eighth Season (Warner Home Video, 2004), DVD.

187 "walking a line": Ibid.

187 "well-placed sources": Gary Susman, "'Friends' to return for one more season, with raise," *Entertainment Weekly*, Feb. 15, 2002, http://ew.com/article/2002/02/15/friends-return-one-more-season-raise.

187 "The neat thing": Matt LeBlanc, interviewed by Jay Leno, *The Tonight Show with Jay Leno*, Jan. 30, 2002.

188 "They'll be there": Josef Adalian, "NBC staying with 'Friends,'" *Variety*, Feb. 11, 2002, https://variety.com/2002/tv/news/nbc-staying-with-friends-1117860562.

188 easiest deal: Jeff Zucker, quoted by Josef Adalian, "NBC staying with 'Friends.'"

188 "It's no secret": Ibid.

188 "thrilled and relieved": Jeff Zucker, interviewed by Michael Starr, "NBC NEARLY LOST BEST FRIENDS,'" *New York Post*, Feb. 13, 2002, https://nypost.com/2002/02/13/nbc-nearly-lost-best-friends-inside-story-of-sudden-deal-that-saved-the-day.

188 "Friends Not in Need": "Scoop," *People*, Feb. 25, 2002, https://people.com/archive/scoop-vol-57-no-7.

188 "We are enormously": Friends cast joint statement, "Entertainment

Today: Showbiz news," *United Press International*, Feb. 13, 2002, https://www.upi.com/Entertainment-Today-Showbiz-news/98861013593500.

189 "We will devote": Marta Kauffman, David Crane, and Kevin Bright joint statement, "Ninth season of 'Friends' gets go-ahead," Digital Spy, James Welsh, Feb. 12, 2002, http://www.digitalspy.com/tv/ustv/news/a6217/ninth-season-of-friends-gets-go-ahead.

Chapter Ten: The One Where It Ended, Twice

191 "everyone knows": Matt LeBlanc, interviewed in "Friends Final Thoughts."

191 "playing with fire": David Crane, interviewed by Beth Cochran.

191 "We knew that": David Crane, "Producers Commentary," *Friends*: The Complete Ninth Season (Warner Home Video, 2005), DVD.

191 *not* in love: Marta Kauffman, "Producers Commentary," *Friends*: The Complete Ninth Season (Warner Home Video, 2005), DVD.

192 never have sex: Ibid.

192 "redress issues": Aisha Tyler, interviewed by Matthew Gilbert, "Colour is not the issue here, girlfriend," *The Age*, May 1, 2003, https://www.theage.com.au/articles/2003/05/01/1051382028069.html.

193 nothing in the script: Ibid.

195 "I say we": "The One with Phoebe's Uterus," *Friends*, Season Four, Episode 11.

196 more than enough: Bill Carter, *Desperate Networks*, 290.

197 with Aisha Tyler: Eric Deggans, "Swerving again," Mar. 12, 2004, *St. Pete Times*, https://web.archive.org/web/20090719091936/http://

www.sptimes.com/2004/03/12/Artsandentertainment/Swerving_again.shtml.

197 "You can't keep": David Crane, interviewed by authors Warren Little-field and T.R. Pearson, *Top of the Rock*, 373.

197 "I don't want to": Jeff Zucker, quoted by David K. Li, "FRIENDS' FINALE WILL BE A VERY SPECIAL CAST-OFF," *New York Post*, Jul. 24, 2002, https://nypost.com/2002/07/24/friends-finale-will-be-a-very-special-cast-off.

197 "nails in the coffin": Ibid.

198 "We have the feeling": Marta Kauffman, quoted by Scott D. Pierce, "NBC exec is slow to bury 'Friends,'" *Deseret News*, Jul. 27, 2002, https://www.deseretnews.com/article/927773/NBC-exec-is-slow-to-bury-Friends.com.

198 "If this was not": David Crane, quoted by Stephen M. Silverman, "'Friends' May (or May Not) Stick Around," *People*, Jul. 24, 2002, https://people.com/celebrity/friends-may-or-may-not-stick-around.

198 "we all get along…not": Lisa Kudrow, quoted by Stephen M. Silverman, "Kudrow Unwilling to Write off 'Friends,'" *People*, Aug. 16, 2002, https://people.com/celebrity/kudrow-unwilling-to-write-off-friends.

198 what it would take: Bill Carter, *Desperate Networks*, 289.

200 "last season for *sure*": Jay Leno, *The Tonight Show with Jay Leno*, Aug. 7, 2002.

201 "We got nothin'": Jay Leno, *The Tonight Show with Jay Leno*, Aug. 2, 2002.

201 "I say that": Jennifer Aniston, interviewed by Jay Leno, *The Tonight Show with Jay Leno*, Aug. 7, 2002.

201 "an *Emmy* nomination": Jay Leno, *The Tonight Show with Jay Leno*, Aug. 7, 2002.

201 "It didn't work out": Matthew Perry, "The 54th Primetime Emmy Awards," NBC, Sep. 22, 2002.

202 "Jennifer Aniston has": Roger Ebert, "Reviews: The Good Girl," RogerEbert.com, Aug. 16, 2002, https://www.rogerebert.com/reviews/the-good-girl-2002.

202 "morose...television's *Friends*": Elvis Mitchell, "FILM REVIEW; The Catcher In the Texas Chain Store," *New York Times*, Aug. 7, 2002, https://www.nytimes.com/2002/08/07/movies/film-review-the-catcher-in-the-texas-chain-store.html.

203 "Are you Lloyd": Cameron Crowe, "Commentary," *Say Anything...* (20th Century Fox, 2002), DVD.

205 "damage is done": Matt LeBlanc, interviewed by Dan Snierson, "The untold story of Matt LeBlanc," *Entertainment Weekly*, Jul. 16, 2012, http://ew.com/article/2012/07/16/untold-story-matt-leblanc.

206 "I was also feeling": Jennifer Aniston, interviewed by Matt Lauer, "A Farewell to Friends."

206 twelve episodes: Bill Carter, *Desperate Networks*, 300.

206 on the phone: Ibid.

206 de facto negotiator: Kevin Bright, interviewed by Jenni Matz.

206 "what was happening": Ibid.

207 network threatened: Bill Carter, *Desperate Networks*, 301.

207 clip show: Michael Schneider, "NBC still 'Friends' for $10 mil per

seg," *Variety*, Dec. 21, 2002, https://variety.com/2002/scene/markets-festivals/nbc-still-friends-for-10-mil-per-seg-1117877795.

207   end of the Must-See TV years: David Zurawik, "Era of smiles fading away," *Baltimore Sun*, May 2, 2004, http://www.baltimoresun.com/bal-as.friends02may02-story.html.

207   gave up on comedy: Bill Carter, *Desperate Networks*, 352.

207   "procrastinate the end": Kevin Bright, "Producers Commentary," *Friends*: The Complete Ninth Season.

208   "JOEY DOESN'T": "The One with the Birth Mother," *Friends*, Season Ten, Episode 9.

209   "toughest episode": Marta Kauffman, "Producers Commentary," *Friends*: The Complete Tenth Season (Warner Home Video, 2005).

209   "very important": David Crane, "Producers Commentary," *Friends*: The Complete Tenth Season.

209   hallucination: retrieved from @strnks Twitter, Aug. 24, 2015, https://twitter.com/strnks/status/635783320517931008.

209   Rachel's dream: retrieved from @lovetherobot Twitter, Jul. 7, 2017, https://twitter.com/lovetherobot/status/883379164388175873.

209   "So there was just": Marta Kauffman, "Producers Commentary," *Friends*: The Complete Tenth Season (Warner Home Video, 2005).

210   in the snow: David Crane, "Producers Commentary," *Friends*: The Complete Tenth Season.

210   "not as difficult": David Crane, interviewed by Beth Cochran.

210   "Do you realize": Matt LeBlanc, quoted by author David Wild, *Friends 'til the End*, 272.

210 "total breakdown": Kevin Bright, quoted by author David Wild, *Friends 'til the End*, 272.

210 world's oldest: Marta Kauffman, "Producers Commentary," *Friends*: The Complete Tenth Season.

211 "everybody found...ending": Kevin Bright, "Producers Commentary," *Friends*: The Complete Tenth Season.

212 "We almost didn't": Marta Kauffman, "Producers Commentary," *Friends*: The Complete Tenth Season.

212 "watched it go": Ibid.

212 "The memories": Greg Grande, quoted by author David Wild, *Friends 'til the End*, 274.

212 Aniston had been designated: David Wild, *Friends 'til the End*, 258.

212 video camera: Gary Susman, "Here's what the cast of 'Friends' is up to this week," *Entertainment Weekly*, Feb. 4, 2004, http://ew.com/article/2004/02/04/heres-what-cast-friends-this-week-42.

212 "yearbook": Ibid.

213 doing a little Janice: David Wild, *Friends 'til the End*, 279.

213 "Lots of people ask": Maggie Wheeler, "'Friends' Janice: Being Recognized Was An Honor" Where Are They Now, Oprah Winfrey Network, YouTube video, Aug. 24, 2014, https://www.youtube.com/watch?v=lBW9QqXhlR4.

213 "The hell with it": Marta Kauffman, "Producers Commentary," *Friends*: The Complete Tenth Season.

213 "a lot of debate": David Crane, "Producers Commentary," *Friends*: The Complete Sixth Season (Warner Home Video, 2004), DVD.

214 ambiguous reunion: David Crane, interviewed by Dan Snierson, "'Friends' finale: Marta Kauffman and David Crane look back," *Entertainment Weekly*, Apr. 16, 2014, http://ew.com/article/2014/04/16/marta-kauffman-david-crane-friends-finale.

214 "We had dicked": Ibid.

215 they go to Paris: David Crane, "Producers Commentary," *Friends*: The Complete Tenth Season.

215 "Can't something go": Ibid.

215 "Somebody is gonna": Matthew Perry, quoted by Gary Susman, "Here's what the cast of 'Friends' is up to this week."

215 "it all came out": Kevin Bright, "Producers Commentary," Friends: The Complete Tenth Season.

Chapter Eleven: The Comeback

216 "We're throwing": retrieved from @ComedyCentralUK Twitter, Aug. 11, 2015, https://twitter.com/ComedyCentralUK/status/631238676471611392.

216 "experiential event": Comedy Central's FriendsFest, The 8th Annual Shorty Awards, http://shortyawards.com/8th/comedy-centrals-friendsfest.

216 renewed its license: Mark Sweney, "Friends repeats to stay on Comedy Central in UK after new deal," *The Guardian*, Aug. 12, 2015, https://www.theguardian.com/media/2015/aug/12/friends-repeats-comedy-central-uk.

216 "colossal": Mark Heritage, "Still there for you: will we ever tire of Friends, TV's eternal comfort-watch?" *The Guardian*, Aug. 12, 2015, https://www.theguardian.com/tv-and-radio/tvandradioblog/2015/aug/12/still-there-for-you-will-we-ever-tire-of-friends-tvs-eternal-comfort-watch.

216 significant investment: Comedy Central's FriendsFest, The 8th Annual Shorty Awards.

217 Thirteen minutes: Rhiannon Evans, "FriendsFest: the one where fans wander around Monica's apartment," *The Guardian*, Sep. 16, 2015, https://www.theguardian.com/tv-and-radio/shortcuts/2015/sep/16/friendsfest-exhibition-one-where-fans-wander-monicas-apartment.

218 one hundred and thirty: Martha Bayles, *Through a Screen Darkly*, 69.

218 forty languages: Michael Starr, "NBC Nearly Lost Best 'Friends.'"

219 K-Pop group: Aurelie Corinthios, "K-Pop Boy Band Phenomenon BTS Learned English by Watching *Friends*," *People*, Nov. 17, 2017, https://people.com/tv/k-pop-boy-band-bts-learned-english-watching-friends.

219 far more helpful: James Wagner, "'Friends,' the Sitcom That's Still a Hit in Major League Baseball," *New York Times*, Sep. 18, 2017, https://www.nytimes.com/2017/09/18/sports/baseball/friends-tv-show-baseball-spanish.html.

219 "In photos": Wilmer Flores, interviewed by James Wagner, "'Friends,' the Sitcom That's Still a Hit in Major League Baseball."

221 "a little lowbrow": *Lyle v. Warner Bros. Television Prods.*, 38 Cal. 4th 264, 42 Cal. Rptr. 3d 2, 132 P.3d 211 (2006).

221 gagging: Ibid.

221 coloring book: Ibid.

221 tampons: Ibid.

221 fertility problems: Ibid.

221 "dried-up pussy": *Lyle v. Warner Bros. Television Prods.*, 117 Cal. App. 4th 1164, 12 Cal. Rptr. 3d 511 (2004).

222 "constantly being exposed": *Amaani Lyle v. Warner Brothers Television Productions, NBC Studios, Todd Stevens, Adam Chase, Gregory Malins, Andrew Reich, and DOES, 1 to 100, inclusive, Los Angeles County Superior Court, No. BC239047, Declaration Amaani Lyle,* Jan. 4, 2002, republished by The Smoking Gun, http://www.thesmokinggun.com/file/friends-writers-lewd-talk-about-aniston-cox.

222 frequently fantasized: *Lyle v. Warner Bros. Television Prods.,* 117 Cal. App. 4th 1164, 12 Cal. Rptr. 3d 511 (2004).

222 "It was very hard": Amaani Lyle, interviewed by Jami Floyd, "Designing the Harassment-Free Workplace," *Beyond #MeToo,* WNYC, Jan. 22, 2018, https://www.wnyc.org/story/episode-1-designing-harassment-free-workplace.

222 "doing a good job": *Lyle v. Warner Bros. Television Prods.,* 117 Cal. App. 4th 1164, 12 Cal. Rptr. 3d 511 (2004).

222 "spaced out": Ibid.

223 "There is a word": Ibid.

223 "had called Kauffman": *Amaani Lyle v. Warner Brothers Television Productions, et al., Declaration Amaani Lyle,* Jan. 4, 2002.

223 regularly: *Lyle v. Warner Bros. Television Prods.,* 38 Cal. 4th 264, 42 Cal. Rptr. 3d 2, 132 P.3d 211 (2006).

224 "Lyle says she was": Michelle Kung, "Celebrity news for the week of May 7, 2004," *Entertainment Weekly,* May 7, 2004, http://ew.com/article/2004/05/07/celebrity-news-week-may-7-2004.

224 "little evidence": Writers Guild of America, West, 2007 Hollywood Writers Report, "Whose Stories Are We Telling?" http://www.wga.org/uploadedFiles/who_we_are/HWR07.pdf.

225 "because 'Friends deals": *Lyle v. Warner Bros. Television Prods.*, 117 Cal. App. 4th 1164, 12 Cal. Rptr. 3d 511 (2004).

225 "creative necessity": Ibid.

225 "unique in the annals": Ibid.

225 amicus briefs: *Lyle v. Warner Bros. Television Prods.*, 38 Cal. 4th 264, 42 Cal. Rptr. 3d 2, 132 P.3d 211 (2006).

225 "destroy the free": Greg Lukianoff, quoted by Joyce Howard Price, "State's High Court Hears From 'Friends,'" *Washington Times*, republished by The Center for Individual Rights, Jun. 22, 2004, https://www.cir-usa.org/2004/06/states-high-court-hears-from-friends.

225 "Group writing": *Lyle v. Warner Bros. Television Prods.*, 38 Cal. 4th 264, 42 Cal. Rptr. 3d 2, 132 P.3d 211 (2006).

226 "There is ample": Prof. Richard K. Robinson, "In the Case of Lyle v. Warner Bros. Television Productions, et al.: A Brief Amicus Curiae," https://docplayer.net/72634413-In-the-case-of-lyle-v-warner-bros-television-productions-et-al-a-brief-amicus-curiae.html.

226 "repeated sexual conduct": Ibid.

226 "sexual antics…themes": *Lyle v. Warner Bros. Television Prods.*, 38 Cal. 4th 264, 42 Cal. Rptr. 3d 2, 132 P.3d 211 (2006).

227 "go at times to extremes": *Lyle v. Warner Bros. Television Prods.*, 38 Cal. 4th 264, 42 Cal. Rptr. 3d 2, 132 P.3d 211 (2006), Concurring Opinion by Chin, J.

227 "Audiences want": Marshall Goldberg, interviewed by Maura Dolan, "High Court Dismisses 'Friends' Harassment Lawsuit," *Los Angeles Times*, Apr. 21, 2006, http://articles.latimes.com/2006/apr/21/local/me-friends21.

228 "will continue to": Jeffrey Winikow, quoted by Maura Dolan, "High Court Dismisses 'Friends' Harassment Lawsuit."

228 "This sets way back": Mark Weidmann, quoted by Maura Dolan, "High Court Dismisses 'Friends' Harassment Lawsuit."

229 "I'd pretty much…there": Amaani Lyle, interviewed by Jami Floyd, *Beyond #MeToo*.

229 "Looking back": Amaani Lyle, interviewed by Dana Goodyear, "CAN HOLLYWOOD CHANGE ITS WAYS?" *The New Yorker*, Jan. 8, 2018, https://www.newyorker.com/magazine/2018/01/08/can-hollywood-change-its-ways.

232 "haven't even left": Jennifer Aniston, quoted by Lynn Elber, "'Friends' cast prepares final episode of NBC sitcom," *San Mateo Daily Journal*, Jan. 14, 2004, https://www.smdailyjournal.com/news/local/friends-cast-prepares-final-episode-of-nbc-sitcom/article_8bd5de13-5b8e-5e90-ab6b-f9be4d4669f8.html.

233 exaggerated version: Matthew Perry, interviewed by Gordon Cox, "Matthew Perry on His Edgy New Play — And Why He'd Say No to a 'Friends' Reunion," *Variety*, Jun. 5, 2017, https://variety.com/2017/legit/news/matthew-perry-friends-reunion-play-1202452798.

233 "People still see": Ibid.

233 "pretty jarring": David Schwimmer, interviewed by Scott Feinberg.

234 "That scene is": David Schwimmer, interviewed by Peggy Truong, "David Schwimmer Launches New Campaign to Fight Sexual Harassment," *Cosmopolitan*, Apr. 3, 2017, https://www.cosmopolitan.com/entertainment/celebs/a9215169/david-schwimmer-interview-sigal-avin-harassment.

236 "A lot of times": Matt LeBlanc, interviewed by Dan Snierson, "The untold story of Matt LeBlanc."

236   let people think: Ibid.

236   "fuck-you money": Matt LeBlanc, interviewed by *Us Weekly*, "Matt
        LeBlanc: I Love My 'F— You Money' From Friends!" Jan. 13, 2011,
        https://www.usmagazine.com/entertainment/news/matt-leblanc-i-
        love-my-f-you-money-from-friends-2011131.

236   "Let me just": Matt LeBlanc, interviewed by Dan Snierson, "The un-
        told story of Matt LeBlanc."

238   "I mean, *something*": Lisa Kudrow, interviewed by Conan O'Brien,
        Conan, YouTube video, Jan. 25, 2018, https://www.youtube.com/
        watch?v=k3CKK58KWQE.

239   "I just don't know": David Schwimmer, interviewed by Megyn Kelly,
        "David Schwimmer talks about 'That's Harassment' PSAs, 'Friends'
        reunion," *Megyn Kelly Today*, Jan. 29. 2018, https://www.today.com/
        video/david-schwimmer-talks-about-that-s-harassment-psas-friends-
        reunion-1148359235845.

239   "wish we could": Courteney Cox, interviewed by Glenn Whipp, "A
        look back (and ahead?) at 'Friends.'"

240   "Someone asks me": Marta Kauffman, interviewed by Shirley Li,
        "'Friends' reunion will never happen, says co-creator," *Entertainment
        Weekly*, Apr. 30, 2015, http://ew.com/article/2015/04/30/friends-
        reunion-will-never-happen.

240   "We ended *right*": David Crane interviewed by Beth Cochran.

240   "a possibility": Jennifer Aniston, interviewed by Ellen Degeneres, *The
        Ellen Show*, YouTube video, Feb. 2, 2018, https://www.youtube.com/
        watch?v=FD66nOy0WCU.

240   "that show was": Matt LeBlanc, interviewed by Matt Wilstein, "Matt
        LeBlanc to 'Friends' Fans: You Don't Want a Reunion," The Daily
        Beast, Aug. 7, 2017, https://www.thedailybeast.com/matt-leblanc-to-
        friends-fans-you-dont-want-a-reunion.

INTERVIEWS

Sarah Beauchamp, February 2018
Toby Bruce, February 2018
Kimberly Chrisman-Campbell, February 2018
Tyler Coates, February 2018
Dizzy Dalton, October 2017
Nancy Deihl, February 2018
Elana Fishman, October 2017
Akilah Hughes, February 2018
Chuck Klosterman, February 2018
Elaine Lui, February 2018
Tijana Mamula, October 2017
Ryan O'Connell, October 2017
Anne Helen Petersen, January 2018
Mey Rude, February 2018
Connie Wang, October 2017
David Wild, February 2018
Lauren Zalaznick, February 2018

INDEX